Some Way Home:
A Memoir in a Myth

David & Barbara Kenney

David & Barbara Kenney

<u>Dedicated to:</u>

My Father, who told me stories
And My Son, who gives me reason to tell them again.

Table of Contents

Prologue: Adam and the Untamed Fury

Crouching at the bottom of the stairs and peering into the smoke, my eyes adjusted to the dark. I couldn't see the boy or any movement in the shadows, but I knew he was there, somewhere. So I called his name, demanding and coaxing both at once. This basement was familiar but seemed much larger than I remembered. The blazing fire in the far right, back corner was toxic. Its crimson glow illuminated the labyrinth of stacked furniture, boxes and bulging trash bags piled between me and its consuming flames.

Dylan was my client, a foster boy on my caseload, and I couldn't be responsible for his death. So, shaking, I stood enough to shuffle forward with my knees bent deep, keeping low to the cement floor while covering my mouth and nose. The flames slid up to the unfinished ceiling and rushed laterally along the heavily laden shelves that lined the back wall. If I hadn't played hide-and-seek with Dylan many times there, I'd be completely lost. I fought my instinct to run away and moved toward the flames as swiftly as I could manage.

I knew he was there. That basement was a playground to Dylan and I. To Mona, his foster-mother, it was a storehouse of personal treasures. Burning it was the most traumatic wound you could inflict upon her. The fire would be a disaster for us all, if we survived.

The speed with which the flame moved was terrifying and I knew the piles all around had cans of cleaning and painting products, aerosols and other combustible things. Would I have time to find Dylan and get out before I was overcome by smoke

4

and heat?

Turning past a stack of boxes; I saw his thin, muscular shape facing the rising bonfire. His arms held high, his fingers, like feathers above his head, extended up and out. He began to bounce and then dance before the inferno. His face was wild as he encouraged the flames like a shaman in the untamed fury of a ritual fire.

I lunged toward him. I had to grab forcefully to turn with him and run, but when he felt my grasp, he jerked forward and then back with huge force, hitting the bridge of my nose with the back of his substantial skull. The pain was a bright flash. My knees buckled and I went over, hitting the back of my head against something hard. For a moment without time, I thought I might be slipping into darkness, for I saw nothing but black.

#

I startled awake full of dismay, drenched in sweat in the warm, wet tangle of my bed sheets. For a second in confusion, I wasn't sure if I'd been there that day of the fire. But then I remembered I was and this is what happened. Was I also with Dylan years before that, on the night his aunt was beaten and her blood shone dark in the moonlight like spilt and pooling ink? No, I realized I wasn't, but I'd imagined it completely and so saw it in other dreams.

My name is Adam MacDonnell and, long ago, I chose Social Services as a career. For the most part, I've worked hard at it and hope I've done some good. But of late, my thoughts return to all my mistakes as I search for causes to blame for the effects I didn't want. The consequences of my work are beat out in the lives of the most vulnerable and I know I haven't always kept true to the maxim: First: Do No Harm. Sometimes hurt and abandoned children suffered as the result of my inadequacies and miscalculations. But of all the disappointed and hurt faces I remember, nothing pierces me, nothing accuses me, like my thoughts of Dylan.

In many ways, Dylan was an ordinary foster kid on my caseload. He matched the normal statistics and background demographics of the typical disenfranchised child in America. But in my life, he was anything but normal. He was a primal force,

5

disastrous in both scope and impact. The wide path he cut through the landscape of my past devastated my self-concept, mocking my rationalizations. Above all other failures, Dylan plays repeatedly in my mind.

I don't even know if he's still alive. That's why these images return to me in troubled sleep ten years on. I often dream of a drunken, Bad-Daddy Bruce, who staggered, hit and burned the boy. I see the sweetness of Aunt Patti trying to provide comfort before slipping permanently into unconsciousness and witness the hospital staff doing their best with a broken little boy. I dream of Mona's sweaty face falsely welcoming us at the front door of her over-stuffed house, soon set ablaze. I recall the joys and the bitter disappointments of Dylan's brief time with the Blanchard's and even scrutinize my social worker's slight-of-hand in monotonous reiteration. Had his adoptive parents taken care of or dumped him? I didn't actually know.

Awakening, I untangled myself and sat outside on a lawn chair in the still sticky night air. I listened carefully as if I might hear the answer to my questions in the sounds of an outlying breeze shuffling through the dry trees or in the buzz of the seven-year cicadas.

To save myself from the gloom of regret, I needed to put all these memories in perspective. To understand my true culpability before I could seek forgiveness, I had to review what happened to Dylan and face the results of my efforts as honestly as I could.

So this was my task: I was determined first, to review Dylan's story to my understanding and second, to find out what became of him and how the adoption turned out. I was resolved to search for the person who knew and interview him until satisfied. I had to go and find the truth because only in Dylan's complete story could I find my hope for release.

Book 1: Broken Wings

A Beginning of Sorts

So . . . almost unnoticed, a boy named Dylan was born. He was born into chaos and handled roughly when handled at all. At five months of age, he was placed into foster care. I didn't meet him during that initial foster-go-round. First other things came.

According to the reports, he entered the system after he was abandoned in his crib, malnourished and naked, covered with dried excrement and hot shingles. The police found him as they responded to calls concerning feral children down on Telegraph Avenue, children who'd been seen playing reckless, demanding food from neighbors and generally making trouble.

His mother didn't think she'd abandoned them. She'd simply made a long trip to the market and things happened along the way. That was all. Tricks and trade-ups for a bad crack habit had led her on in an updated quest for the Holy Grail: puffing incense to the homeless.

Her six children were rounded up from the efficiency apartment, little ones from the front, older ones from the alley in back, and Dylan from his crib. Like seed spilt out along the highway, the brothers and sisters were scattered into the child protection agency. All became temporary foster children, some later adopted by separate families, while others became long-term wards of the state. No one was sure who would be the lucky ones, those less damaged.

8

Before the police came, in Dylan's mind there must've been only one long, exhausting wail. The fierceness of hunger, cold and infection must've converged in the infant's pre-verbal mind to form one constant cry of distress. Therefore, the first thing Dylan learned was that this world hurts.

#

In Dylan's first foster home, there was a regular routine. Warm and dependable, a nameless woman's arms swept down to change and provide him with an efficient bath and clean pajamas. He was part of a schedule. His basic survival needs were met but nothing more came to him as he was most often left alone in his crib, while the T.V. buzzed somewhere else.

But babies need the human face and the rich communication of touch. In the foster-home, Dylan's world was sterile and anonymous. He stared at the blank ceiling for endless hours.

The foster-lady reported him to be a quiet baby who didn't require much. The pediatrician noted he was listless but clean. And Dylan's brain was imprinted without any reflection of how he might matter to anyone. He was alone.

Then, inside himself, Dylan felt some preverbal kind of No! response to the world. It came sharply into his awareness. Although unspoken, it was surely a word and with it he rejected whatever it was that'd rejected him. This new No! response was as loud as a cathedral bell and as firm as an anchor as it sustained and steadied his mind. It stopped the draining of his soul that began with his birth and clarified his surroundings as different and distinct from himself.

What a powerfully sweet little concept, "No!" It was as sharp as a razor and as insistent as scissors. With it his mind snipped himself off from the rest of the world and made him separate from all the things that had caused him pain. It removed him a sweet distance and insulated him, giving control and protection.

9

As months passed and the internal No! grew, Dylan heard it finally become a sound. At first his lips couldn't form it properly. All that came out was a breathy but angry "Ah!" But still, he chopped the air with it. When the woman came to bathe him, he spoke up. He slashed into her neatness with "Ah, ah, ah!" and beat her with his scrawny arms and legs. Each time she entered the room he battled her, fighting as fiercely as he could.

When he became strong enough to push her hand away, it took her longer to complete her chores of caring for him. Consequently then, the second thing Dylan learned was that if you pushed hard enough and long enough, the world couldn't dismiss you so quickly or completely. As a result, he would push into and against this woman and pull away from her simultaneously.

The records said Dylan was a good-natured and loving baby at five months of age when he was removed from his mother's efficiency in poor physical health. But by the time he left his first foster placement at fourteen months of age, in relatively good health, his temporary mother described him as a "live-wire," a toddler who couldn't settle down. "If you pick him up," she remarked to the caseworker, "he'll push you away. If you try to put him down he'll cling to you for dear life."

#

Then things seemed to take a positive turn when Dylan's Aunt Patti volunteered to take two of her sister's children. She chose the youngest ones since she'd always been partial to very small children. In exit interviews with the agency, Patti said everyone thought the little boys were the luckiest of all.

However, it turned out that her good intentions paved an unwitting path to hell, as through romantic love she delivered them to a man named Bruce. Later, Dylan remembered him only as the "Bad Daddy".

But things didn't begin as horribly as they ended. When Bruce wasn't drinking, things weren't too bad. There was actually a time when Bruce believed he was a good father to his old lady's nephews, but his tie to the boys was too weak and the turmoil he carried inside too strong. Eventually, he came to see them as rivals for Patti's attention and as blocks to his own potential success.

To set the scene for the boys, you need to know about Bruce and Patti and how they got together. To see Bruce on the street you'd probably not think of him again. To meet him at a party, you might be superficially receptive to listening to his litany of "dreams and schemes". You see, Bad Daddy Bruce had only a small character flaw. It didn't show much until it broke everything up.

Usually, Bruce got by on charm. He loved its smooth, slick feel and enjoyed the things it got him without much effort. With it, he disarmed customers down at the store and got them to buy more appliances than they could afford. Charmer was the role he relished playing and was his main approach to taking from the world. But the effects of charisma inevitably fade with age. There are always new, fresh faces to replace those growing old and corrupt, tangled up by their own cons.

About then, Bruce met Patti and, for a while, she was taken in by his singular vortex. She became his favored audience and then his stage. He loved to see himself sparkle in her eyes. And as for her, what if he was becoming a bit frayed at the edges? So what if he drank more than he should? She forgave those things. After all, hadn't she been around, a time or two, too?

The only real problem with the relationship between Patti and Bruce was that it was mainly about Bruce. But as such, it was remarkable for him. With her feminine roots and nurturing power she lifted him up and became a living stage upon which he performed his life. She didn't mind letting him have the spotlight. She never wanted too much attention. In fact at first, he kept the social pressure from her. She liked the way he talked and he was still cute when they first met.

The problem was that, for Bruce, the first blush of their love was too good. To be the center of her attention, simply awed him. It seemed to be everything he wanted. Consequently, he forgot himself and soon got carried away the day he told Patti all his "dreams and schemes." Every one of them from beginning to end! He'd never done that before. It all just tumbled out in a rush one morning over coffee.

When he was finished, he was shocked to hear how different his plans sounded spoken out loud from thinking them in his head. As long as he never told anyone them all at once, they were a work in progress and seemed to glitter in his imagination, full of promise. He could confidently drop a casual mention of his plans into a conversation and people seemed to respect his ambition and vision. But by being genuinely interested and listening to his plans, Patti had somehow stripped them naked. Once everything was said, Bruce stopped with an odd, frightened expression.

Patti had never seen him at a loss for words before and it shocked her. Concern showed on her face. For Bruce, the doubt and pity he thought she felt consumed the magnificent image of himself he had carefully cultivated there in her eyes.

Graciously, she turned away, giving him time to think of something to say and finish things off.

He saw this gesture as a rejection and a lack of faith and therefore began to hate her.

She smiled and said it all sounded just great.

He grabbed a couple of beers and went for a drive wishing to take everything back. But he couldn't.

The incident didn't really matter much to Patti and she forgot about it quickly. She suspected not much would ever change with Bruce and his job. But it was good to be with a man who put up with her with little fuss, who seemed safe, who could tell a good joke and who brought home a regular paycheck.

But for Bruce, that conversation changed everything. He thought Patti now saw him as fake and a fear, a feeling that nothing different was ever really going to happen, settled into his gut. He drank more beer every day and watched his dreams burst like amber bubbles.

Some Way Home

13

The Ghost

Patti never really understood that something shifted that day in Bruce. And for a while thereafter Bruce was more affectionate to her. She got caught up in romantic fantasy. But the truth was: Bruce began to blame her for each little failure or setback he had, real or imagined.

It was just about then the boys came to live with them at Bruce's apartment. Patti and Bruce had already been living together nine months. Without foresight, anyone would've seen the arrival as great good fortune. It certainly seemed that way to Dylan's older brother, Casey.

The long hug Aunt Patti gave them in the hall said they were home. And she kept repeating, "Welcome home. You don't need worry no more. You're safe now . . . welcome home." There was cake and ice cream together, a sloppy mess in their bowls and on their faces. There were two fresh single beds to lie down on.

Late that night as Casey slept, Dylan fell in love. It started when he began to fuss. He cried and Patti was there at once. Dylan was small for his age at fourteen months. Patti, as petite as she was, could easily pick him up and comfort him. But with all his well-hidden might, he pushed her away. He became rigid and poked at her with elbows, knees and toes till he no longer felt like a little boy in her arms. He resembled more barbed wire tightly coiled around blocks of wood nailed shabbily together. He was unnaturally twisted and contorted. She startled and laid him

14

back down. But then he began to fuss again and grabbed angrily for her hair, which hung down over him like a baby's mobile.

She thought for a moment and then picked him up once more. He pushed at her but this time she was prepared. When his body stiffened and twisted she spun him about in her arms so fast his eyes widened in surprise. She stopped him, face-to-face and began to push against him. She held him with one arm and pushed against his hands with the other.

Caught, Dylan was uncertain what to do. He didn't know whether to cease opposition or to try to force her to put him down. He looked at her mouth but it was her eyes that caught him up. Dylan and Patti were soon in a game of blink-don't-blink.

She pushed against him firmly. He was held out and suspended like a frozen figurine. Her force remained constant and matched his exactly. Then a deep, insistent hum rose from the back of her throat. The noise grew until it was loud enough to wake a soft sleeper. To Dylan, Patti had transformed into a big, mamma-bear growling as if to say, "Who's sleeping in my bed?" Then her expression changed, this time, into an exaggerated and comical snarl.

Not in a way he could've explained but intuitively, Dylan suddenly understood the simple elegance of what she was doing. Not with words but in the more primitive language of behavior, he knew that she wouldn't hurt him nor leave him alone. In the face of his opposition, she had chosen to play with him. You see, her behavior was an exaggerated version of his attitude. She was imitating him and he got it.

This realization took him by surprise and his defenses broke down. Something loosened deep in his middle and a giggle was let loose from an unknown spot inside his belly. It bubbled up his throat, cool, crisp, and playful. No longer were the muscles in his body entirely at his command. They moved and jiggled about, convulsing into joy. She heard the giggle move inside him like gas. She felt it, tumbling up from his belly and pop in his throat near her ear.

At that moment, Dylan fell in love. He and his Aunt Patti were in love together. After that, there was no distance between them.

#

The next months raced by as Dylan turned one-and-a-half, two and then two-and-a-half. He and Patti and Casey were inseparable.

Bruce was still working, consequently Patti had every day, all day, to spend with the boys like the proper mother she wanted to be. She was completely engrossed in the work of being a mom. There was something to it that was solid and filled her deeply. When she was with the boys she felt connected to something that anchored her to the north, south, east and west of her life. She was no longer drifting and no longer alone.

Bruce noticed Patti's happiness and despised her more for it. Often the apartment was empty when he came home from work all knotted inside with stories of the bosses who didn't show him proper respect and the idiot-loser customers who drove him nuts while he baited, hooked and reeled them into providing their signatures on his form.

He needed to unwind but no one understood his struggles or cared. When Patti and the boys were at home, he could hardly get a word in edgewise with all the laughing and goofing around. The apartment was bedlam. Bruce was high-strung like he knew most talented people were. He needed time each day to unwind and unload. But that wasn't possible. And to make it worse, he was sure Patti and the boys were mocking him when he left the room.

#

Bruce sulked most of the time the boys were with Patti. His salary, however, allowed her to pay all the bills, save a bit, and spend time with the boys. Every day with Patti and the kids was an adventure and every activity became a game the three relished. Baths were expeditions into a menagerie of rubber animals that squeaked and burped and splashed rudely about.

16

Brushing teeth became monkey time with their faces mugging in the mirror. But whatever adventure each day uncovered, the evening was the best time of all. After their typically messy but hearty dinner was finished and set aside, the boys waited. They stood in the living room anticipating what would happen next, while Patti banged a few pots and pans in the kitchen to divert their attention.

When the boys' concentration finally, drifted away, Patti would pop out from around an unexpected corner. Usually she emerged in the guise of one animal or another, bouncing, leaping, prowling, or slithering. The boys were endlessly surprised and delighted. The three of them flew around the living room propelled by flapping arms, or lifted high by Patti to soar overhead. Finally, they would collapse into a writhing, tumbling mass of laughter and pretend growls, barks, woofs, meows and chirps, as suitably fitting.

It was in this way, with play, that Dylan learned to walk and then to run. Much later, he began to talk in fractured sentences. With the exception of a few single words, Dylan talked much later than most children and even then, his words were garbled and inarticulate. Patti made a report to a social worker about his speech during the only follow-up visit from the agency. She was referred to a doctor who diagnosed recurring ear infections with intermittent hearing loss, which was a surprise since Dylan never fussed about his ears at all.

#

When Dylan was about two and a half, almost three, the struggle for Patti's attention between the boys and Bruce began in earnest. It began slowly and in little ways. Since it was initially petty and childish, it isn't surprising that it was Bruce who started it.

No longer being the center of the apartment's attention, Bruce spent most of his time in the back bedroom watching re-runs of COPS and brooding. He left his den only to get a beer and snacks or to make a pit stop. However, more and more often, he was able to end the fun by demanding Patti attend to him.

The boys were surprised the first time he insisted Patti join him. She and the boys were in the middle of a game. Bruce appeared at the end of the hall and stood with his knuckles pushed into his hips. "How can I stand up to that asshole tomorrow if I'm wearing wrinkled pants?" he chided. "What are you trying to do, beotch, ruin me?" and then he smiled as if this was a charming thing to say.

Patti slid passed him to fetch the ironing board.

Bruce strode after her, leaving the brothers with their hands slack at their sides like broken wings.

Casey looked down and kicked softly at the corner of the couch.

Dylan caught Casey's eye as he whispered, "Bad Daddy."

This struck Casey as funny. He laughed.

Dylan started to march around the living room imitating Bruce, all puffed up and full of swagger, knuckles pressed deep into hips.

They laughed and scowled for half an hour.

#

Bruce's motives for interrupting soon became clear. He wanted Patti to himself. One night, Bruce stormed into their room to demand of Patti. "You, now" pointing to the open door. "I've had enough of this bullshit!"

Patti protested, trying to figure out what was wrong. She didn't want to argue in front of the boys so she left in a hurry with Bruce.

Bruce slapped her bottom hard as she passed him and scowled at the boys.

Dylan sat upright hearing the crack of Bruce's flat hand against her jeans. At that moment, Dylan wished Bruce could be crushed by a giant's heel and smashed into the dirt like a squished berry. The boys heard Patti ask Bruce what's "wrong with you,". This made him angrier still.

He yelled that there was nothing wrong with him but there was "sure as shit" something wrong with her.

The fight got louder when Patti yelled back.

Then something came back to Dylan's mind, something from long ago. He remembered his first foster placement, run by that faceless lady who'd taught him to say No! He heard it again inside, No!

Yes, it felt good to remember.

"No!" he said out-loud. Yes, it felt so right!

"No," he turned to Casey and repeated.

Surprised, Casey looked up high over his head, lost his balance, and fell back onto his bed.

But Dylan wasn't in the mood for a joke. He turned to the hall, no, he thought and while his lips said "no", his heart pounded yes. He breathed sharply through a partially opened mouth. His eyes narrowed as he looked towards the loud voices barking from down the dimmed hallway. His stomach grew momentarily queasy. Then, resolute, he marched out of the bedroom.

Dylan had never seen adults fight before. He'd heard Patti and Bruce shouting but it was always from behind the closed door of their room. As he approached, Patti and Bruce didn't notice him.

"I'm not your slave!"

"You ought to be. I pay enough for it, you fucking bitch." Bruce barked.

The snap of his words made Dylan involuntarily jerk.

Patti saw Dylan standing there. The menace in her body melted. A moment before she was strong, even arrogant, but now her strength dribbled away. Dylan's chagrin undid her.

Bruce noticed this immediately. He looked and saw Dylan's expression pleading to Patti, Please, Aunt Patti, don't. Bruce, knowing how to put two and two together to get an easy answer, found Patti's weakness. Instinctively, he knew where to strike next.

He was on Dylan in an instant. "Get out of here you creepy little freak!" he yelled, spraying Dylan's cheek with saliva. His breath smelled of old food and warm yeast. He pushed Dylan hard and the boy's neck and shoulder hit the wall with an audible crack.

Pain pounded in Dylan's head. It muffled the shouting and confused him.

Patti jumped and pulled on Bruce's shoulder, "Don't!" she shouted.

"DON'T?" Bruce retorted. "Don't you tell me what to do in my fucking house!" Bruce slammed the door of the bedroom.

Dylan was left on the floor in the hall. After a time, Casey came to help him. They heard the sound of several blows from the room but heard no more from Patti.

In a while, Bruce came out of the room and smoked himself to sleep on the couch. Later still, Patti emerged from the bedroom bruised and quiet. She put the boys to bed without a word. Dylan lay awake for a long time. His head and shoulder hurt as he listened to his aunt move about the apartment.

20

She went into the bathroom and stayed there for a time. By the tinkling sounds made when she inadvertently bumped things together, he knew she was moving small glass bottle about. Then, she came out from the bathroom and went to the kitchen. She opened a drawer and shuffled some papers. He wanted a get up and hug her but his arms were frozen at his sides again like broken wings. So, instead, he listened to the sounds of the house until he finally fell asleep.

#

The next day was misery. Everyone was awake long before they got out of bed. Patti was first to stir to visit the bathroom. When she came out, Dylan stood looking up at her, his mouth set into a tight, angular frown. The hurt in his eyes was the worst thing for Patti and overpowered her.

She'd failed at the one thing she wanted more than anything; she'd failed at protecting her child, at being a good mother. She collapsed to her knees and grabbed him, crying softly as he froze like a board. They stayed like that for a long time in the hall until he softened to her. They connected without making a sound. When Patti ran out of tears, they stood up, became separate and started the day.

Later in the morning, Bruce got up trembling from a hangover and guilt. He had Patti call him in sick, but after that she wouldn't talk to him. She treated him like a ghost and turned her back when he entered the room, partly out of anger and partly out of shame. She'd let herself be marked by him and hadn't even defended herself. She felt too embarrassed to let him see the bruise his knuckles had left high on her cheek under her right eye. When he came near her, her stiff back said that she despised him and was determined not to let him hit her again.

Bruce was glad she turned away from him to hide the evidence of his eruption. It was easier to apologize to the back of her head. He thought he'd get sick if he had to say sorry directly to that mark. For the rest of the day, Bruce worked to tempt Patti out of her righteous anger by doing thoughtful things and promising gifts.

21

He was relieved when it became clear Patti didn't have the intention of moving out immediately. In this, he read her accurately but incompletely, for she was really thinking she needed time to plan a move with two children. She was determined to become a better mother. There'd be no next time. Besides, she still needed a place to stay in order to look after the boys. A job, she would need to get a job right away. Then she'd be rid of Bruce and be on her own.

In this way she spent the day, sending Bruce clear messages that he was "out" with her and that she was in control. Every muscle in her back and neck twisted and strained away when he entered the room. With a quick turn, she'd leave. In her mind, he was a phantom that flitted about, whispering in her ear "So sorry! So sorry!" He was less than nothing. She would train him like a pup. She'd house break him and he would never lay hands on Dylan again.

Dylan and Casey were on edge and watchful all day. Dylan studied the situation but didn't like what he felt. Patti seemed not to be as angry as she should have been. Was she forgiving Bruce? What was happening? Bruce had hit them both and Aunt Patti wasn't fighting back. Dylan hated Bruce most for this.

Patti and Bruce were engaged in an intricate dance that's common to adults, negotiations which Dylan didn't understand. The two were fully occupied telegraphing messages to each other and even though they weren't getting along, the mood in the house began to soften. As the boys watched, Dylan felt increasingly betrayed, mad, distant and inconsequential. In reality, it was he who was becoming the ghost. He needed to push against something to feel real. He leaned into Casey and, for a moment, could remember how the lady in foster care had smelled. So, he pushed harder still.

Just You and Me, Kid

During the next few months things changed within this make shift family. Patti got a job, spending more time away. When home, she needed to do many chores. At the same time, Bruce drank heavily and needed more mothering from Patti. Between the two, the boys were effectively squeezed out of Aunt Patti's time.

The more Patti worked the less Bruce did. In effect, the two adults changed places while basically keeping their financial status quo somewhere in the range of the working poor. Bruce called in sick more often until one day he stopped calling in at all and just stayed home. He drank earlier in the day and when Patti came home, he took her into the bedroom for a while. During this phase of their life, the boys could barely say hello to their Aunt. Bruce's needs came first. When satiated, Bruce would palm a handful of bills from Patti's tips-of-the-day and head off for a night at the bar.

All this happened fast. Patti didn't register the full meaning of it right away. She was exhausted and mired in the situation and couldn't work it through completely. As Patti tried to better their situation, Bruce removed an equal or even greater amount of financial support from the family making her even more dependent on him than she'd been before. Patti had no extended family that was worth much and she couldn't afford to pay for daycare for the boys. If for nothing else, Patti needed Bruce for babysitting. Bruce hadn't planned this change consciously but felt it through raw instinct and implemented it with sloth.

For a time, all Patti knew was that she was getting tired. She was working as hard as she could to get away from The Bruise, a name she began calling Bruce to herself. But she was getting nowhere. When she came home from work each day, Bruce pounced. She really had no desire to be with him, but with the loss of energy went her ability to do anything but placate him as efficiently as she could. And then send him out like a bad dog to play in traffic.

Patti knew the boys were missing their games but she had to get a little bit of everything done. The boys didn't understand, but tried to adjust. They knew nothing about bills. All they knew was something had gone out in their lives and a hint of danger always lurked in the apartment where they were effectively confined.

There seemed to be more shadows in the rooms. Dylan began to like the shadows and the hidden corners under and behind furniture. He sat in dark spots and watched what occurred in the light between Patti and Bruce. When Bruce told Patti they needed to discipline the boys for their own good, Dylan didn't know what he meant. He didn't know what Bruce was asking for, but found out the day after Patti agreed the boys needed proper training to be ready for pre-school.

The next day, Bruce got up early when Patti left and, after an eye-opener, started to work with the boys. He made them stand at attention, side-by-side with their eyes forward.

"You boys aren't getting any younger. You need discipline. That means you do what I say, when I say, with no sass. Understand?"

The boys didn't. They turned to each other to see if the other did. The timing of their heads turning was so precisely matched and their expressions so perplexed that it surprised them and they began to laugh out loud.

Bruce didn't appreciate that.

"Oh, I see," he said. "I thought we might get through this friendly, but if you want it that way." He smacked each of them once hard on top of the heads with his knuckles.

The boys winced and leaned their upper bodies away from Bruce.

He repeated, "You'll do what I say, when I say!" This felt good to Bruce; to see the effect he had on them. He'd teach them all right.

Bruce marched one of the brothers to the bathroom and locked him in with a sliding bolt he installed high up for that purpose. He forced the other into a corner, nose touching. He taught them how he wanted them to stand. He made them learn several postures that day: at attention, at ease, corner punishment posture and kneeling on a broomstick. He made them practice these for several hours until he got tired and they stopped whining and then he made them take a nap while he relaxed.

In celebration, Bruce drank several extra beers and kept Patti in the room for more than an hour that day. He told her he'd achieved a big breakthrough with the boys and that if he kept working with them they would definitely be ahead of the other kids when they started school.

Patti took his words at face value because she couldn't possibly do anything else. It was good if the boys and Bruce could get along; it would make living together on a short-term basis easier and their transition out of the house smoother. If the boys could learn something they would need anyway, well then, that was good too. And who knew, if Bruce began to feel better about himself, perhaps he would even go back to work and help out financially.

When Patti tucked the boys in bed that night she thanked them for behaving well for Bruce and said she was happy about what they were doing. She asked them to please do whatever Bruce said and then told them everything would be fine if they did.

26

As he practiced the new discipline in the house, Bruce felt more and more powerful. Curiously, he also felt more certain that what he was doing was right. In his ignorance, Bruce was practicing rage and attack.

Something had happened the night he hit Patti. Bruce realized he was more powerful than he thought before. With this realization he began to feel liberation. His confidence grew. He felt more than good, he felt virtuous. Yes, that was it. It was as if Bruce somehow knew whatever he did was right, just because he was willing to fight for it. To him, might made right. This was true even when he was completely capricious. Indeed, it was when he was the most arbitrary that he felt the truest and, therefore, was willing to fight even more. For example, he was soon able to get Patti to give Casey back to the adoption agency and was convinced that he was absolutely correct in doing it.

Circumstances arose shortly after his training sessions had begun that threatened to hurt Bruce. But with his new confidence, he was able to change it to his advantage by pushing Patti into sending Casey back into foster care.

It started one day with Patti rushing out to work in a half conscious state and continued with a negligible breakfast and then a consequential training session. But the day took a complete about-face around 10:30 a.m. when Dylan went to the right after Bruce had told him to go left.

At over three years old now, Dylan had had enough and figured there were more important things than touching his nose to some corner for an hour, or pulling his legs high as he ran in place, or how straight he knelt on the broomstick. What was wrong with Aunt Patti? Why wasn't she here?

Dylan was past most of the pain that was being inflicted upon him by Bruce. The exercises he was made to do, "just like the big boys," no longer exhausted or made his muscles stiff. They just turned his body and feelings harder. The stings of pinches, pokes and slaps placed where bruises wouldn't form became a thing you could adjust to . . . like mosquitoes. But, even though he was used to these things, he was in a constant state of agitation because he could not stand submitting to

27

Bruce's whims any more. Dylan couldn't sleep, couldn't eat and was often constipated for days at a time because he just couldn't stomach Bruce's smug, smirking grin when he believed he'd won a point with the boys.

On that particular day when Bruce told him to go left, Dylan understood it meant he was being ordered to his room for another long nap spent staring at the ceiling. He just couldn't bring himself to do it. Anything was better. So instead, he turned right and ran down the hall. Then, in the kitchen, he panicked when he could run no farther.

Knowing Bruce would be there for sure, Dylan didn't know what to do. Surprisingly, Bruce was taking his time. Dylan heard Bruce lock Casey in the bathroom. Dylan listened to the slow footsteps approaching and grabbed Bruce's plastic lighter from the counter by the sink and held it out in front of him with both hands.

Already on fire, Bruce entered the room and found what he thought to be amusing, a little boy holding a Bic as if it were a light saber. He grabbed Dylan's forehead and slammed him against the wall hard enough to rattle his brains but not hard enough to leave a bump. He banged his head again and again with practiced certainty.

"You want to burn me?" He asked the shocked boy. He grabbed Dylan's useless hand and took away his weapon. "You want to see me burn? You'd like that. You'd like that a lot, huh?" Bruce knelt down, grabbing Dylan's jaw in his hand. "But you shouldn't play with fire, little boy. Little kids shouldn't play with fire. They might get burnt," he looked deep into Dylan's eyes, searching for something there. Bruce let go of Dylan's face and forced him back to the wall with a hard elbow.

At the same time, he grasped Dylan's right wrist with his left hand. Bruce forced Dylan's hand out stretching it in front of them both. In his right hand Bruce lit the lighter. He paused a long moment then burnt Dylan.

28

He took Dylan into the bedroom and covered the cries with a pillow. He seared Dylan on three fingers and the thumb of his right hand over and over again.

In the bathroom, Casey heard muffled cries but was afraid to wonder what was happening.

Afterwards, Bruce knew he needed a cover story. He lit a fire in Dylan's room, using a wooden waste basket. He burn Dylan's hand over it and then jammed the trembling fingers down into ash covered coal.

Bruce backhanded Dylan across the mouth, just for fun, and then called Patti at work to play out his game.

Bruce told everyone at the hospital the same story he told Patti. The boys had been playing with a lighter in their room. Dylan had gotten stuck between the dresser and the wall, next to his bed where the fire was started and couldn't get away. He must've shielded his face with his right arm and then passed out from the pain, his right hand falling into the basket.

Casey had gotten a small glass of water from the bathroom but hadn't called Bruce at all. If it hadn't been for Bruce's vigilance the whole place might've gone up. Bruce told everyone he'd grabbed an extinguisher kept under the kitchen sink, put everything out, and called for help.

However, what Bruce didn't tell anyone was how he threatened Casey with "worse than what Dylan got" if he ever contradicted this. Then Bruce waved his lighter in Casey's face.

#

For Dylan, the following days and nights were all pain. The suffering started with a surrealistic feeling as Dylan's body went into shock. He saw and felt everything from a distance as if he were looking down a long, dark tube. Way at the other end, he could see the things that were happening to him. They were clear but miniature like crystals. Sharp corners cut into flesh.

29

Someone screamed. At some point, everything went empty-white into darkness and Dylan passed out.

Being burned was like stepping into the gravity field surrounding a black hole. It felt as if he were being stretched inside and dragged down into an enormous darkness by vast power, falling inward fast. His sense of reality was distorted by this inward feeling of falling into darkness. His perceptions were twisted and lengthened by forces not under his control. Something unimaginably strong had taken possession of his internal life and now turned it into something different, something wrong.

Dylan's life lost its continuity and became a series of spotted traumas. It lost the feel of linear flow. Ordinary time had been cracked and couldn't be smoothed again. It flowed like random video clips mixed and badly spliced together.

When he woke up next he was in a universe of pain. Oddly enough, it was then Dylan first felt shame. It felt as if something was wrong within him and that something was making everything else bad happen. Then he passed out again.

When he woke next, it was dead night. From out of the dead of night, he heard a woman's voice say "Poor thing, I guess he won't be playing with fire again."

Then there was bright light, a sharp ray that cut through his eyes and into his head, morning came through the hospital window bright white. It was a world of agony. Everything was filled with pain, especially Dylan's right shoulder and hand. It wouldn't stop. A blinding throb made his breath hiss in, around, and passed his small, chattering teeth. "Gotta hold," was all he could think, "gotta hold."

He had to make it stop. He had to get out. In this world, agony began in him and spread out from there in all directions to infinity. It was a distress that consumed everything and wouldn't go away.

Since the pain wouldn't go away, Dylan did. He went within himself, far away, far beyond the pain. Since all that filled his senses was anguish, he squeezed himself until his senses began to compact and shrink. When he did this the pain grew smaller because his willingness to be aware of it was constricted. He traded the bright hot feeling of fire to his bones for the deep, cold black of inner space and unconsciousness. He slid into the black. It cut him off from the world around him but eased his pain. He slept.

He slept for a long time. For how long, he never learned. This sleep wasn't really sleep but a combination of different levels of unconsciousness that were accentuated by dreams and intrusions from the world outside. But the outside world was still on the other side of his pain and only came through in bright, sharp snippets, out of context, hard to interpret. Soon as they passed, Dylan worked hard to get away from them.

Later, he awoke to see Aunt Patti looking sad and confused. She kissed his forehead and stayed with him. Something wasn't right. She was trying to tell him how she was worried about what Dylan had done. She said that Casey needed to stay somewhere else for a time to be safe. Dylan thought, fault, all my fault.

Dylan remembered Casey standing by the bed saying something. Something was wrong with him too. He was dressed in outside wear and was going away. Dylan didn't understand but Casey was there, standing and looking sad. He was saying goodbye. But that didn't make sense. "What?" Dylan managed.

"You're next." Casey came clearly into focus for a moment.

"Next? What next?"

"Be careful." Casey said and repeated, "You're next" and left.

#

When his pain lessened, Dylan found that he liked the hospital. He was able to rest and play video games for days. He was able to lie lazily in the safety of his sunny bed by the window

31

and watch the Ninja Turtles on TV. He had time alone with Aunt Patti, who came by every day after work to visit. Once, she even spent the whole day with him. They visited the colorful hospital playroom filled with toys, little plastic chairs and short, round tables. Patti told him that this would be like going to school. Dylan thought this odd, looking at all the children in hospital robes and pajamas.

Even though his hand still hurt and there was a heavy, unspoken melancholy between them, Dylan was happy playing with Patti.

Bruce didn't visit the hospital because he was taking care of things at home. The day Dylan was released from the hospital, Bruce was standing at the kitchen sink holding a mug of coffee. He didn't turn from the window but said in a sweet and relaxed tone, "Hey, Patti babe," but Patti continued on to Dylan's room. Dylan froze in the hallway just a few feet from where Bruce stood. After Patti left, Bruce turned, smiled, and said coolly to Dylan, "Welcome back, kid. It's just you and me now." Then he winked.

#

When Patti was home, Bruce played the perfect significant other but when she wasn't around he terrorized Dylan. Dylan learned to be invisible, to disappear under the table or behind the bed for the hours when Patti was away. It was the only way to stay safe when it was just the two of them in the place. Dylan knew there was nothing he could do about it.

This new way of living seemed just right to Bruce. He was more self-assured than he'd been before. He was a man apparently at peace with himself. If Dylan looked like he was about to step out of line, he got the punishment he deserved and didn't even cry when he took it. Bruce was fine letting his relationship with Patti become more platonic. He enjoyed his television programs and didn't drink as much or go to bars. Sometimes he helped Patti out with her chores and every once in a while he made her laugh again.

On the outside, Dylan seemed to absorb everything and show nothing, but inside he turned to sabotage when these days wore him down. Things around the apartment began to turn up missing or broken or sticky. Dylan began to pee secretly in small controlled spurts around the apartment. Bruce never understood why things were often slightly wet in his favorite spots and Dylan developed such good control he became expert at not leaving enough to incriminate himself. Once, Bruce found something spilled in his shoe, but when he sniffed his fingers he couldn't identify the source of the acrid scent.

Often Dylan imagined he'd turned into a fox. He would be good for a long time and then one day he would be a fox and run as fast as he could from room to room, not stopping until he was caught by the bad hunter. Dylan made it his private rule never to stop or give in until he was completely trapped and couldn't get away. Then he would bite, scratch and kick the best he could. The punishment hurt less when he'd run enough to tire Bruce out. Hence, Dylan ran and ran and ran.

When he was caught, he would just go inside into the darkness he'd found at the hospital and then nothing Bruce did could hurt him.

Patti asked, "Why won't you speak to me anymore, sweetie? Are you still mad at me for going to work?" He didn't say anything because he didn't know anything to say.

#

From the account the lady in the next apartment gave the police, things had gotten loud between Patti and Bruce for five days before the final incident. It started on the day Patti announced she and Dylan were moving out at the end of the week. At first, Bruce didn't believe her but when she showed him the deposit receipt for her new apartment; he saw she really meant to leave.

The neighbor could hear the yelling through the walls but was afraid to intervene and worried everyone would be embarrassed if she called the cops and then it turned out to be nothing. But just passed 10:00 in the evening, when everything suddenly became quiet, she stopped what she was doing and listened. The silence was more dreadful than the yelling, but she didn't move until she heard the child's voice screaming outside. Then she dialed 911, put on her robe and went out to the little boy.

that child screaming in his pajamas and covered with blood on his hands, face and hair. He was wild eyed and screamed at the top of his lungs. She'd tried to comfort him but he pulled away with force. He wouldn't stop screaming until the police arrived and took over. Then he collapsed in the back of the patrol car.

Bruce was gone. He'd left quickly out the back door, taking the car and slipped into the night. Sometimes, I think Dylan still wonders if Bruce will come to get him again. In this way, Dylan continues to be a hostage to fear.

Patti never really recovered from the multiple blunt-force traumas to her head. The monkey wrench he used was recovered in a bush out the back. She was like a small child in a big body. A sister took her in and then moved her out of state. This was all done before Dylan saw her. Perhaps that was best. How could he have made any sense of the shape she was in?

#

That night Dylan became a long-term ward of the state. By now, he was almost four, didn't speak, was described as almost always out of control, fearful, incontinent of bowel, oppositional, defiant and given over to fits of uncontrollable rage, both violent and destructive. And the responsibility to help him, on behalf of the state, came to me, a stranger. If he was to have any sort of future, it was for me to find. At the children's protective services where I worked as a clinical case manager, the question was what could be done with Dylan.

Shell Games at the Crossings

On a sunny day in the fall, you might not have known where you were heading, as you made the lazy looping turn off Hawthorne Drive. It's easy to get confused. Shortly after sunrise, the autumn trees at the top of the hill blazed red and orange in the sun's nearly horizontal rays. At the entrance to the Crossings Psychiatric Hospital and Foster Care Facilities a certain stand of maple seemed to lick the blue and white sky like a bright red tongue of fire. When the wind blew just right the whole hillside caught, ignited and danced in a flame that didn't burn.

But when you got over that first small knoll and saw the mature psychiatric facilities, all doubts were removed. You understood clearly that for half of the last century this was the place for nightmares. It was where those who couldn't awake from bad dreams were confined in the hopes of healing their impaired reasoning.

The facility wasn't built by malice nor was it intended to punish but in the end it became little more than a weigh station on the highway to hell. At the time it was built, it was thought to be a great commitment to the compassionate treatment of the sick by the scientifically enlightened.

During those days, across our country, great facilities like this mausoleum to the living dead arose, erected by medical specialists who sought to rescue people from their insanity. They were built in the country for leisurely walks intended to enrich those lost in spirit, while behind the buildings' granite facades, doctors sought to recover sanity with the edge of a scalpel, through the contact of an electrode, or with the prick of a needle.

Most of these facilities have now been abandoned due to the development of powerful sedatives, anti-psychotic medications; along with political leaders who believed hospitals were no place for the sick. The ill have now been sent back to the streets leaving only their haunted souls behind.

Across the U.S. today, you can find ghettos of Adult Foster Care homes slouched together in the poorest parts of cities' decaying infrastructures. Places abandoned by the poor years ago are now cheaply refurbished for schizophrenics, who are then left to smoke cigarettes on warping porches and pound cracked concrete in search of their lost and sometimes forgotten sanity.

However, this old psychiatric hospital, suitably situated to serve southeast Michigan, was spared the common fate of her sister establishments. She wasn't abandoned. Some clever bureaucrat enticed a patchwork of loosely related and semi-autonomous social service agencies to inhabit her emptying halls. She is now a quilt of human suffering knit together by well-intended mental health and protective service professionals.

This hospital was built on a grand scale. Her many halls formed a labyrinth. During my first months working at The Crossings, I spent considerable time lost within it. My boss, Maggie, made several veiled threats concerning my "horrid" waste of time. That was when I decided to stop being lost and start wandering on purpose.

I spent more and more time strolling and visiting with people. The back-wards, where the severe mentally ill were confined, became one of my favorite places. Initially, I liked the children's wards best but that was too much like work. All the while I wandered; I'd stop and visit as much as possible. Listening to these confined strangers fascinated me.

Through my wandering ways, I memorized the layout of the facility but, more importantly, I learned about the stories everyone keeps inside, their personal mythologies that heal when they are discovered, reshaped and retold. To search for and study these stories, I spent more of my time in the back wards of the hospital. By now, my boss was livid. So I began to work longer hours and made sure my caseload was cleared before those of other case managers. Besides, turnover of line staff was high at our agency. In the end, she let me be.

Talking to people in the hospital taught me to listen with an active ear by focusing on only them and crawling in behind their senses. It was hard at first but when I developed the skill, I found a new tool with which to influence people. When done correctly, in total passivity, I actually had more control than previously possible. It's an odd phenomenon, a paradox. If you try with all your conscious might to eliminate your presence in a conversation, if you eradicate every vestige of your ego, you will discover a place of increased potency. You gain greater control over both others and yourself when not rooted in your own identity.

After this realization, my job became more than a job to me. It became a mission. I used my new talent to place foster children in homes that matched their needs at a new and unprecedented rate. Thinking about how my placement numbers had risen, I realized I was already using my new ability to match couples with children. By finding suitable children on our list server and connecting them to the unspoken needs of potential parents, I was able to make new bonds. By repeating what I heard deep inside their words, I was able to positively frame a potential parent's first encounter with a child.

#

After only two years of agency work, I was the senior member of my department. My numbers continued to rise and the younger members of our organization were treating me with too much deference. By now, because of our high turnover, I was near the top of the seniority list, save for a few old timers hanging on until retirement. My boss had stopped her scrutiny of my work completely and now let me do and say what I wanted; I was untouchable or at least I thought so.

Little did I know my life was about to change when, one day in fall, I stepped up to my secretary's desk to retrieve my messages.

"Got a new one for you, hot-shot," Rose snarled in what I'd learned was a playful manner. "Emergency placement! He's been over in Psychiatric for a while. We're pushing the limit on days he can continue one-to-one."

"He's still on one-to-one? How long has that been?" I asked as I took the file from her outstretched hand.

"Hey, you got the file, hot-shot." She lowered her head and returned to sorting paperwork.

"He must be in bad shape." I said to myself and began quickly thumbing through my new assignment.

"Must be," agreed Rose. "He was to go to Rick by the normal rotation but Maggie had me hold the file and not put him into play until your name came around."

I stopped my search and looked fully at Rose to see if she were kidding. Clearly, she was not. I then looked over to Rick who was writing a report at his desk in the bullpen, a large open room with islands of desks that served as our office.

My desk was on the other side from Rick's. He always seemed to be writing reports by hand whenever I came into the office. I began to wonder if he ever left. Did he ever meet the children and parents on his caseload or just write reports? He whined a lot, however, and his stories were all boring. "Whaaa, whaaa, whaaa," I never felt sorry for him and the stories went on and on and on. I'd taken to making subtle comments like: "Not now, I'm busy" to fend him off. But he just continued to whine about the problems he was having with his classic corvette convertible or the rainwater that dripped into his new, uptown home. Now in his forties, I guessed I knew why he'd never married. Who could stand to hear such a long and sad litany of mundane trivialities? His placement rate was always near the bottom of the list. Rick was clearly coasting on a long slope toward his retirement, still years away.

"Why, is it something she thinks he can't handle?" I turned back to Rose.

"A real red ball" she said without turning from her work. "Maggie got a call from the Board. They're making an inquiry. The word is they're afraid this one might hit the papers. The boy, his name's Devon I think, was with us before. He was placed with his Aunt for adoption but his adoption worker dropped the ball and didn't follow-up per standards. Later, Devon turns up beaten and possibly tortured. His Aunt was found near dead and her significant other vanished. It'll make the agency look bad, especially if the press gets wind of it. Maggie's hoping you'll make it go away . . . fast."

"He's been in psychiatric fourteen days?" I raised my volume a bit. "That means I've got to find him a temp-spot in foster care by tomorrow." I gave Rose my most incredulous expression.

"Hey, don't give me your two dollar looks" she said. "Rotation was slow this week. And you started near the bottom of the list."

"Jesus, Mary and St. Joseph..." I uttered an oath my Grandmother saved for special occasions. Then I continued, "Only one day..."

"Better quit complaining and get on it. We're counting on you." She raised two hands which held make believe pom-poms and cheered, "Go team, rah! Fight team fight!"

I looked at her again and she began to snicker. "Oh, you just wait. I'm going to dictate a long report on this one. You'll be typing with nubs before you're through." I said in mock threat.

"Ooooo ..." she returned in fake and artificial horror. "I said go team, GO team, so go . . . go away!" She repeated and waved me from the front of her desk.

#

"Not now Rick, I'm busy," I said as I sat down at my desk.

"Ha, ha, very funny!" He replied.

I grabbed my electronic organizer and turned on my computer nearly simultaneously. Predictably, Rick began his litany but I didn't wait to hear today's list. "I'm going to key your Corvette," I said over him in response. "I'm serious - shut-up. I've got no time for you today."

But Rick just shrugged off my words and continued with his own.

I did my best to ignore him while I waited for my computer to boot up. I opened the agency's shared hard drive and searched the list of homes with empty beds. There were miserable, slim pickings, just a few extra beds in the whole agency.

At first, I couldn't find an empty spot in a house that took emergency placements. My eyes raced down the list, frantic. If I couldn't find a spot in a home already on the emergency placement list, I was screwed. I'd never make my newly discovered deadline. I'd have to talk one of our other foster parents into changing their designation to an emergency placement home with all the extra scrutiny that is required. I had to document it all and file before I could move the boy in.

"Oh . . . come on come on come on . . ." I said as I flew down the list. "Ah ha!" I said when I found what I'd been looking for. "Mona, you lovely lady!" Mona hardly met my description. She was old, massive and stingy. But she owed me a favor or two and when her beds were open she'd take just about anyone, as long as they didn't damage her property.

Mona was one foster parent who was clearly in it for the money. In foster care, there are two unambiguous groups of parents. The first group was dedicated, loving and committed to helping children. The other group wasn't, at least not as a priority. Mona was part of that second half. But she was reliable

41

and definitely had a bed available for the boy. I could move him out of psychiatric today and start looking for a better placement tomorrow if it didn't work out at Mona's.

I picked up the receiver of my phone and glanced over at Rick, who'd stopped talking at some point and returned to his report. I dialed. Mona was home. I could hear a loud TV in the background.

"That's not Springer, I hope." I chided her in a familiar manner before identifying myself. She knew who I was immediately.

"Adam McDonnell, you ought to be ashamed, bothering a helpless old woman like that."

"Mona, you're anything but helpless. Don't run that tired trick by me. I'm on to you now." I could hear her cackle a bit on the other end of the line. "Listen, I need a favor."

"Oh no, I know I'm in trouble now. I know about you and your favors," she interrupted.

"No, no, I'm serious. The bosses down here have set me up good this time. I've got an emergency placement I must move today."

"Oh, oh, sounds like trouble. Only the testy ones are held back to the last day. I've been around too long for you to pull that one over on me. I ain't going to have no lowlife delinquent in my home tearing things up. No way, no how, Adam McDonnell! You can forget it. Forget it right now..."

I half-listened while letting her normal tirade run its usual course. Then, I began to say the things that I needed to get this boy placed in her home. "Now Mona, you know I would never do that to you. That'd be like giving a scorpion to my mother instead of bread," I added the scriptural tone intentionally as doing this always had a good effect on her. "I wouldn't think of placing a delinquent in your home. It wouldn't be right. No, no, he's a good boy. A fool has just hurt him, that's all. Poor, little, hurt boy.

Needs a good home like yours, that's all, you'll see. Someone good to look after him! You'll do him right."

"Adam McDonnell, you'd lie to St. Peter himself if you thought it'd get 'cha through them gates. I don't believe a word you say." She held firm.

"No, I swear, I've seen him, he's great . . . adorable," I lied.

#

I was able to talk Mona into taking Dylan by telling her good things and giving her promises. The next thing I did was to go to our in-house, psychiatric ward to meet the boy and see if any of the things that I'd said about him were true.

I checked in at the nurse's station, where a middle-aged woman was charting medications. I introduced myself, showed her my badge and asked about the boy, "Devon." She said she had it down in her records as Dylan but said she'd double-check the court papers. Then she came out from behind the counter and led me away to a locked door.

"He's in the playroom," she said officiously. "We asked him to wait for you in there." With that and several efficient moves from her hand, (the jab of the key, the quick sharp turn of her wrist, followed by the echoed clunk of the door bolt snapping open) she deftly moved me into the playroom.

"How will I know him?" I turned and asked.

"He's the only one in there," she replied and disappeared.

As I turned away, the metal door behind me closed with a thud. I always hated the sound of the door being locked and not having a key. I hated feeling trapped. I stood for a moment to let my eyes adjust to the light of the new room. I looked about as familiar objects took shape with increasing focus and regularity. The couches and chairs, the orange and yellow plastic play structure, the TV set with a solid, blue screen (Nintendo on but nobody home), the boxes of teddy bears and dress-up play

43

clothes, all these things I remembered from the many play places where I'd worked with kids in the preceding years. There were a lot of things in the room but there was no boy.

Where could he be? He was clearly not, like she said, in the room waiting. It would've been easy to see him if he was there but he was nowhere to be seen. I began to feel annoyed at being locked in an empty room. So, I went back to the door and pounded a few times. The nurse came.

"Someone must've moved him." I said, flatly, to the woman's straight face.

"No, they haven't," she said back in a superficially polite tone. "He's in there," she motioned me back with a nod and shut the door again.

I turned around and continued to search. I was careful and systematic this time, looking under every table and couch. There was no child! I was certain. I could feel my Irish rise steadily inside as I headed back to the metal door for a second time. I know a boy when I see him and I know when I don't see him, too! This time I knocked indignantly on the dark-green door.

"You've made a mistake..." I began but was interrupted.

"No, you have. Try again, please" she insisted and closed the door in my face without waiting. For a moment, while standing with my head dropped slightly low and my face to the locked door, I remembered my third grade teacher, Miss Gene. I wanted to scream but resisted the urge. I took a deep breath and turned about. Just then I heard, or thought I did, something: a sound somewhat like movement ahead and to my right. I turned with a natural motion but nothing was there. The disturbance in the playroom had been small; I dismissed it quickly.

That was when I heard the boy's voice for the first time. A small animal sound came to me from the other side of the room. I spun in the new direction and maneuvered around the few intervening obstacles that lay between me and the noise. But when I reached the place where it'd come from, there was nothing there.

"Yeeeet!" There . . . there it was again ... to my right. It was the sound of a small animal or . . . no . . . a baby bird in distress. The sound was brief and sharp but indistinct as well. This time it was a little louder and held for a bit longer than before. I stayed still. I slowed my breathing but heard nothing more. There was no discernible movement in the room except mine. When I got to where the new noise had come from, it was empty too.

I'm embarrassed to admit that I could feel my blood beginning a slow, rolling boil. I still had a lot to do that day if I were to meet my deadline. The last thing I needed right then was to have my boss come down on me about technicalities. She never really cared about the big things but trip up on a piece of paper and she was all over your back. "Oh," I thought out loud, "I don't need her all over me" I said shivering at the image I held in mind.

So when I couldn't find Dylan after five or six tries, I began to lose it.

"Damn, I don't need this," I whispered to myself in a low voice. Just when I was about to shout, I heard a giggle. It was tiny, not much more than a quick tee-hee. It made me mad at first but then I understood that this was a game. He was playing hide-and-seek with me and I was losing big-time. Being mad might be a personal problem. After all, wasn't I standing in the middle of a playroom?

"Oh, that's the game?" I said consciously adjusting my attitude. "Hullo!" I declared to the dust in the air, "The games afoot then. Call out the dogs." I barked in an exaggerated imitation of an English nobleman. Then I howled over my shoulder and to the rear. I got down on my hands and knees and played a hunt out for my unseen audience. I buffoon'ed as well as I could and each time I made a good joke, I was rewarded with a giggle slightly louder than the one before. When my hunting dogs got all crazy and out of control, I heard a full guffaw.

With each new laugh, I moved closer to my real prey and, in this manner of misdirection, was able to zero in on him, my true quarry. When finally I shouted "Hey what, boys!" and play-acted the English gentleman falling from his horse into a mud puddle, landing, splash, on his royal bum, the boy burst into open laughter. Fast, I moved in on him. I found him under and behind a short table. But when I reached out to grab him, to say: "Gotcha," and to poke at his belly, I was stopped still.

I'd gotten to him in time to see his smile. It was bright and drew me in at once but, in a flash, when he realized that he was really trapped, a look of panic overtook his features. In fact, it seized his entire body. He tried to get away as his stocking feet back-peddled rapidly on the tile floor not gaining a grip. He was trapped. I'd put him in a real corner. He began to scream.

At first the sound was horrific but then his scream became almost silent. It was terrible to see him swallow his shriek. I watched those piercing, tearing tones and the pains they anticipated disappear into him as he gulped hard for air. They became guttural, drowned by his throat, pushed down. The noise fell away to nothing.

To hold it in, however, took all of his might. He stiffened every part of his body. He closed his eyes, curled into a ball holding his knees to his stomach with both arms and rolled over to face the wall. His eye lids wrinkled as he clenched them shut. Then he hid his head but the muscles in his back screamed, silently, way down deep inside.

Hurriedly, I stepped back to give him room and said "It's okay. It's okay." I made myself small and talked softly. "It's okay; I'm not going to hurt you. I was only playing. It's okay." I opened a way for him to leave by stepping out of the area. "It's alright, Devon." I said, still mixing up his name. But I wanted to reach him, to let him know that he was safe.

He didn't move from that spot next to the wall. I sat down ten feet from him and continued to talk in as comforting a tone as I could. But he didn't move. He became rock and stillness.

After a while, when I was pretty sure that he wasn't going to hide again I got up and went back to the green door to talk to the nurse. She told me that she had double-checked and his name was "Dylan" for certain. She also said that what I'd just seen was

46

a patterned behavior. The staff put him in the playroom to show me that his ability to hide was exceptional. They could hardly believe it. And if you found him, he acted as if he were being violently beaten. The terror on his face was ghastly and repulsed most people.

He'd run away when he could but if trapped, he'd fall limp then curl into a fetal hardball. He stiffened and stayed like a dried leather orb for several hours, then fell into a deep, still state from which he couldn't be roused. Much later, he appeared out of nowhere, calm, rested and oblivious to what had happened.

"You can't take him to a foster home like this," she said to me directly. "We never leave him in the playroom because we can't find him when we do. Here all the doors are locked. Don't you see? We can barely find him in a locked room. How could you expect to keep tabs on him in a foster home?" She asked and waited for my reply.

"You know the state guidelines mandate a placement." I started. "He'll be all right." I continued but she was clearly not buying my line. "How about this:" I began again. "You say that when he has one of these episodes, he will stay asleep for a long time and can't be stirred, right?" I asked and she nodded. "Well, what if I were to go back in there and get him to come out here in . . . say . . . ten minutes . . ." I looked at my watch to confirm. "Would you say that I knew what I was doing? Could you give me that much?" I asked while really not having a clue to what I would do.

I knew that I had to do something to move this kid quick. Not only because of the limited number of psychiatric days but also because children who stayed longer in hospital didn't do well in the end. Foster care, with all its faults, was still better than long-term hospitalization.

She thought for a moment then nodded, "Alright then!"

I moved back to the playroom door once more. Back inside, near Dylan, I didn't know what to do. I sat down on the floor close enough to him. He could see me if he turned from the wall but I was not in his direct line of sight. And, in no way, did I block his

47

path to freedom. I held my head low and drew with an index finger on the cool, tile floor. After what seemed a long time I began to talk again.

"Dylan," I said softly, reassuring. "Dylan, I know that I called you by the wrong name, I'm sorry." I waited for nothing. "Dylan . . . I know that I scared you but I didn't mean to, I'm sorry about that too."

After another period passed, seeming longer than it was, I continued but in a new direction. I needed him to respond . . . respond to anything. "Hey, what kind of things do you like? Do you like playing games? What is your favorite kind?" It was a cheap trick but I had to get him to start talking somehow. I felt confident that if I could, I would be able to get him up. "I like make-believe myself. I'm nuts over imagination. I bet you are too."

I looked around, somewhat frantic and saw a little play kitchenette with pink plastic dishes and bowls. I reached over and grabbed a bowl and a big serving spoon. "Hey, what's this? Ah, a big bowl of my favorite dessert!" I made an exaggerated and sloppy show with the bowl but to no effect. Dylan's back remained undisturbed.

I sat perplexed. I knew that he liked to play, at least one game, namely hide-and-seek. I had to find another game he liked and quick. My time was running out. I sat and thought but my mind continued to be blank. I looked about hopelessly for an inspiration.

Just when I started formulating the excuse I would be giving Maggie for my missed deadline, my eyes landed upon a large, red plastic play phone. Maybe he might play-act, long distance with me. I picked up the phone and opened it. I dialed loudly. "Ring ... Ring," I said, "Hello. Hullo, is anyone there? Ring ..." I looked over to Dylan. Evidently it was going to take more than that as he didn't budge.

"Ring . . . Ring . . . Hullo! Harvey Horse? Oh, I'm glad to see you are home," I continued and turned away from Dylan. "I thought you might be out at the store buying treats for the party.

Yes, that's right, cake and ice cream, games and toys, stuff like that. What else do you have on your list? . . . Uh oh . . . okay . . . that sounds great. I can't wait to come over."

I looked over to Dylan, he hadn't moved but something had relaxed in his body a bit. It was subtle but something seemed less stiff. Encouraged, I continued. "Well, who are you planning to invite? Oh, I see. Teddy and Holly Bee and the rest of the gang . . . And what? You can't get a hold of every one. They're not answering their phones . . . Oh, no! People are coming over already. Ah, ooh! Do you think they might miss the party? That'd be terrible. Hey, how about this . . . how about if I give them a call before I head over. I might be able to get them to answer the phone. Do you think so? Do you think it might be worth the try? Okay! No, I don't mind. Sure. Sure. No problem. Should I bring anything else? Oh . . . I see . . . we'll have fun . . . that's right. Okay! I'll see you in a bit."

I hung up the play phone and got to my feet. I walked away, stopped in the part of the playroom that looked like a bedroom. "Oh, where did I put Dylan's phone number? I just can't remember." I messed about, looking around for an imaginary piece of paper with Dylan's pretend phone number written on it.

I knelt before a trunk of play clothes and started to grab at them and toss them high into the air, all about the room. Out of the corner of my eye I thought I detected movement. But I didn't turn around. "Oh, where did I put it? I don't want him to miss the party. Where, oh, where!"

Near the bottom of the bin I stopped suddenly, "Oh, there it is. I knew it was here somewhere." I reached into the bin and pulled out a piece of rumpled air. I unfolded it and read nothing aloud. "Aaahh, Dylan: (434) 555-D-Y-L-A-N," I said continuing to improvise. I picked up the toy telephone again and dialed loudly, "(434) 555- D-Y-L-A-N. Oh, please be there, please," I repeated and turned directly toward Dylan. But when I looked to where he'd been laying, he was gone.

Oh, no, I thought, he's hiding again. Now what? I gestured to the air.

49

Just then I heard, "Ding" behind me. I turned to see Dylan standing right there close enough to reach out and touch me. He delighted in my surprise. He was holding up his right hand to the side of his head, a thumb to his ear and pinky extended toward his mouth. His face was bright and set off by a great, self-satisfied smile. "Ding," was the only noise he made, "Ding." I took a mental note, evidently, Dylan liked many games.

Mona's World

After that, I got to know Dylan extremely well. Before convincing Mona to take Dylan, I had to give her my home phone number. And she used it lavishly. A day and a half after Dylan left the hospital I heard her voice, cracking over the phone at three in the morning. It was the first of many late night calls I received from her.

She told me that she'd thought she'd heard an intruder downstairs. Determinedly, she rumbled down into the darkness with a flashlight in one hand and a stick in the other. She would fight to keep her things from the hands of robbers. Mona wasn't afraid of "no sneak thief." But when she entered the dining room, where her fine, plated silver was kept, she found what she couldn't beat with her stick. It was Dylan relieving his bladder on her simulated Persian rug. His water piddled and splattered in the middle of the main pathway to the kitchen. It splashed onto her real cherry wood hutch. When she screamed, he disappeared through the kitchen into the basement.

The basement was his. My job that night was to get him out of there and back to bed. Then I had to listen to Mona rave about "that creature" being immediately removed from her home.

Placing Dylan with Mona was a bigger mistake than I could've imagined. I think that all of us, Dylan, Mona and I, would've been better off if I hadn't rushed his placement. But not knowing the extent of the mismatch and its consequences, surely I can be forgiven my error.

But after his placement with Mona, the damage to Dylan would've been much greater if I'd sent him back to the hospital. Although Mona, her house and my caseload would've fared better, returning Dylan would almost certainly have ruined his chances for adoption. Children who are taken out of foster placement and put back into the hospital are rarely returned to the community in any meaningful way.

Infrequently these children escape their childhoods without being scarred from not belonging or without feeling that they were unlovable. Most often, they spent the rest of their childhood bouncing back and forth between large, institutionalized group homes, little more than old fashioned orphanages and psychiatric facilities. No child on my watch had yet ended up at that dead end. I wasn't going to let Dylan be the first.

So I spent most of my time in the next five weeks, at Mona's, putting out allegorical fires and waiting for a better placement to come along. By herself, Mona was unable to find Dylan in her home. With all three floors finished, Mona had 3,520 square feet of space in which she stored all her worldly wealth.

Before she'd owned her house, it was owned by a wealthy auto man in the thirty's and forty's. The combination of many square feet, much clutter and Dylan's ability to disappear was quite remarkable. I still admire his ability to simply vanish. This was a situation that'd never occurred in Mona's home before and was one that she couldn't have imagined. The only solution she could think of was to lock the deadbolts on the front and back doors with keys and secure the first floor windows. This way she'd be somewhat assured that, at least, he'd remain indoors.

She couldn't get him to bed at night, or rather more correctly; she couldn't keep him there for long after the inevitable struggle each bedtime brought. The first opportunity he got, the first time she turned her back on him, he'd slip away.

In his time at her house, Mona was uncertain whether Dylan ever used the bathroom at all. In this, he was a bit like having an untrained puppy in the house. Only he was more subtle in the placements of his deposits. If you forced him into the bathroom, he'd put up such a fight that one night the neighbors three doors down complained about the screams that reached them. The police were bemused by the size of the noise that came from the undersized boy. Consequently, he never bathed.

His eating habits were just about the same. He wouldn't sit at the table. And he only ate what he could steal from another's plate. At night, after everyone else was asleep, he would raid the kitchen. One time, he emptied the entire contents of the refrigerator and kitchen cabinets onto the floor. I was impressed by the climbing, agility and strength that this must've required.

In the morning when Mona came down from upstairs all of the food, dishes, glasses, cups and other containers were randomly placed on the kitchen floor. There was hardly a space big enough for an adult foot to fit on the entire floor. She had to pick up everything and place it in the dining room before she could get into the kitchen to put it away. That day she bought locks for the kitchen cabinets and refrigerator. After that it was uncertain just what Dylan ate.

Things were so bad that I practically lived at the house. I took short naps on one of Mona's couches and showered in the upstairs bath. The rest of my caseload went pretty much unattended, as I became a virtual stranger in the office. I faxed and e-mailed most of the work in.

After a few weeks of this, however, I grew impatient with Mona's ineptitude towards Dylan. I started to react more slowly to her calls. Once I'd determined that Dylan was safe, I let her deal with him more and do her own work while I hustled to catch up on mine. However, Mona, feeling that I was ignoring her and not living up to the promises I made, began making calls downtown without my knowing.

In trying to manage Dylan's behavior, we were in a bit of a predicament. There was no hope to teach him new, less maladaptive responses to his environment, if we weren't able to keep him in a place where we could see him, where we could talk to and reinforce him. But we couldn't force him to stay and restraint was out of the question. With children who have been severely abused, our office had a strict hands-off policy. In no uncertain terms, I told Mona that neither she nor her staff should touch Dylan in anger.

So we were in a bit of a quandary. I suggested and modeled the use of positive reinforcement and shaping as a means to teach Dylan more pro-social behaviors. But frankly, when damage was done to Mona's property I saw more revenge in her eyes than unconditional, positive regard. But I was there often and could run interference. The two older women, heavy and thick, who constituted Mona's "staff", weren't proponents of our hands-off policy, hence, as representative of that policy I became "persona non gratis". The whole atmosphere became tense and quietly antagonistic.

Dylan, still my biggest worry, reacted to this change by becoming more skittish and hyperactive. At times, he seemed to be little more than a frightened, under-fed, large-eyed, nut-gathering mammal moving about at night, hiding during the day and squealing when confronted. I spent what time I could with him but it was awfully inadequate. More and more of my time was spent interceding on Dylan's behalf. More often I had to explain Dylan's behavior to everyone at Mona's. More often I played on their sympathies. Then, what little time I had left was filled with paperwork. But whenever I could, I found time to be with Dylan.

Often we started our time together by a few rounds of hide-and-seek. Dylan took delight in finding new places to hide. I thought it would be good if someone could find him in the house; therefore, I called it staff development on my activity log.

He'd invite me to play by sneaking up on me while I was working. He'd position himself on the periphery of my awareness (he was good at knowing where my blind spots were) and then he'd dart from the corner of my eye into full view, catch my attention and then vanish. Often I followed. After a few rounds of his hiding and my seeking, we sat and were quiet. It was at these times that I thought Dylan might speak to me. It felt as if he wanted to anyway.

One day while sitting on the floor in the basement I got the call to go down to the office immediately; my boss wanted to see me right away. I left thinking that Dylan and I could spend more time together when I got back. It wasn't likely that my boss would take all day. She probably just wanted me to capitalize my 'i's' or sign some form. But I couldn't have been farther from the truth.

When I got to Maggie's office, her shoulders were stiff. Her face was red, her manner formal and she may've been slightly out of breath. When I asked her, "What up?" she nodded to the ceiling and the offices of the county's mental health governing board, which were on the floor just above us. "The bosses, that's who,"

"No, I mean, what's that important that I had to come down right away?"

I suppose I could've put it a better way, for after I finished talking, something seemed to have come unhinged within her. She began to sputter and shake her head, tightly, rapidly from side-to-side. Then she opened her mouth and began in earnest. "What's so important?" she mimicked in mock amazement. "I told you, the bosses, THAT'S WHO! And I've been spending far too much time talking . . . no, I should say: listening . . . Yes, listening intently to them. And do you know what they are talking about? No, don't guess. You! You, that's WHO!" She extra exaggerated this last part.

"What are you talking about," I managed to stammer with insufficient grace. This'd taken me totally by surprise.

"I'm talking about you . . . that's who. You, who discharged a child against medical advice; you, who misrepresented that child's status to one of our long-term home providers . . . you, that's who. You broke your promises in effect setting up a situation where the child is underserved and the provider's property is being damaged," she scolded me like a third grader, her fingernails rapidly and sequentially rapping her desktop.

Evidently Mona had been busy talking to her local politicos, who'd been busy talking to their friends at the mental health board, two pay grades above my boss. It wasn't unusual for

56

home providers to have political connections but I hadn't known this about Mona before. Anyway, I hadn't been thinking of much else other than Dylan for a while. Obviously, I hadn't thought it all out but everything came into clarity during my boss' tirade.

Instead of requesting a transfer for Dylan through me, the case-manager, with the normal procedure, Mona had decided that it would be more effective to discredit me with her buddies and have Dylan transferred from top down.

"Get him out of there . . . now," Maggie continued in my face. Her eyes locked on mine in her best impression of Rambo's drill sergeant.

"But I need time to find another . . ." placement, I was going to say but didn't have the chance.

"You've no time but the present! I mean today. If he isn't gone today, you are on suspension tomorrow. Disciplinary leave follows! You're lucky I'm not taking you off the case right now." I didn't feel lucky just then. After further raving and berating, she let me escape her office.

I sat at my desk for a while staring, not knowing what to do next. The bottom line was that there wasn't much to do. I couldn't get around both Mona and my boss . . . And my bosses' bosses too, for that matter. If it were just one of them I could've figured a way out. I'd get a delay. I'd find an alternate placement. But with everyone united against me and Dylan, it wasn't possible. I couldn't think of any way to avoid placing Dylan back into the hospital.

At my desk, I delayed a long time before I picked up the receiver of the phone. Slowly, I dialed the number to the hospital's in-take department. I mumbled some information concerning identity but then changed my mind.

I could at least see Dylan one more time and tell him myself that I'd made a mistake. And that he needed to go back for a while because of my mistake. "It isn't because of you," I could tell him. "It's because of me. You'll be out in no time." I'd heard that one before from other case workers. To me it had always sounded like a lie. But I still had enough arrogance in me to believe that I wouldn't break my promises.

After I hung up on the intake worker, stopping my potential betrayal, I got in my car and headed back to Mona's. The traffic seemed to take forever getting out of the parking structure but things sped up unexpectedly as I rolled off the pot-holed exit ramp from the Lodge Freeway and headed into the heart of northwest Detroit. When the traffic opened before me I saw smoke in the sky. It was still low to the ground. It hadn't yet turned into the thick, black column of smoke that fires become when out of control. But still, it was foreboding as it was in the direction of Mona's.

After a few turns of the road, foreboding became distress, as the smoke signal drew me closer and closer to trouble. I had to park a block from the house. I hesitated when I saw the old structure leaking smoke from all sides. Grey billows flowed out of cracks and crevasses on the first and second stories. I parked illegally but it didn't matter as I ran the buckling sidewalks between me and Mona's.

I had to show my ID to enter the inner ring around the house. I was surprised to realize that there was less chaos closer to the burning building. This wasn't to say that there was little activity. It was just less random than the crowd, now encircling the calamity. Both the fire and police departments were already busy on the scene. No water was flowing yet but preparations were being made.

A small group of officers coordinated half way between the crowd and the fire. A number of senior team members were inspecting the house. At the Elm Street side, I recognized one of Mona's staff huddled up with a small group of three or four frightened children. She was having trouble keeping them all together. They were moving about on the neighbor's grass. I went over to them.

The lady was bent to one knee and embraced two of the most frightened children in her arms. She tried to keep the other children near her with her voice. But she needed to shout at them to be heard, which only increased their anxiety. She had sweat on her brow and was panting for breath. She wanted help. She needed help. I didn't want to give it to her. It was then that I wished I remembered her name. I knew that I had heard it on several occasions. Sylvia, I thought, but was unwilling to guess and be wrong.

"Where's Dylan?" I said and kept up a visual scan of the scene.

"What do you mean? Where's Dylan?! Can't you see, we saved these," she replied quickly. And then unexpectedly: "You and that devil-boy starting fires." She said the last with such vehemence that it grabbed my head and turned me back to her. Evidently, the fire burning in the house wasn't the only one set. Her head shook and trembled from side to side as if filled with dry timber at the height of combustion. At any moment, I believed that her skull might split open and send glowing embers blasting towards me.

Just then an emergency worker came over and told us to move back and then passed on.

In our current position, we could only go toward the back or the front to get farther away. We couldn't move more to the side. The decision was quickly made that the front was no good because of the chance that a child might get lost in the crowd. The worker and I started laboring together to get the children to a new spot of greater safety. We headed our group into the neighbor's back yard. Its fence had been knocked down in the confusion.

As we moved 15 or 20 feet, Mona's backyard came more fully into view. Between giving a young boy a comforting pat on his shoulder and loudly whispering comfort to another's fright, I suddenly saw Mona. I'd only a moment to look but took in the whole scene in a flash, as you do when you unexpectedly realize that you are in danger.

Mona was in the center. Her massive form gesticulating wildly, formidably. I couldn't hear what she said even though she was, apparently, shouting. The noise of fire and now spraying then hissing water blasted it away. But the movements of the group told the whole story. Mona was surrounded by relatives, supporters and friendly neighbors that were being emotionally whipped up to the proper consistency for a mob. Like Cassandra amid the fires of Troy, Mona bemoaned her unheeded prophecies. Her entourage currently acted as a chorus, bemoaning her sorrows as refrain. But soon that the scene would turn on a target chosen by Mona. I didn't want to be it.

I looked back to the child I was attending but was really trying to hide from Mona when turning my face away. If I went any further, she would surely see me. But I couldn't leave the group without first knowing where Dylan was. I could not leave him.

"Stop!" I yelled to the lady with me. She froze for a moment. "By State Guidelines, you must tell me where all its wards are or be legally liable for their safety. Now, tell me: Where is Dylan?" I stood straight up for the last part of that.

She looked at me with disgust. "He's in there," she pointed. "In the house. . ." It was my turn to freeze. "I saw him run downstairs after. . ." she halted abruptly.

"After what?" I insisted.

"After Mona slapped him . . . you know, she was fed up . . . And . . . well, hit his face. He ran off into the basement. Later, the smoke started coming up from down there, all around. We all got out, as fast as we could. No one has seen him as far as I know. Most likely, he started it. Most likely, still down there . . ." she trailed off. My insides jumped at her last statement. You can't believe the trouble . . . if Dylan started that fire. I was already in the soup for discharging him too soon.

"Did you see him start it? Did anyone?" I insisted. "No, you didn't," I could see it in her face. "Then let's not go jumping to conclusions." I turned away. But then I saw someone pointing at me. It was Mona. A moment later, I saw her crowd turn in unison. Their expressions are forever etched into the fear centers of my brain. I needed to do something but still didn't know what.

I moved along the side of the house. Then I remembered Mona and had to get out of there. But I couldn't leave Dylan behind. I was stuck, I couldn't go forward and I couldn't retreat, indeed, I was dead in the water. It was the last place I wanted to be. I stopped abruptly, took three steps to the right then stopped again. I stood facing Mona's side wall, jumping and shouting inside myself. What was I going to do? If Dylan were downstairs, it was unthinkable. If something were to happen, I'd be finished ... my career ruined. I might even get sued. Could I be criminally liable? I was desperate as I saw my life changed in so many wrong ways.

Just then a man in a long, yellow-rubber coat burst from the house's side entrance. He ran to the front yelling, "She's going . . ." The noise of the banging side-door and the feet that rushed passed shook me from my thoughts.

Abruptly, without a plan or clear thinking, I hurried forward and grabbed the aluminum handle of the screen door and jerked it open. I put my shoulder hard to the wood door inside until it gave way. Then I went in and left the door partway open behind me. I ducked under the rancid, black smoke that backed up, then welled in the landing a moment, before it continued winding its way to the top of the building.

I wasn't thinking of anyone but myself when I entered that burning building. It wasn't the act of the hero but the confusion of a man caught in a trap made by his own cleverness.

Once inside, I stood for an impossible moment on the worn linoleum of the back landing. I was immediately dumbfounded by the absurdity of my action. I was too afraid to go farther but still more afraid to leave without Dylan.

I bent low to avoid the hot, foul air that flowed up the stairs. If he were anywhere he'd be down there. I might not have left that landing but for the sound I heard of someone approaching outside. I thought it was the fireman returning. I was embarrassed when I imagined him coming in and finding me hunched over and frozen with fear. It was this thought that finally stirred me forward.

I made a decision as I descend the stairs. I needed Dylan to survive; I wouldn't without him. I couldn't leave the house alone.

When I ran out of steps I stopped.

As in my dream, I searched for Dylan and found him by the furnace. When I reached for him he nearly knocked me out with the back of his head. I lay on the floor, almost unconscious but determined to remain awake by strength of will, if nothing else. I was struggling to save myself by way of saving Dylan.

"No!" I screamed inside at the enfolding darkness and willed myself back to my senses.

I was lying on my back, turned around and could not, at first, recognize what I was looking at. Then I realized that I was looking up into the blackened wood of the second floor. The space we occupied was a contrast of light and dark, yellow and bright orange flames and dead-black, burnt wood and smoke. There was a thin red strip that separated the two. Dylan was bathed in that intense, red light as he had been bathed in his Aunt Patti's blood on that night now long ago but still present. His image became sharp in my sight; then began to blur again. I was fading.

"No!" I shouted out loud enough to make Dylan startle. He turned to me with an exalted look of delight still glazed on his face. But his face changed quickly when I bolted upright and dove at him in a single movement. It was now or never.

The flames having reached the ceiling of the second floor and finding no easy way out, paused in their rising but then began to move out in all directions. If we didn't get out now we would be trapped forever. We had to get to the side door before the fire did or we'd be lost.

I rushed at Dylan and grabbed him up the best I could. I wrapped my arms around him and held him tight. At once I began to move across the basement, still wobbling from Dylan's blow to my head.

His face to my chest, Dylan bit down on my breast muscle two inches to the left of my nipple. His teeth sunk into my heat-stung flesh. This was his revenge. But I dared not take time to stop him. Besides, I probably deserved it. I let him bite and held my scream as the pain that it built inside me made me focus and propelled me toward our escape.

I've no idea how long it took. Part of me will stay in that basement forever. I deserved to die in that hell for all the damage I'd caused. But I didn't die. People, I'm told, don't die in hell; they remain alive to their pain and shame. So, I continued to live and brought Dylan from that pit because he didn't deserve to stay there. Even though there was no doubt he'd lit the fire, I believed that he was the only complete innocent in the whole affair. Dylan never really had a chance in life. It wouldn't have been right for him to stay there, so I kept moving. I remember, if only vaguely, trudging up the stairs with all the speed my shaking legs could muster, still holding my breath. I thought we would never make it, until we did.

And then we were out in the cold, fresh air. Life! We collapsed on the lawn ten feet from the door, a bundle of pain and anger. Whose was whose, I'm still not certain.

"We made it, Dylan. We'll be alright." I said for my own relief.

He bit down in response. Then the pain pushed me out of consciousness and oblivion embraced me.

A Good Go

I was told that rescue workers came and separated us on the lawn next to Mona's exuding ruins. I don't remember our burns being tended or lungs treated but our wounds were neatly field-dressed by the time our senses came around. The workers, whose names I'll never know, had treated and quickly tented us in loose, white gauze by the time we rolled into the hospital's emergency room. I can't recall the sporadic flashing lights but our pictures made the local papers the next day. I still have copies though I'm not sure why. But I do know the exact moment that I saw Sharon and Dan Blanchard in the hospital. It was as I rolled on a gurney along the long, terrazzo'd corridor from emergency to radiology.

Without delay I called out, "Sharon" and again, "Sharon! Wait!" This last phrase I addressed to my attendant. Effective and self-assured, Sharon reacted in her typical manner. Almost as if a vision, she appeared immediately near. The clearness of her being there struck my senses and roused me from my stupor.

You see, Sharon Blanchard and her husband, Dan, happened to be legends at the Crossings. Clearly they were the best of the best foster parents that the agency contracted with. I'd been privileged to work with them on various cases. And we worked well together.

If I believed in providence, I'd be obliged to say that it was evident in Dylan's story here. What was the chance that I'd run into them at that precise moment, when I needed them the most?

The strength of the moment's impact on me was immediate. My head cleared, time slowed to a comfortable pace and I began feeling a rhythm in the flow of my perceptions. "Sharon, is everyone alright? How are the kids?" I asked, oddly out of context with my back on a gurney.

"Yes," she replied. "We're just here for a follow-up down the hall. But . . . what happened to you? Are you alright?"

"Not important, I'm fine. I'll tell you later." I refocused her onto what was most important to me, "Do you have any open space at your house?"

"Just a temporary spot," she intoned inquisitively. "We might get one back from medical soon. Why? What's up?"

"I've someone for you. You've got to take him."

"Why?"

"Because this one can be saved," I replied on instinct. But as I heard my words, I knew that they were exactly the right words for Sharon.

I conserved my energies and listened to her think for a moment. She asked several questions in fast report, "What's his name? Why is it critical? What condition is he in?" But I was too tired and about to swoon again.

"Can you take him?" I asked.

She turned to her husband who nodded and then turned back to me, "Yes, I think we can. Do we have a day or two?"

"He'll be in the hospital a couple of days, could be more." It was hard to stay focused. Now knowing that I had a new placement for Dylan, I let myself drift. And what a placement it was, the Blanchard home! When Dylan was discharged from in-patient he wouldn't go to a group home. I smiled. He had a NEW placement and with the best of the best foster-parents in the system, no less.

This meant that Dylan would soon be getting an abundance of social services to help him along his developmental way. The Blanchard's weren't rookies; they knew how to make phone calls and ask the right questions. They weren't political like Mona but neither were they naive. They had a more scientific and dedicated approach to fostering. It also meant that I could write behavior plans that would be followed by Sharon's helpers. Dylan would be in a house prepared for children with special needs.

The Blanchard home was far less cluttered than Mona's. Unlike Mona, they didn't need a pile of treasures to feel secure. The Blanchard home was already child-proofed and a child friendly environment. Sharon's house could also provide one-to-one care from time to time. A person could be with Dylan all the time as he transitioned into the home.

In both structure and impression, the Blanchard home was as much like a well-adjusted, nuclear family as possible within the Child Protection Agency. I was pleased to know that Dylan had found a new home, maybe the best one yet.

It wasn't the disastrous step down I thought it'd be but a step up into a home that really would meet his needs. Dylan's past could start to heal. I took a deep breath and let myself resolve into that warm thought.

Besides, I've finally followed orders, I laughed to myself, I moved Dylan today. I snickered and slipped into darkness.

#

When I awoke, our fortunes had changed completely. My boss was at my bedside assuring and encouraging me. This was a shock. She was almost jolly in her presentation but close . . . too close.

66

"All's well that ends well," she repeated to herself, placing flowers on my bedside table. "We're all worried about you down at the office. You've got to take whatever time you need. I've got you on full disability, so take time . . . if you need more you can get days from the sick bank."

For some reason, she was courting my favor. I needed to know why. I had to watch and not commit myself to anything. There were motives and agendas still hidden that I needed to know before I acted. If she wanted me to "take my time", it was almost certainly in my best interest to move fast. It might be that I had some extra political influence downtown currently. If I did, she didn't want me to use it. That much was sure!

So it was probably best to get out of bed and back to work ASAP. I had to verify the real situation for myself. Besides, after reaffirming Sharon's arrangements, I was excited. I really couldn't hold myself down. The burns, cuts and contusions which traced my recent past soon disappeared and I was able to fast-talk a doctor into discharging me after "only" 48 hours without restrictions.

Even when I couldn't find my car, which a friend had left for me in the hospital's parking lot, I was elated. I didn't mind . . . at first. Happy to be moving on my own outside, I searched up one aisle then down another until I'd nearly covered the whole lot. After going around almost once, my enthusiasm had wearied.

When I found my car tucked behind a red minivan, I went home to shower quickly, change clothes and eat. But I was back at the hospital within two hours. Record time, no? I needed to see Dylan, right away, from the outside. I visited Dylan in hospital gowns for a day and a half but I now wanted to visit in street clothing to encourage him that life was still a good go. As always, he was mute but interactive. I did all the talking.

Later that day, I visited the Blanchard's in great anticipation, but fatigue caught up to me and I took a short nap on their lazy boy. Later, I woke and went home to my neglected apartment and slept a long time.

67

When I awoke, I set to work with vengeance. By the luck of the draw, Dylan's case received new life. I wasn't about to blow it through neglect of details. I was astute with the technology that social science gave me and used all the tools in my arsenal. I left no behavior plan unwritten, no insight uninterrupted and no developmental milestone unmarked.

It was great to work with Sharon again. She was a real pro and had a real heart for children. The Blanchard's were veteran parents. They had twin biological daughters 25 years ago and, after raising the girls, the Blanchard's became foster parents and nurtured several dozen children, frequently with specialized needs. They adopted their foster children who didn't return to their biological families. They'd never turned a child away in need.

Currently, one adopted child and three foster children stayed with them. State guidelines determined that Dylan filled the last open spot in the house. The Blanchard's older daughters, who didn't live at home anymore, helped care for the little ones and kept the household running.

There were many hands at work in the Blanchard home but the busiest were Sharon's. She was a dynamic pure force working through distance. She appeared ageless and, in a paradox, rose to her 5'2" stature like a giant earth-mother incarnate. She cared and tended for everyone in a way that made each feel special. She organized the household schedule for six to eight people and made it look easy, always performing with grace under pressure.

I enjoyed being in their home and, like sunshine on a winter morning, I felt immediately welcomed. I took an extra cup of their coffee. After the highly chilled circumstances at Mona's, this was a relief. Since being at the Blanchard's was like being at home, I played with all the children incessantly.

Kyle and little Nikki, both younger than Dylan by a year and then two, ran to me to continue our play whenever I arrived. Upon Dylan's arrival, the three became inseparable. Ryan, an older foster son, played with them at times but most often was busy trying their parent's collective willpower with pranks and rude behavior. Colleen was the oldest child now living at home. She was in high school and acted more like an aunt than a sibling to the younger children. Jennifer and Anna, biological twins, lived with their own families but stopped by daily bringing their children with them. This was the Blanchard home that welcomed Dylan.

While still at the hospital, Dylan delighted in playing video games, watching movies and being brought treats by smiling nurses. When I visited, he always seemed happy even though he was undergoing treatment for breathing problems. All the smoke he inhaled at the fire had given him respiratory difficulties, potentially with a long-term risk for asthma. While hospitalized, it was noted that he measured below the second percentile in both height and weight for children his age. He spoke not at all and, at some point, lost bladder control, becoming nocturnally incontinent.

Sharon and I met several times in the following days and I outlined the medical and behavioral plan Dylan would need to have in place as he made the transition. Sharon agreed they could take him and, as she signed the documents, I kept my emotions in check.

In these first days after Dylan moved in with the Blanchard's, he seemed like a child who was seeing a beautiful parade for the first time. He appeared captivated by the energetic comings and goings of this happy and noisy household. There were many new things for Dylan to experience and learn. When I stopped by to check on him, after his official move, he'd often be sitting and watching the show go by with a shy, almost imperceptible smile.

Frequently, Sharon hugged Dylan and he loved to follow her around the house watching everything she did, at first staying at a safe distance. He tried to keep out of her sight and she pretended not to notice him at times, letting him become familiar with the routines of the household, the other children and her presence. Sharon understood how important games were in connecting with Dylan. She sometimes pretended to sneak up and surprise him but always with gentleness and an elaborate, slow set-up.

Dylan wouldn't actually be startled or frightened. He was delighted.

The fact that Dylan was enthralled with Sharon was significant because it might indicate that he was still able to emotionally bond. Children with a history like Dylan's often suffer from Reactive Attachment Disorder and are unable to connect with others. Many psychiatrists think this is how killers, torturers and various psychopaths are made. But Dylan seemed to have survived with this part of his humanity intact. The connection he established with Sharon could expand and grow, allowing him to trust and forgive.

Early in those days, Sharon understood it was best not to focus on Dylan too much. In an instant, he could be over stimulated and then become a bundle of jumbled, reactive nerves. When something triggered him, he became extremely hyperactive, running nonstop up and down the stairs and through the rooms of the house. He crackled like static electricity jumping from couch to chair, snapping from shadow to sun, running and turning in mid-air. Sharon videotaped him to show the professionals at The Crossings just what she and Dan were dealing with, but no one had any ideas beyond the treatment plan we were already working with.

When these spells of hyperactivity overcame Dylan, his energy seemed maniacally boundless. Eventually, long after he tired everyone else out, he began to settle down and then would stay almost catatonic for periods of time, hiding. Sometimes late at night, he'd drag a blanket into the living room and fall into a fitful sleep stretched out along a hidden baseboard. Sharon would find him like that during regular nightly rounds. She'd gently lift him into bed and stay with him until he drifted into a deeper sleep.

If Dylan was even mildly confronted by one of the children, Dan or Colleen, he'd curl up behind a piece of furniture, most often between the heavy drapes covering the large plate-glass window in the living room and the oversized green couch. Dylan would twist into a ball with his head tucked into the center of his skinny body. His back was curled outward, his vertebrae extending like the teeth of a chain saw blade. He could stay like

70

that for a long time, well defended and nothing could coax him out.

Dan and Sharon insisted on letting Dylan come back to the family on his own after he'd processed things in his own way. I agreed with this approach. We all thought there was nothing to be gained by using overly intrusive interventions right now. Dylan would show us how to support his healing process if we paid careful attention to what triggered his distress and what soothed his traumatized psyche.

As the weeks zipped by, Dylan's burns healed and he seemed to feel better all around. I suggested that Sharon use Dylan's interest in being near her as a positive reinforcement. That way we could shape his behaviors and improve them. When it was time to eat, Sharon made sure there was an empty spot near her. Dylan would slide in and begin to awkwardly use his fork and spoon. He wasn't eating enough to gain weight yet, but at least he was eating and at the table with the family.

In the evening, if Dylan took his bath without a fuss, Sharon let him pick a story and help turn pages to show Kyle and Nikki. On pages long with words, Dylan would lean into Sharon and begin to breathe deep. With these simple rituals and after only a few months, Dylan re-learned how to eat, bathe and go to bed routinely.

#

It was an odd phenomenon but after Dylan adjusted to life in the Blanchard family his activity level in the late afternoon to early evening hours didn't decrease but grew even more pronounced.

"He's like the wind," Sharon said as Dylan tore by us on his circuit through the house.

"Are you sure he's only one boy? It feels like we've got a house full of Dylans," Dan retorted and we all laughed.

71

But the Blanchard's persevered hoping for the behavioral breakthroughs that'd make living less problematic. In the meantime, Dylan giggled at the antics of Kyle and Nikki and at the cartoons the three of them watched together. He laughed when Colleen danced to her music, trying to look cool. As the Blanchard's understood the magic of a child's laughter; they noted what a wonderful sound it was, especially since surviving what Dylan had experienced.

This gave them all hope.

#

It was an honor to be invited by the Blanchard's to attend the sealing of the adoption orders for Kyle and Nikki. It was a big day for the family and, if they thought of their case manager as an adjunct member of the family, that was fine with me. We all dressed up for the hearing before the judge at the county court building. I asked to drive Dylan so I could have a little private time with him. I watched him in the rear-view mirror. He was strapped into his booster seat in the back of my car, looking up and out the window. He seemed sad and withdrawn. Did he feel left out?

At his age, Dylan could hardly be expected to understand the legal ramifications involved in the differences between foster care and a legal adoption. The rules about these distinctions seemed Byzantine even to me. For instance, one of the Crossing's official policies was that foster parents weren't supposed to get emotionally tied to their foster children. They were asked to create a relationship structured to be temporary. It was a hard policy to measure, enforce or even understand in terms of how it actually played out in the million details of family life.

What would be a warning signal that you were becoming too attached? How could you intentionally treat one child differently than others in the home simply because they fell into the category of a foster child rather than an adopted one? When a child's wounds came clearly from a lack of attachment, how could you consciously work to maintain distance?

If Dylan felt left out, it was because in a legal and literal sense, he was. But the adoption of Kyle and Nikki was still a windfall for him. He couldn't appreciate the difference but the change in their legal status made a permanent space available for Dylan as a foster child at the Blanchard home. He could stay indefinitely. And eventually they might even adopt him too.

As Dylan and I walked around the fountain in front of the county court building, lagging a bit behind the rest, I tried to explain his new status, but it was a stupid thing to do. I should never have said anything but he looked too sad. Dylan suddenly stepped into a flower bed in front of the court house and picked a bloom from its stem. He held it cupped carefully in both hands.

When we all stood together in the judge's chamber, the older twins, Colleen and Ryan were all clearly as moved. Sharon and Dan stood with the two small children up in front of Judge Williams. In his long black robe, he bent forward at the waist to meet the children at eye level and read the order that made it all official. Along with the essentials, Judge Williams added a warm dose of pomp and circumstance. We all cheered and hugged and then Dylan shyly offered his torn flower to Sharon.

Later, as a celebratory lunch got underway, she pressed it in a large picture book as a keepsake of that fine day.

The symbolic significance of accepting Dylan's flower made Sharon wonder about the no emotional ties policy of The Crossings. We talked and shared our mutual confusion concerning this rule. We couldn't think of how to explain the need for distance to Dylan. He had no-one. How could we turn him away or stifle his affection? Therefore, we decided to do nothing. That may've been a mistake.

#

With Dylan's adaptive behavior improving, we took on the challenge of encouraging him to speak. He was enrolled in Head-Start. In addition, a speech teacher from special education came to the house once a week to work with him. I also saw him twice a week to try to help increase his expressive language.

73

Once, we were playing Mutant Teenage Ninja Turtles downstairs. It was his favorite game. He transformed me into the wise, old sewer-rat who taught him karate before sending him off to fight the forces of evil. Kyle and Nikki threw themselves into being enthusiastic turtles as well. As their orchestrated chaos and many rescue missions unfolded, I tried to get Dylan to speak to me, the rat, or to his turtle companions.

I flopped onto a beanbag in the play room, stretching my legs across the carpet, watching Dylan, who was still accosting some criminal element in a corner. Kyle and Nikki were slowing down and had moved to a T.V. in the corner. Then I remembered the first game I'd played with him and I extended the thumb and pinky of my right hand, holding them to my ear and mouth, respectively. With the index finger of my other hand, I dialed a number in mid-air, humming a tone for each button. This caught Dylan's attention. He looked my way. "Hello, hello? Is Dylan there? Hello?"

Dylan giggled in recognition. He remembered the game too. He stuck out his thumb and little finger, putting them to his head.

"Dylan? Are you there?" I asked, but he only continued to hold his finger phone to his ear and smile dumbly. "Dylan, I can't hear you. You need to talk on the phone." He met my eyes. "I'm pretty sure if you say the first word all the other words will come out too. I know you have them all lined up in your head. I can see them there." I waited.

But he didn't interrupt the silence and I didn't want him to feel he'd failed. I continued, "Perhaps I'll call you later."

I hung up my hand with a smile but Dylan recognized the disappointment under my assurance that everything was fine. I could see it in his bright green eyes.

He pointed to my hand and shook his head. When I didn't understand, he reached out and took my hand, pushing it up against my head.

He jumped, nodding yes with his entire body when I turned my hand back into a phone. He held up his forefinger and thumb forming the shape of a circle, as if to say okay and offer me encouragement. Then he pointed to me and held up his hand to his ear again.

I understood. "I'll call you," I said.

He repeated his two previous hand signs and pointed to himself. Then he gestured to me.

I spoke for him again. "You'll call me."

He then pushed his fingers to his lips to form an exaggerated smile.

"I'll call you. You'll call me. And we'll both be happy."

He clapped.

I was thrilled.

Dylan had communicated in whole sentences.

"Yes," I said, "you are close to chatting away like a little chick-a-dee!" I offered him in a bad imitation of W. C. Fields. Dylan zipped away before I could say, "I'm so proud of you!"

In the end, Dylan spoke to Sharon first, only a couple of weeks following our phone game. She was icing a cake in celebration of his birthday. As she finished, with a flourish to surprise him, she pulled a bright plastic Ninja Turtle figure out of the kitchen drawer to her left.

Dylan exclaimed in excitement, "The turtles are coming to my party!"

Then it was everyone else's turn to drop their jaws. Dylan said a full sentence. What more could be celebrated in one day. They all laughed, jumped around and then blew up balloons. What a happy way in which to turn four.

While the Weak Ones Fade

I was wrong in being exceedingly confident that we had Dylan on the right track. But in the "best of the best" of foster care at the Blanchard's, the expected norm was growth. What a way to turn four! Dylan hit the ground running, directly on his way to five.

He began to talk a lot but he talked too fast, mumbled, and misarticulated. Only two people could understand him completely, Sharon and Sis. They seemed to get his every word. In a friendly piece of advice, Sharon told me to "hear it as a whole". I tried for hours, until both Dylan and I were worn out in my frustrations. When I gave up, Dylan said nothing but evacuated the area quickly, while I sat and shook a disgruntled forehead. After weeks of trying, I still couldn't make much out of his noises. In time, my not "understanding" him became a sore spot for both of us.

I just didn't have the ear for it. I'd never been good at understanding mumbling. In elementary school, I was the kid who never ever got a whispered secret, even when said right into my ear. Consequently kids stopped passing them to me. They knew that I'd end up questioning loudly, "What! What did you say?" thereby giving the whole thing away.

I had a history. I simply could not understand misarticulated speech; that didn't make me less of a social worker, did it? But when I couldn't make out what Dylan was saying, he acted as if he had somehow hurt me. He began to be a stranger to me before we actually, officially, said goodbye.

However, the tableau at the Blanchard's at this time was quite sweet. Hence, I accepted the fact that Dylan was growing closer to Sharon and away from me. I thought, at that time, that he would stay with her indefinitely. I had visions that she'd raise him to healthy manhood. I saw it in my head and it felt so sure.

#

At Sharon's, Dylan grew in many ways, not just in language, although this was the most noticeable and dramatically improved area. His mood was generally good and stable, except for short periods of time each evening (and these were still manageable). His growth on the height and weight charts started to gain a percentage point or two. Everything was going and growing in the right direction. His social behavior and self-help skills, "activities of daily living" to be precise, were picking up at a very rapid pace.

Academically, he was way behind other children his age but I figured he would catch up once we dealt with his basic survival and emotional needs. Later, he would catch up on reading, 'riting, and 'rithmetic. All we had to do was to keep him stable and sailing the current, positive course. If we did, Dylan had a chance. He would be able to salvage a normal life from the wreckage of his infancy and young childhood. He would be a survivor. All that had happened before now would seem like the far off rumble of yesterday's bad dreams. It would fade away as he woke to a reconstructed life.

Dylan was four and then turned four-and-a-half before I knew it. During this period of dynamic equilibrium, I began to spend less time with the Blanchard's and re-focused on other cases. My boss was acting up again. I missed the day that Dylan turned "and-a-half" but managed to play with him the day after.

That was when I actually became aware of his rapid growth. On the Blanchard's front lawn, I took him by the hands and spun him in the air. I spun him until he was nearly horizontal to the ground. His eyes squeezed against the speed, his mouth popped open in laughter. I saw a blurred Kyle and Nikki dancing and skipping in a larger circle around us, shouting in unison, "Me next, me next!" After spinning them all, I led them in a duck line to the small park down the street. When I got back, I went into Sharon's kitchen to get my traditional cup of coffee. I sat awhile nested between my thoughts and my paperwork, two distinctly different messes.

Sharon and Colleen came in discussing something intently and, uncharacteristically, didn't acknowledge me. It occurred to me then that I was no longer in touch with this family. I had lost its pulse. This was good as it allowed me to continue the job I had to do. I wanted to be closer to Dylan but was restrained by our situation and my position.

Everything was currently stable except that Dylan still showed an increase in hyperactivity. Sharon continued to video him and took the tapes to the psychiatrist who diagnosed him with an Attention Deficit Hyperactivity Disorder (ADHD) and placed him on Ritalin. This was a problem as the drug made matters much worse. Dylan took it for only three days but that was enough. It increased his activity to a level higher than I thought possible. I don't believe that Dylan slept at all in those three days.

Luckily, Dylan's mornings were filled with school-type activities. Even on his worst days, he did better with these structures. But as the day wore on and people around Dylan began slowing down, he typically switched over to his energy afterburners. And, day after day, his energy level increased. Each boost was greater than the boost the day before. These upsurges in action weren't without consequences to the entire family. They were no longer simply harmless periods of hide-and-seek or cute, crazy times. They were more than just noisy and annoying disruptions. Soon there was a cost in physical destruction to the house, to its people and to their possessions.

Dylan began to break things in these up-states, which now resembled frenzies. Among numerous things, he broke two of Colleen's favorite glass figurines. They were her oldest treasures, given to her by her birth father with a story from Sharon. Dylan busted them up while he was trashing her bedroom "looking for something". This began significant animosity between the two.

Dylan's energy crested for the first time only a day after he turned four and a half and only shortly before Sharon and Dan's 25th anniversary. Dylan's energy was like a great wave. It had been building up, day by day, driven by the sympathetic surges of excited reinforcement from his new family, pushed forward by the steady rhythmic beating of morning, noon, and night. It ebbed in the morning and rose in the afternoon. Dylan's wave had grown to a point where its force could no longer stay in a unified fluid form. Nature required that it fall apart and come crashing down in chaos and exhaustion.

A crash was inevitable but it was unfortunate that it came two days before the big anniversary. Dan had made elaborate plans to celebrate. Dan was more than nervous. He wanted everything to be perfect for his quarter century bride. But when Dylan's hyperactivity reached its crescendo, it gave no thought to Dan's plans. When the limit of Dylan's furious state achieved its ultimate, he just fell, dead to the world. "Just like a sack of potatoes," Sharon said later.

The minute before, Dylan was agitating Ryan. He held something belonging to his foster brother. He held it tightly and tucked near to his chest as he climbed the living room furniture. He escaped Ryan's stronger but slower grasp. Sharon and Dan couldn't see what Dylan gripped as they turned toward the squabble. By the time they got within twenty feet, Dylan had climbed high onto the back of the couch and halfway up a bookcase, high above the older boy. He shouted in what was now known to be his war-cry, "No, No, No, No!" He was still moving. His momentum was still carrying him up when "the light just went out". He swallowed the last "No!" and then his face went completely blank.

For a moment, Dylan just fluttered at the pinnacle, seeming to pause in mid-air. Dan tried to get to him but only managed to close the distance a little by the time Dylan was free falling. During the six or seven foot drop to the floor, Dan was able to reach out and push him in the direction of the couch. It was all he could manage. Dylan bounced off the taunt cushions of the new couch, arched up again and fell back to the ground. He landed with a thud, his skull banging the stiff-napped carpet.

The sound of Dylan hitting the floor echoed like one strong stroke on a kettle drum. It bounced off the back of Dan's mind as he awoke to a new thought: "All he does is stir things up." Dan hadn't known that he'd felt that way but, really, all Dylan brought was constant turmoil.

Dan stood stunned over the prone boy's body and knew that Dylan did not belong. And from that time on, Dan's home was no longer Dylan's completely. Dan began to treat and think of Dylan in a temporary manner. And for the first time, it became possible for the Blanchard's to turn away a child in need.

An ambulance soon came and hurried Dylan to the hospital where he underwent an E.E.G., blood work, and various other clinically diagnostic procedures. Everything came back negative, even the E.E.G. showed no abnormal brainwaves. This definitively ruled out seizure activity.

Sharon stayed with Dylan every moment. She went along as the emergency med-tech's strapped him onto a gurney and tucked it tightly into the back of the ambulance. She stayed with him as they raced through the city streets, staying by his side straight through to the next morning when Dan lifted him out of the sliding, side door of the family's van, back home again. She never left.

Dylan was released the next morning after the short overnight observation. His stay at the hospital was a Medicaid Special: short, both in and out. Dylan was administered a large dose of Haldol and sent back home before Dan went out to work the next morning.

Sharon received two prescriptions and a referral for a follow-up psychiatric consult. She was worn out and not yet relieved. No one could explain to her satisfaction why Dylan had blacked out. And without knowing why, she was left to wonder when it might happen again; with Dylan that was dangerous.

Dylan slept all that day.

The family was collectively grateful for this break. After work, Dan and the older members of the family sat around the kitchen table with large mugs of coffee. The girls had come over to help. Again and again, they asked themselves what made Dylan fall. Sharon was relieved that it wasn't caused by some neurological thing that might deteriorate like an exotic, genetic disease or something. Colleen was just happy that nothing was broken. Dan was mostly quiet until Sharon started talking about changing schedules on Friday to cover a one-to-one for Dylan. Then he perked up quickly and jumped in.

"We don't have to change everything around because of one falling spell, do we?" Dan asked, mostly of Sharon. "It was just one episode. We have no idea that it will happen again." He looked from one surprised face to another at the table and then added, "The doctors gave him medication and you said he was sleeping soundly."

Friday night was the big night and Dan was fighting to keep his anniversary surprise for Sharon. The plans were made at great expense in time and money. He'd worked everything out to the tiniest detail. Dan knew what "changing schedules" meant, and everything could be screwed up if they were changed.

After a quiet moment, Sharon said, "I suppose we shouldn't disrupt things too much ..." and paused another moment, this time wondering. Slowly, she started to think aloud. Like a train on a single track, her thoughts built up momentum as a compromise came to her, "Especially if he does have another fit," Sharon said "and this turns into a long term thing. We will all have to be well rested and ready to work then. Okay, I think Dan is right, let's not do anything right now ... just keep a watch. If everyone pays a little more attention to him, then that will be enough for now."

Dan breathed.

Later, Sharon and the older girls went upstairs leaving Dan and Colleen at the table.

After he was sure that they were gone, Dan reminded Colleen of her promise to baby-sit Friday night. It was her gift to him. Dan extricated this promise earlier from Colleen.

Colleen tilted her head and scrunched up her nose on its left side. "Awe, Dad, I don't know," she said. "What if he goes nuts again and no one can stop him. I don't want to be in charge."

"No, no." Dan reached out across the wood table top and touched the back of her hand. "You promised. Everything depends on you … that's your gift."

Colleen looked doubtful and, slowly, shook her head.

Dan continued, "Come on, you got to. The plans depend on you. He won't be a problem. He'll probably still be sleeping." He nudged her hand. "You got to, for me."

Colleen finally relented, reaffirming her promise.

Dan scooted out of the kitchen satisfied that he'd avoided simultaneous disasters on two fronts. It was what he called a chess solution, an elegant move. He saved his plans and was now eager to make more. He invited Sharon's parents and brother and sisters and his brothers and all his friends and hers too. Everyone knew about the big party except Sharon. Their family and friends were loyal and would show-up. I was glad that I was included too.

Dan had scheduled three celebrations for Sharon; first, a surprise party with a ton of family and friends, then dinner in a swanky restaurant and, finally, a night in the grand suite at the fanciest, downtown hotel. In addition, he planned a trip for her to a neighboring health spa in the morning. Dan was to go home to do her chores. She would be household drudgery free for the entire day. "Domestic-less bliss", she would exclaim when Dan announced the plans with a toast at 4:35 p.m. on the nose that Friday.

It was a sweet plan and one well worth saving, Dan thought to himself over and over again.

#

With Haldol pumping through his veins, Dylan slept all that night and most of the next morning. When he awoke, his foster family was well rested. He, however, was groggy. He remembered nothing of the last two days. The last thing he recalled was playing Lego's with Kyle downstairs. The doctor at the emergency room expected this and had forewarned Sharon. So she did not panic. The doctor also told her to be vigilant of any possible side effects from the medication. There was a laundry list of things, from tics, a swollen tongue to stupor, nausea, and vertigo. Some of the side effects were transient, others were potentially permanent.

By the early afternoon, Dylan was starting to come around. While everyone was facilitating some part of "Dan's Plans" and watching how all played their parts in the unfolding ruse, Dylan was waking up. Later that afternoon, as Sharon was pulled from the house by another charade thought up by "devious Dan", Dylan began to hit his stride. When a busy throng streamed in to set up the party, Dylan became over-wound.

He ran about and hid under the folding tables with their over-hanging table cloths. Crepe paper and balloons dangled from the ceiling out of the reach of the children, which made them their favorite targets. The kids jumped and jumped. Dylan almost hit a low hanging blue balloon. Nikki jumped from the couch but still couldn't get as close as Dylan. When Dylan saw her efforts, he thought it a good idea and jumped on the couch. He began bouncing to achieve good altitude then launched out towards his prize. Kyle lined up behind him for a go. But when these efforts failed, Dylan found things to throw at the dangling streamers and balloons.

The other children, now numbering five under the age of five, were caught in their assault on the decorations and were exiled to the playroom downstairs where they were ordered to stay until Sharon came back. The five were left to themselves but their numbers grew as more people arrived for Sharon's party. Although there was a constant low rumble of adult voices above, the noises that filtered down to Dylan were mainly bumps and thumps on the floor. Its pattern was a random and non-rhythmic pounding of multiple feet. Occasionally, then more often, Dylan recognized some familiar footsteps in the uproar above the growing tumult below. The first footsteps he recognized were Colleen's.

It was Colleen who had ordered the gang of five to the basement. With his ears, Dylan followed Colleen's footsteps. He traced her movements on the floor above. Then he wondered, "Why could she be up there and he had to stay downstairs?" He lived here too. He thought about this and he began to dislike Colleen more than ever. Anger and frustration built up in Dylan for an hour.

He let her movements and rhythms soak into his mind until he seemed able to bounce ahead of her and guess where she would go next. For instance, at one time she was working at the kitchen sink. He could hear the water flow. "Next she will go to the refrigerator," he guessed in his thoughts. "She'll stop, and then go to the table." And she did. For nearly another quarter-hour, he went ahead of her in his mind, growing in confidence and anger.

Then, suddenly, he was ready. He moved across the playroom through the increasingly agitated children. Some began to cry. Mothers were drawn down from above by the large wailing from little ones. Dylan slipped passed the wild milieu and snuck to the top of the stairs. He knelt and squatted with his hip brushing sideways into the second step from the top, leaned in with his left shoulder, inched open the kitchen door, and peeked out.

The house had become a single entity growing in excitement. Everywhere everyone anticipated Sharon and Dan on their twenty-fifth anniversary. At first, when Dylan opened the kitchen door, all he could see was a living tangle of swinging shinbones and flapping feet like an ambling mass of jungle vines. If he were to escape the dungeon below, he would need to employ all his Ninja Turtle prowess to pass through the forest above. He settled his stomach and set his eyes. When he felt the readiness within him rise, he slipped into the beat of the heavier feet and, without brushing a vine, swung back and forth through the living forest as if he were flying instead of gliding along the floor. When he reached the quiet carpet of the dining room, Dylan knew that he had made it. He had escaped.

He slid under the formal oak table centered in the middle of the dust-settled room and lay on his stomach. He hid in its shadow and peered back into the vibrant light from the kitchen. His eyes squinted, momentarily adjusting. A growing, distant commotion still flowed up from the basement. He watched as more mothers went down to find their particular weepers. He watched the rapid motions of people arranging food and beverages. Then he saw the working groups dissolve into conversations, to jokes and jibes and finally laughter as all was ready.

But he didn't see me watching him from behind the table, back near the window. I'd arrived at the pre-party about forty minutes earlier having been given the instructions to arrive early in order not to "spoil the surprise". Since I had no part in the preparations and knew only a few people there, barely a few, I found myself shifting, lamely from spot to spot as workers buzzed and droned about me inevitably needing to work in the exact place where I stood. I gave them a quick nod, said a small "sorry", and stepped aside. I was displaced like this numerous times. When I grew tired and foolish from making weak apologies for occupying space, I withdrew from the growing crowd into the relative tranquility of the dining room.

I wanted to say something to Dylan but I didn't want to startle him. So I remained quiet. Then I thought how awkward it would be if I said, 'hello' and then didn't understand what he said back. Would I just pretend to understand him, smile, and nod? In my current melancholic mood I didn't think that I could carry that off. So I decided that it was probably better to watch him unnoticed. Besides, I'd always enjoyed the opportunity to watch Dylan without him knowing.

Dylan seemed to be viewing the scene as a whole, not focusing on one thing or the other. His gaze remained steadily concentrated on the middle of the room, floating neither this way nor that. He rested his chin on his paired knuckles and then suddenly perked up. His interest had been grabbed by something in the kitchen. I looked and saw Colleen taking a relish platter from the white refrigerator and carry it to the serving counter that separated the kitchen from the breakfast nook by the big bay window. She removed the plastic film that sealed the tray tight, while laughing inconsequentially at something her

85

uncle had said. Unconsciously, she adjusted a stack of pink and blue cocktail napkins and then left the kitchen for the living room.

Dylan came up into a squat as she disappeared, hidden by the kitchen crowd. He shot forward into the kitchen and slipped through, only stopping a moment at the snack counter to grab a bowl of pretzels and mess up the napkin display. Then he followed Colleen into the belly of the beast, bursting silently into the living mass of the farther room. Then he too was lost to my view. This was the last I saw of him that night although later I gathered several reports from party people in order to piece the whole story together.

Still not knowing that I'd been his silent witness, he left me. I thought that I should follow but couldn't bring myself to enter the accumulation of the bio-mass, which now pulsed further on. I stayed where I was, wondering about the pretzels that Dylan had snatched. Eventually, I found out how he used them.

Evidently, he followed Colleen and caught up to her in the large family room. He saw that she was headed towards the stairs. Accordingly, he circled around some people, cutting a more direct route to her destination in order that he might get there first. In effect, he cut her off at the pass. He waited a second for her between some large bodies and a decorated card table until she was nearly upon him. Then he took a pretzel and tossed it in front of her footfall, directing it precisely, timing it succinctly. Her stocking foot came down on it with a crunch that stopped her dead in her tracks. She pulled back a step and looked down at the crumbs and the broken pieces that littered the carpet and clung to the fuzzy, white threads of her sock. She did not know who'd dropped the pretzel but was disappointed that someone would leave it after all her cleaning. She shook her head from side to side and pursed up her lips.

Dylan enjoyed this effect so he repeated the ploy again when, after picking up the debris, she moved on towards the far end of the room. He slipped away from her when she bent to clean. Hiding further on, he was able to deploy another pretzel to greet her before she went upstairs. This time, when the pretzel broke, a sharp piece poked into the soft skin of her foot's arch. An irritating pain shot up past her ankle. She said, "Ow!" and pulled up dead in her tracks. Someone asked if she was alright but she paid no attention to anything but the fragments on her foot and the floor. What ticked her off , more than the pain or her surprise, was her annoyance at her house being messed up by some inconsiderate guest. She had worked all day to prepare the house. In her mind, one pretzel was a sloppy accident, two were a trashing. She turned to the man who had asked if she needed help and looked close to see if he were holding any snacks. But he was holding only a drink,. She bent to clean the carpet again and then straightened herself to move on.

But again, Dylan had gone around to the front and slipped undetected up the stairs. He left a trail of pretzels neatly placed in line. He laid a path for her to follow and follow it she did. Her hands swooped down like Hansel's birds and snatched up every crumb. Her temperature rose as she ascended the stairs. The trail led her, inexorably, to the door of her own bedroom. She stopped picking up pretzels and marched straight through the door.

The door burst open from her weight hitting it. And Dylan popped into view in the center of the yellow shag carpet. He was smashing pretzels in the bowl, tossing the crumbs high into the air over his shoulders and calling, "Smash Colleen! Smash Colleen's stuff!"

She was enraged. Huge, she stood with hands on her hips, elbows bent to the side, feet set in wide stance and ready to pounce this way or that. Clearly, her posture said that she was ready to "smash" Dylan. She was at least twice as tall as he and two and a half times his weight and every ounce of her wanted to get every little bit of that brat back.

But, "You ...!" was all she got to say because as she leaned forward to snatch him, Dylan dashed through her legs, a direction she was not prepared to follow immediately, and then down stairs.

He escaped her.

It seems that for the better part of that night Dylan was able to conduct a successful gorilla war on Colleen. He lay in wait inflicting pain, confusion, and mayhem on her time after time.

One time, he snuck up on her from under a clothed table and poured fruit punch over her foot. She fumed when she had to change socks. Because of this she wasn't there for Sharon and Dan's 'Bon Voyage' speech as they cast off on their sea of love. She couldn't believe she missed the big send off. She still fumes over that. And it was all Dylan's fault.

So by the time all the friends and acquaintances had slipped out, when the party was folded but not yet put away, and the last of the loyal cleaners had departed for home, Colleen had had enough. She could take no more. So, she determined that while she couldn't actually catch him, she could keep him confined. She could close down his access to all floors of the house if she blocked the upstairs staircase and let nothing pass. He would get bored up there. She could control him by confining and ignoring him. To her that was a manageable victory in their war of attrition. If she could hold to her plan, she would prevail.

"I'm off duty," she said to herself, resolute now that she found the way to shut down Dylan's games. "I don't have to watch you anymore," she continued by talking up to the apparent darkness above her. But she knew he was listening.

Because she "owned the stairs", she could move up and down them at will. This extended her sphere of influence, for without leaving her post for long, she was able to build a look out station at the top of the stairs and a home base at the bottom. She had turned the TV on and turned it in the direction of her home base. Also, she placed a blanket and two of her favorite pillows there for her comfort. She made a few quick dashes into the family room to get a book and fetch the remote control. But it was only when she was convinced that everyone upstairs was asleep, that she felt safe enough to scurry to the kitchen for a snack and a drink.

However, when she came back, she found Dylan doing a dance with her favorite pillow. Dan called it the "Bootie Dance". It was a step that Dylan and Kyle made up to annoy Nikki when she wouldn't play their way. It definitely included a move of disrespect, which included rubbing his derriere on Colleen's pillow in a particularly disgusting fashion. Colleen was already mad at a distance but when she saw that he was using her favorite pillow case on which to rub his rear-end, she became enraged. In response, he stuck out his face, his nose wagging high in the air, gloating. The sarcasm and smirk dripped off him and sloshed all over the strategy she'd developed.

This was the final insult. She had nothing left. She charged him.

But he was not going to back off. He stopped what he was doing, dropped his head low, ramming into her oncoming form.

Dylan took the worst of the collision as they collapsed backwards onto the lower stairs. But he managed to slip to the side just enough to begin wiggling away from underneath Colleen the moment they hit carpet. Colleen quickly realized that she was about to lose her advantage. She reached out and snatched at him, quickly grabbing his wrist before he was able to extricate himself from her sphere of immediate influence. She knew that she'd lost control of all but his wrist. Consequently, she focused all her malice on it. She squeezed it with both hands and all her might. She was determined to hold on until the end.

But Dylan was just as determined to get out. He wiggled and squirmed in different directions and in opposite turns. For a few minutes, they were a mass of writhing, angry flesh, convulsing at the bottom of the stairs. The writhing only subsided as they grew tired. Colleen still held on to Dylan's wrist. She held the side of his hand for leverage. Dylan twisted his whole body in order to apply an equivalent to Colleen's two fisted force. Both their efforts were being focused on and applied to Dylan's wrist.

It hurt so she figured he'd have to stop soon.

It hurt but he wouldn't stop.

Just when they began to grow weary and watch their efforts fail, their eyes met. Their tired and distorted faces came around and lined up eye-to-eye. Each, seeing the other, maddened and encouraged them again. They could win if they tried just a little bit harder. The anger had burnt low and become weak and weary, little more than smoke and ash. But now it was kindled afresh. So, hot breath tanned cheeks and foreheads once more.

Animosity burnt like Cain's rage. One last push, simultaneously applied, did the trick. Dylan's wrist snapped in a spiral half way up to his elbow.

Colleen felt it all, every crack, every breach. For a moment she was uncertain that it was not her own wrist that had been broken. In some odd way, they had begun to feel as one. But that sensation, as slow as it was, passed. They reacted quite differently to the injury.

Colleen felt the snap of his bones pass into her hands and vibrate inside her arms all the way up to her shoulders. Its pulse continued down her back, sinking into and softening her bowels. The feeling as a whole made her uncontrollably nauseous and stole any strength left in her. Her eyes widened, her breath held back, her expression froze in shock, as if saying 'what have I done?'

Dylan, however, never blinked. Even as the burning in his wrist exploded into red pain blasting up his arm, the muscles of his face stayed still. The pain gave him focus; it brought clarity that was a source of energy and power, not weakness. The pain, like enraged rock, scorched all paths that led away from his heart, sweeping along any pretense of civilized life. It all turned to ash and ruined any hope for all but the most primitive of his thoughts.

Dylan had no more concerns. The pain tolerated no obstacle in its way. It destroyed Dylan's life at the Blanchard's but it never overwhelmed his mind. He hated Colleen and that was all that mattered. He hated her. Accordingly, he smiled in her face and dangled his broken arm as if he were returning a borrowed piece of jewelry, a tangled, golden chain.

Her resistance collapsed, broken by the curving of his lips. Bent over, she fled the scene.

He thought he'd won.

Not With a Bang But a Whimper

The doctors at the hospital submitted their reports to protective services; it was a spiral fracture consistent with abuse. Legal wheels began to turn.

By chance, the whole scene between Colleen and Dylan had been recorded on the video camera Sharon had been using to tape his episodes. Playing with it earlier, the children had turned it on and left it running. The scene was dark and the action a blur so the features were unclear. Nonetheless, it was all there. Temporarily, things looked bad for Colleen.

However, it didn't take long for Colleen's pleading glances to have an effect on Dan. She caught his eye at every turn and produced an expression guaranteed to grab any father's heart. It was a cross between helpless pleading "save-your-young" and "I-did-what-you-wanted-even-though-I-didn't-want-to-do-it-so-keep-your-bargain" kind of look. These pleadings from Colleen struck straight home with Dan. He felt guilty about forcing her to watch Dylan and even angrier that he hadn't been able to take his wife away from the house for one evening without something like this happening. So Colleen and Dan had a common foe, namely Dylan.

It was probably good that when Dylan first met up with Dan, he wore a cast too big for his small stature, held large and high out in front. It acted like a big blasted sign around his neck saying, Don't touch me, I'm broken! It caused Dan to halt and hold his anger back but, at the same time, it infuriated him even more. Dan decided to support Colleen no matter what.

That morning, the first full day of their twenty-sixth year together, Dan told Sharon that Dylan must move out. Lit by the bright daylight that baked the breakfast nook, their coffee mugs steamed on the table in front of them. Ten to twelve a.m. this time of year, the big, bay window in the kitchen acted as a sideways greenhouse, bouncing intense light around the cubby. The yellow of the nook burst out in response. Dan and Sharon sat, mostly quiet, together, shocked and squinting.

Dan re-stated, "We can't keep him, Hun! He's got to go. If the State pulls our license, we'll lose our other children. I can't let that happen. You know the State. To them it'll be either him or her to blame. Fault will be found. It wouldn't be fair to blame Colleen. You know how much he's badgered her. And you know we've been overly fair to him. You know I've never said no to you. But this time I need say it and mean it: No! He can't stay here."

They came to my office that afternoon and made their request formal. I was in a meeting with another family's child when Rose poked her head into the small conference room around the corner from the bullpen. I asked her to have the Blanchard's wait at my desk for a minute. I'd meet them there.

I'd every intention to talk them out of transferring Dylan. I'd done it many times with other children and foster providers. It mostly required schmoozing, a little glib and a little gloss.

A few minutes later, I was still preparing my approach when I sat down, triangulating them across my "desk-mess". I reviewed it again in my head before I finalized the details to my approach: I'll let them vent a bit, sympathize but not too much and then positively redirect them to the child from a different vantage point. Out with the bad . . . in with the good; I'd saved many a placement for the agency by such a psychological slight-of-hand.

But Dan didn't blink. He sat unmoved. He was a big and quiet man and I'd obviously mistaken his acquiescence to Sharon as a weakness. I now saw I'd been wrong in that.

"Damn," this was the first time I ever swore in front of a foster-family. "Don't do this!" I pleaded finally. "Don't do this to him. It isn't fair . . . not right . . ." the last I added weakly to

93

Sharon.

She was clearly devastated. I could barely stand to look at her that day. She was pale, like she hadn't slept. Her eyes were red-glazed and her look far off. She was clearly anguished by the circumstances and grieved for more than one of her children. I saw this as I spoke to her. So, I appealed directly to her, only weakly. She was too brittle to play psychological games with.

#

I never went back inside the Blanchard's home again. I never placed another child there. As for Dylan, as for the contacts I had with him that next month, we met at the Crossings. For Dylan, the focus had shifted from the home to the agency. There were many procedures to be conducted and many reports to be filed.

Because Dan's request wasn't revoked, Dylan was on the State's clock again. By regulation he had to be transferred out of the Blanchard home within thirty days. This was a disaster I couldn't avoid.

It all happened too fast. Dylan was out of our hands before we had the chance to fix him. We would have been successful. If we could only have held on, we'd have made him all better. But he was slippery. He was in and out of our reach before we could finish grasping.

By regulation, finding a new placement for Dylan wasn't a choice but a duty. The whole system needed to work for the good of the majority and not for just one little boy. Since he was going to be moved under these particular circumstances, his Medicaid status was officially upgraded to "specialized care" and was given therapy twice a week at The Crossings.

I made it a point to see Dylan in the playroom while he waited for his appointments and also talked to Sharon in the lounge where foster parents waited. She was obviously emotionally distraught about Dylan, but was reconciled to his moving out.

When I saw Sharon two weeks after Dylan's arm was broken, she still looked devastated. Clearly, she was anxious.

Colleen and the rest of the Blanchard's were okay. The investigator from Child Protective Services had interviewed everyone. The video recording hadn't been mentioned and, in the end, Dylan was identified as the person responsible. In the report there was also a hint that his psychiatrist may've been under medicating him. The investigator filed her report and that was that. I read it later. There would be no legal action taken against the Blanchard's.

But because of this finding, no obvious placements were available for Dylan. There were always openings at the Long House, but I wasn't willing to consider that option yet. The Long House was one of the last stops for children who were completely abandoned. If you went to the Long House, an orphanage, you were sure to end up in the MEER book, a list of children who, in the eyes of the state, were least likely to be adopted or placed in foster care again.

The MEER book was compiled monthly with an update sent out to the surrounding counties. It served as a catalog of the State's most available and hard-to-place wards. The state was willing to offer valuable special incentives to the counties whose agencies placed MEER children in adoptive homes. I was cynical about these incentives since the chances were slim-to-none that any county would actually collect on them.

Being sent to the Long House and being placed in MEER were two of the three dead ends in the child protection agency. The last was long-term psychiatric hospitalization. I had helped Dylan avoid that future, thus far, but there was no guarantee he wouldn't end up institutionalized. He was certainly headed straight for MEER and the Long House unless I could find him a home. Except for a few severely and multiply impaired children, those who were nearly in a permanent vegetative state, no one on my caseload had come to that fate. Almost any home would be better than none, but I had to find it soon.

But Sharon wasn't so worried about Dylan's ultimate placement, which was clearly my problem, as much as she was about his current emotional state. No one had actually come out and told Dylan he was moving yet, but with his keen ability to read the situation, Sharon believed Dylan knew something was up. No doubt there'd been many small changes in the family since his return from the hospital, little things meaning big shifts were underway.

Dylan must've felt he was no longer a close family member but was more like an unwanted guest who'd stayed past his welcome. He was now a nuisance to be endured for a bit longer.

The sixteen months Dylan had lived with the Blanchard's had been the best part of his life, the most normal experience he'd ever known. He seemed to be mourning what he was about to lose. I could tell he truly loved everyone in the family, even Colleen. Accordingly, he grieved deeply.

He was sullen and withdrawn. This had the effect of eliminating his hyperactivity almost completely, as well as flattening his mood and emotions. His lips were locked into a small thin line and, most of the time, he stared ahead blankly. He stopped playing with the younger children and became watchful and suspicious. It was uncertain just how much he ate but surely it wasn't enough.

In Sharon's view, things were as hard as they could be. She found Dylan's withdrawal harder to handle than his previous frenetic behavior. She was pained by the change in how they all viewed him. But how could she blame her husband or children for what they felt? Outwardly their behavior toward Dylan remained kind but he was on his way out and the feeling of separation permeated the household.

In her desperation to help Dylan prepare for the transition to come, Sharon told him a story she made up about turtles. It was about the sadness of saying goodbye and was also meant to encourage him about the future. I was supportive of this approach, thinking that perhaps the story would help Dylan cope.

It was a risky move because Sharon had no real idea that an adoptive home would be found. But in the end, I think it helped more than it hurt. Sharon had always enjoyed telling stories to all the kids but in the last few months she and Dylan shared a special story time together. The stories she told him were always about some little boy character who struggled with his life like Dylan. It had become Dylan's custom to ask Sharon to name the character 'Deda'.

The "Three Fine Turtles" was about a mother and father turtle that had no little turtle of their own. They wanted to find a special turtle to raise. They searched high and low and, after looking for a long time and having many adventures, they finally met a little turtle named Deda. Immediately, they knew he was just the right turtle for their family and so they took him home.

Sharon said Dylan didn't like this story. He protested that it wasn't a real story about Deda. Sharon insisted it was real and the turtles took little Deda home with them and the three of them lived happily ever after. For the first time, Dylan ran away from her.

Dylan's therapist believed it was time for Dylan to know what was going to happen and explained the transfer process to him during a session. Apparently, Dylan didn't ask any questions, didn't cry and didn't seem angry. When I asked Sharon how Dylan had been at home that night, she reported he'd gone straight to bed with his clothes on and dropped into a deep sleep without saying a word.

#

In my mind, the only hope for Dylan was to be adopted. He wouldn't continue to survive in the foster system. If he were to make a lateral move at this time, from "the best of the best" of foster care homes to some other, he would most likely be landing in a spot not conducive to better mental health, something perhaps worse than Mona's place.

In fact, when experienced foster parents learn that a child was moving laterally from his first foster placement, they automatically assumed that there was a problem with the child. But if the child were moved twice, most foster parents wouldn't even consider them. Only those foster parents who were either desperate or stashing cash in a big way would take a 'third timer'.

So, needless to say, third placements were in the poorer quality homes. No, I needed to find Dylan a home, a real home, a permanent one, which wasn't especially likely. How many couples were trying to adopt a specialized care, five year old, nearly feral boy? Not many that I knew.

But I searched high and low anyway. I made calls, scanned data-bases, opened many, musty file folders looking for any chance of hope. I talked to anyone and called everyone I could think of and then started calling them all again. I made myself annoying to the point that my co-workers wanted to avoid me altogether. That was the best part of my plan, after a while they'd do anything to get away from me. I had made myself a negative reinforcer. They'd all be on the lookout for what I wanted, just to keep me away.

I stopped people in the halls away from their desks. "Hey did you come up with any?" I asked them just for a reminder. The water fountains were no safe place to hide from my 'P's for D' campaign (that's "Parents for Dylan"). The workers at the Crossings were on high alert. In the next week and a half, I schmoozed, campaigned and spun my way in quest of two fine and willing parents. But the field was bare and pickings were slim to none.

Before I started my campaign, part of me knew that what I was doing had a low probability of success. But now that I was getting nowhere and Dylan's deadline was approaching fast, I truly began to believe that I'd screwed things up.

Four days before time ran out, I sat down at my desk and felt completely defeated. I wasn't going to make it. Dylan wasn't, I mean if I'd no place for him to go, my boss would undoubtedly remove me from Dylan's case and shift him to the Long House herself. I had to act by the twenty-ninth day. I sat at my desk and actually buried my face in both palms; my elbows spread wide, resting hard on the desk. Just then I heard Rick come in and sit next to me. I heard him twist my way and pause.

"Not now, Rick! I'm thinking." I droned.

"Don't you think you'd better do more than think?" he retorted sarcastically. "What I hear is your ass is dried grass and the boss is flicking her Bic."

"Big chuckle, hey Rick?" I lifted my head and focused on the tropical fish of my screen saver. For a moment I let my mind swim along with those fish until I found a dark place, a hole in the bright coral in which to hide. Darkness, I needed to forget everything about that day before I finished living it. "I need to

98

forget about it all until I find something else." I mumbled making no sense even to myself.

"Oh, you're feeling sorry for yourself too. You're not making this any fun at all." Rick intoned smugly.

"You're having fun?" I snapped back and sat, glaring at him.

"Don't get too mad. I'm about to save that grass ass of yours." He laughed.

"What do you mean? What are you talking about?" I stammered.

"I got a couple of names and a phone number you might like."

"No. . ." I elongated the vowel.

"You think not? I guess you aren't interested then." He moved to get up.

"No, wait! I believe you." I was willing to beg. But if he was blowing smoke, I'd kill him later. "Tell me!"

"Jacob and Martha Ebonite at (313) 555-1812; they might be talked into adopting. I've been saving their number as rain insurance but I guess I'm going to waste it on you. Who'd of thought!" he shook his head.

"Hey," I stumbled and then said, "I appreciate it and take back everything I ever said about you." I tried to laugh casually and reached out a hand to him, which he didn't take. He just looked at it and continued.

"I'm doing it for the kid, not you . . . They're already licensed for foster care but aren't on the active list. They were trained about a year ago. I placed two kids with them: a boy and, then later, a girl. The girl was short-term, fairly primitive and was in and out before they got too involved. However, the boy was a different story. He was a cute little guy, curly hair and outgoing. It looked like he was going to stay.

"He and his sibs had been in care for over two and a half

99

years. Even his therapist started to prepare the little boy to be adopted. They were happy and the boy was starting to adjust. But then a judge, who was in a bad mood, shipped the boy and all his siblings back to his mother, who, by the way, was still smoking crack. The Judge sent the whole lot of them back.

"The Ebonite's took this hard. A week afterwards they called in and took their names off our foster parent list. But it's on file that they wouldn't be 'opposed to adopting kids,' they said, but they needed 'something permanent' because it hurt too much to give up children.

"I've kept them in mind in the past months. I think with time and the right approach they would adopt. So, I kept them on the back burner, simmering. Here's their file." He plopped a thin manila folder on my desk calendar and leaned way back in his chair.

I was in shock; I felt many things at once. Easily, I can name three I felt passionately. First, I was relieved from the feeling of being targeted by circumstance; second, I was happy for Dylan; and third, I was angry at Rick because he'd made me wait for this information. He could've told me last week, I thought. He must've really enjoyed watching me squirm, knowing that he'd swoop in and save me at the last moment. So, now I was mad at the one person I'd no right to be mad at, at all. Damn! I hate when that happens.

I called the prospective parents right away. I talked to Martha Ebonite. She didn't know what to make of me at first so she put her husband, Jacob, on the phone. He was formal and stiffer than I'd hoped he'd be, but he was polite and set up a time to talk at the Crossings the next day.

When I got off the line, I said thank you again to Rick and meant it more. Then I just sat a long time and felt the relief. I hadn't realized how much tension I'd been carrying around until I let it go. I hunched my back slowly. I closed my eyes and felt soft warmth inside. I imagined it as gold light. I rested, body and mind, until I felt as if I were filled with the light.

I let it all go. I unloaded my mind, discarding memory after memory. I watched as mental pictures of Dylan and our recent ordeal fluttered and fell away one by one. Backwards I watched all the way to that day when I played an unwanted game of hide-and-seek. I went all the way back and then came forward again.

Knowing him and working for Dylan had been the most intense part of my professional career. In fact, I now saw that it was my biggest failure. As I went over everything in my mind, I really couldn't believe all that had gone wrong. Frankly, I'd made almost every mistake in the book. Almost every mistake that is, but not the worst one, I thought in an attempt to justify myself. I didn't make the mistake of not caring. I cared about Dylan. If I could've taken him home I would have. But I could not; the law wouldn't allow me. I had to do for him what I could in my role as a Case Manager.

Really, when you look at it, it seemed that my biggest mistakes were associated with the times I cared the most. It seems paradoxical but I felt that it was true: the system and its limitations mustn't allow for the saving of someone as damaged as Dylan. Perhaps it was set that no matter how much we did, we were fated to lose him anyway, like destiny or something. The more effort we put into saving and curing him, the more damage we did, only rushing the inevitable.

I'm not certain exactly what it means but it felt like the system had been damaged in Dylan's case. "All the king's horses and all the king's men" had failed in the best of its best circumstances. You see, if all of us in this social service system, from administrator to home worker to foster sibling, cared for Dylan with all of our might; we would still not have been able to heal him. The system had been broken and I could no longer believe in it completely. And it wasn't the parts of the system but the system as a whole that failed him. It is true that some parts were better for Dylan than others but why place blame? It does no good. Even when the best pieces were in place, it failed because, in the end, it let him go. It couldn't hold on tight enough.

It's been said that time flows like a river; if so, Dylan was born during the spring rains in a season of floods. From the first, he was swept along, a victim of fate, powerless to set his own direction but feeling the consequences of every encounter along his way: the crack of Bruce's backhand, the yelp of Mona's anger, or the massiveness of Dan's decision. Along the river's course, he rushed.

101

At some narrow places, we held onto the shore and reached out to grasp him. But the current was too strong or we were too weak because he whooshed by, out of our grasp. Patti and Sharon held him for a bit and if his heart were ever to survive, it is due to their loving touches. But in the end all was hopeless against Dylan's raging river. We couldn't hold onto him.

It is in the nature of systems; the limitations that bring failure in some cases are the same that lead to success in others. Does that mean that the system has failed? This system, our system, has done many good things for children. That much is certain to anyone who has spent even a day in our office. But is that good enough? Have the many small goods outweighed Dylan's one big bad?

It was a tough philosophical question and any philosophy was too much for me right then. I let it go. Our system is limited like all phenomena. Like fate, history, reality, etc., its nature simply needs to be endured. Ultimately, no matter how well intended a governmental agency is, it can't fix a child. All its efforts seem vacant and typically end not with a bang but a whimper. When wounds are deeply dealt, they don't mend, leading to destruction.

This must've been the case with Dylan and perhaps my biggest mistake was in not recognizing that sooner. Perhaps, if I'd been more distant, more professional, I would've recognized it earlier. And then I wouldn't have gone down into that psychological, black-hole with him. No, I wouldn't have tried to save him and I would've served him better. I would've been better at my job.

"It isn't my job to tap the children with a magic wand," I thought to myself. "It is my job to treat them well and place them with others who can hold them temporarily safe until their families can resume their care."

I was a case manager; my job was to manage and coordinate the services delivered to children in foster care. I was to get them connected with the service they needed, not give it to them directly. The majority of my work should be in consultation. Technically, I shouldn't be responsible for any direct service at all. If I do more than that, am I then more responsible than if I'd chosen to do less? Haven't I still met my obligations?

I decided that if the best thing I could be for Dylan was a case manager, then I should manage to get him a home. That was the standard for success. Anything less, I determined, would be a failure.

After much contemplation, I was focused again and decided that I would do whatever I needed to do to get the Ebonite's to adopt Dylan.

I thought of little else in the next 24 hours. I hate to admit it but I even practiced my approach to the Ebonite's in front of my mirror at home; something I hadn't done in quite a while. I went over different strategies and approaches in my mind. I held mock debates taking both sides of the issues. Before I left work, I called and talked to a friend in the licensing department to see if I could get any more information on the prospective parents.

She confirmed what Rick had said and shared with me the impressions she got of them during their training. She said that they were straight laced and not embarrassed to openly admit that they were born again. This wasn't good. They were probably rigid in their approach to children and flexibility was needed in working with Dylan.

I was ready to get Dylan a home but must admit that my nerves were frazzled by the time Rose buzzed my desk and let me know that the Ebonite's had arrived. They were a little early, a good sign of interest, I hoped.

I smiled and extended a warm hand as introductions were made. Martha Ebonite seemed uneasy and uncertain as she took it. Jacob eyed me with suspicion. I directed them to a small conference room and we moved through the narrow hall. I'd reserved conference room B because it'd been a lucky room for me in the past.

Martha was a bit shorter than her husband. She had a rosy complexion and wore no makeup. Her pretty oval face was framed with brown curls. Her shoulders were held high and tight. She was sturdy looking, but not overweight. Jacob's face seemed to indicate he was a bit older. Worry lines were evident at the corners of his eyes and mouth. He was robust and muscular. His hair, cut conservatively, had a light touch of gray at the temples. He was clean shaven.

As we sat across from each other at the well-worn table in the battered room, I felt the weight of the boy's future squarely on my back.

Typically, I like to have prospective parents initiate conversation. It's easier to influence people if you can sense where they are coming from and read their signals. In this case, these two were obviously so wary of the agency, I knew that I needed to warm them up and lead the discussion. I must get them to adopt Dylan but they needed nothing from me. I had to proceed carefully.

"Thank you for coming today," I dove in. "I understand you were foster parents with our agency for a time and you didn't have a good experience."

"That's correct," Jacob said flatly.

"I'm sorry you had a hard time. But I was told you had a special way with children." I was fishing for feedback but when neither responded I continued. "Our conversation today will impact the life of an extraordinary boy. So first, I need to know if you still have any ill will toward our agency as this is important. I'd like to get everything out in the open to start."

Their expressions told me I'd hit a nerve. I continued, "I don't want what happened before to taint what I'd like to propose to you today. I've worked here a long time and I've seen mistakes by inexperienced case workers and by judges who don't have a clue about what is best for a particular child. It breaks my heart when that happens, but we also do have success sometimes and I think I've got a child who could be a wonderful fit for you."

"We're angry," Martha spoke up and Jacob reached over to gently hold his wife's knee.

"Please tell me what happened," I asked with sincerity, hoping my demeanor suggested they could trust me.

"When Martha and I chose to become foster parents, our decision was based on many things. We'd been married for five

104

years and weren't exactly young when we married . . . well, if babies were going to come, they'd have." Here he took a breath and looked at Martha to make sure she felt comfortable with this disclosure.

"It'd have been nice to have a baby of our own." Martha continued but Jacob interrupted.

"I understand that many people who can't conceive want to adopt babies so they can imprint themselves on a newborn. But we felt strongly God had something else in mind for us and that we could serve a child who was older."

"Why did you stop trying through the agency?" I inquired.

"We just couldn't take it," Jacob said. "When we lost Owen after we knew he was so right for us, it was just too messed up to go on."

"I think a terrible mistake was made in your case," I commiserated. "He never should've been taken from you." At this, Martha's eyes filled with tears and she turned her head slightly away.

"There was no excuse for it." Jacob snarled.

"It's clear you loved him very much." At this they both seemed to relax into their sadness and to soften. They needed this acknowledgement. They had wanted to have their pain heard by the system that'd hurt them.

"It happened suddenly. Owen had to be turned over immediately once the judge signed the order," Jacob expanded.

"It was the hardest day of my life. I could never go through that again." Martha added. They had now opened up to me and showed me the way to give Dylan a shot. Their worst fear was losing another child. Dylan couldn't afford to lose again either. That was a shared circumstance that could bring the three of them together.

The Ebonite's were also somewhat older than typical adoptive parents who, in turn, are usually older than fertile people having children. Biological parents characteristically have their first children before the end of their twenties, adoptive parents a little later; after they find out they really can't have their own children.

The Ebonite's were in their late thirties. Time was running out for them as well. Some agencies don't even permit adoptions after the age of forty. Had they been deeply hurt partially because the loss of Owen represented a last chance for them? If so, this was another possible point of connection with Dylan, who was also at the end of the line. The Ebonite's may not have been the best possible parents for Dylan, but I wouldn't have time to find out.

I couldn't let them take him on any sort of trial basis because he was so difficult there was a great likelihood they wouldn't want to keep him. I needed to lock in the adoption and make it happen with them seeing as little as possible. The three of them could work out the details later.

Another selling point was I could streamline Dylan's adoption so they could have as little to do with the agency as possible. They weren't going to trust us again. But that worked to Dylan's benefit too. I talked about Dylan at length, providing selective information and linking his plight to theirs. I made them feel that they and Dylan both had a mutual adversary, namely, The Crossings. Bonding through alliance, that's what I was attempting.

"He's such a wonderful little boy, but because of ridiculous bureaucratic pressures, he's been bounced around in ways that haven't served him. When I found you, it just clicked. I felt strongly a sense of divine involvement that you were the right parents for Dylan." I regretted this crass manipulation. But on the other hand, I was only stretching the truth a bit. If they took him, it'd be nothing short of a miracle.

"What'll happen to Dylan if we don't take him?" Martha asked.

"He'll end up in an orphanage." I explained what life was like in the facility and what a dead end it'd be for Dylan, noting that in using his name Martha had already begun to connect with him.

"What's wrong with him?" Jacob asked the most difficult question. I had to be careful.

"Nothing . . . nothing that's his fault. He just needs the right parents to take care of him, loving, decent parents who can make him theirs from the beginning. As soon as that happens he'll be fine."

They looked into each other's' eyes, clearly trying to read the reaction of the other. Jacob spoke next, "Do his parents have any rights to see him or to get him back for any reason?"

"He was abandoned at five months of age." I said. "The rights of his birth parents were legally terminated years ago. If you're interested in adopting Dylan, you'll need to be willing, soon, to take the adoption through to completion. You'll have to be sure. Dylan doesn't need any more false hopes. He'll have to know he belongs with you forever. And I can assure you, there's no chance he'll be taken from you and you'll deal only with this agency briefly."

"You can guarantee there'll be no interference?" Jacob demanded.

"I can bring our director in this minute to put it in writing if you want," I said emphatically.

"We'd have to meet Dylan and spend time with him before we agree."

I can arrange the first meeting as early as tomorrow." I was almost certain they'd adopt Dylan if there were no major meltdowns during their visit with him. Martha and Jacob asked to be left alone in the conference room to talk together for a while and if what they were doing behind that closed door was praying, I was certainly doing my own sort of praying on the other side of it.

The Ebonite's agreed to meet Dylan and then decide how they felt about a possible adoption. I decided none of us would tell Dylan why he was meeting the Ebonite's and I set the first meeting for the playroom at The Crossings because it was a place Dylan enjoyed and where he likely would feel comfortable.

The next afternoon, Sharon brought Dylan into the room and left him with us. I introduced Dylan as casually as I could. He stood looking at Martha and Jacob for a long thoughtful moment. And then he slowly moved to a sand table in the far corner, and stood tracing the fingertips of his right hand gently on the surface of the sand.

I tried to engage the Ebonite's in small talk. Martha responded politely and Jacob walked over to Dylan and smiled shyly. He knelt a respectful distance from Dylan and started to play with the cars and plastic figures in the sandbox.

When Martha and I had finished chatting about their home and neighborhood, she joined Jacob and Dylan at the sandbox and I sat alone at a table filling out forms. From where I watched, Dylan looked as if he could be a plausible physical combination of Jacob and Martha. Did they notice how closely his coloring matched their own and how easily they looked like a family to the outside world?

I hoped the dynamic between them was working and they'd start running the idea of being Dylan's parents through their imaginations. Thank God, Dylan was calm and well behaved. The meeting lasted nearly an hour and ended without incident.

We arranged the next meeting to take place at the Blanchard house. As I stayed with Dylan in the playroom, I watched out the window as Jacob and Martha walked to their car. They were holding hands and although my view of her face was partially obscured by the branch of a tree, I thought I saw Martha smile.

#

Dylan's deadline at the Blanchard's was up in a couple of days but with the Ebonite's signature on an "Intention to Adopt" form, I easily got permission for an extension signed by Sharon. I set up visitations at the Blanchard's. Then before we knew, all the paperwork had been processed and moving day had arrived.

I got there late. I had a problem at another home. I arrived just in time to see Dylan off. He was walking to the car. It was strange and it happened way too quickly.

Mr. and Mrs. Ebonite were smiling. Mr. Ebonite was carrying Dylan's things in a small cardboard box. Mrs. Ebonite held Dylan's hand in anticipation of crossing the street. Dylan looked completely blank. He walked stiff like the Ebonite's. His mouth formed a tight horizontal line under his nose. Just before stepping into the street from the curb, Dylan stopped without warning, slipped his hand from Mrs. Ebonite's and ran over to Kyle who was on my side of the small group that crowded onto the front walk to wave Dylan goodbye.

Dylan ran right up to Kyle and handed him a small toy turtle. "Be careful . . . don't get taken away", he said and looked at me; his eyes dark and his expression blank and then back to Kyle. "You'll see." He added and then went back to Mrs. Ebonite waiting by the road. They crossed the street to where Mr. Ebonite waited by his car with its doors held open. The Blanchard's waved goodbye and shouted to him but Dylan's face never changed. It was the empty expression of loss.

This was the last I saw of him: the back of his head through the rear window as the Ebonite's drove away. It was just as expressive as the rest of him had been that last day.

Just like that he was gone. It didn't take more than a minute or two. Colleen was the first to leave the group and go inside. The little ones were next, drifting off in different directions. Soon everyone was gone but Sharon.

She looked at me, shook her head and went inside. I went to my car and sat there for a while, wondering what was to happen to Dylan.

Had I stayed at The Crossings I might've known what happened next but just after Dylan moved in with the Ebonite's, I had an opportunity for a promotion if I was willing to relocate to another state. The position needed to be filled immediately and I was qualified, so I left for what I hoped would be greener pastures and lost touch with the boy whose case had been so challenging.

I could've stayed in communication with Maggie to hear updates, but the truth was I felt guilty about Dylan and preferred to imagine that all was well, rather than face a possible darker truth that things might've gone terribly wrong for him once again.

I simply wasn't brave enough to find out where life took him and this cowardice haunted me for the next decade.

End of Book 1

Between Father and Farther

A man in a brown overcoat walks toward the high school. He nods to a student straggling onto the last bus waiting by the curb. The man's head stays down against the rain as his feet slap modest, gray arcs across cold puddles. He approaches the glass and metal doors. He is Adam McDonnell, Dylan's old caseworker. He's come from farther off to see. Ten years and some months have passed since Dylan left the Blanchard's home and Adam comes to ask the questions that he must. He seeks the answers he's been afraid to find.

Jacob Ebonite, Dylan's father, is in his classroom bent over a pile of American History quizzes. His desk sits in the southeast corner of the darkened room. He pretends to concentrate.

A few minutes ago, Jacob turned out the lights except the small, grading lamp on his desk. After the last bell rang, he'd dimmed the room so he could watch the progress of the early winter storm outside. Apprehensive, he wondered about the possibility of ice as the sun sank low. He should go home before it froze.

As the busses rolled away in many directions, Jacob saw Adam approaching the building from his second story classroom window facing west. Although Jacob had hardly known Adam, through the long distance, rain and time, he recognized him at once. There was something in the approaching gait that still remained the same even when drenched in weariness. Jacob moved to his desk and began to work.

The classroom, where Jacob lectures five days a week, is decorated with pictures, maps and drawings of events from America's history. A Civil War theme stands prominent on a wall and a half. These displays cover three walls in multicolored splatters. The fourth wall consists of a large window overlooking Harding Avenue.

Jacob doesn't look up when the wet figure shadows the room from the bright, hall light.

"What can I help you with?" Jacob asks still without lifting his head.

"I'm looking for room 207, American History," Adam replies reading from a scrap of paper.

"You've found it," Jacob states flatly.

"Mr. Ebonite?"

"Again, you've arrived." Jacob looks up, clearly annoyed. "What can I do for you?"

"I'm Adam MacDonald. I don't know if you'll remember."

"I remember . . . remember you," Jacob says and looks back down.

"Well . . . I hope I haven't come at a bad time." Adam glances to the papers on the desk. "Are you busy?"

"I'm correcting papers. That's about as busy as my busy work gets. But come in, it's safe . . . I'm not armed," Jacob adds full of sarcasm.

Adam enters the room and mills about the students' desks at its center. "I hope you don't mind I stopped by without calling. But

113

. . ." Adam nods to the weather outside. "I think I may've already been punished . . . you know . . . with a slogging."

"How bad could it be?" Jacob brushes Adam off, continuing to look down.

"Listen . . . you seem like you aren't in the mood for this . . . perhaps my interruption isn't timely. Perhaps I can come by again later." Adam indicates the door, "But I just thought I'd stop by . . . and see you . . . to let you know that I . . . um . . . I wanted to know how everything turned out for Dylan and you. I just wanted to see how Dylan did. I've been concerned for a long time." Adam's voice trails off.

"Dylan did . . .?"

"Yes, how he did after the adoption? Is he okay? How has he been doing with you? Hell, I don't even know if he's still with you or . . . even alive, for that matter." Adam throws this out nervously then waits before continuing. "Please, tell me what happened to him."

Jacob snorts, "Tell you? Tell you what . . . And why?"

"Tell me he's okay." Adam continues. "That it turned out alright for him. I need to know . . ."

Jacob shakes his head incredulously, "And why? Why now after all this time?" Jacob pauses but Adam looks puzzled. "Jesus, look at you. I don't understand you at all! You fall out of sight . . ." Jacob slaps his hand on his desk then snaps his finger. "Gone for ten years and then just pop up out of the freezing rain, desperate to know what happened. Lord . . . our social service agencies at work!"

Jacob watches Adam lost in the matrix of desks that make up his room. He needed schooling. Jacob continued, "Who do you think you are? Do you think Dylan wonders what happened to you? What right do you have to know? Go away, we don't owe you anything!"

114

"Not even basic news? Can't you even give me that?" Adam's eyebrows arch pathetically high on his forehead.

"Not even . . ." Jacob looks away. "But I'll give you this . . . you sure got nerve. Showing up here after what you did? Amazing!"

"What? What did I do?" frustrated Adam jumps at this.

"Oh, you know alright."

"What?" Adam insists. "I got you the child you wanted. I did that . . ."

"And . . .?" Jacob says his eyes steadfastly fixed.

"I got you a child. How did I owe you anything more than that? You and your wife came to our agency seeking an adoption. You came to us . . . you got one . . . so what? You got what you were looking for."

"And?"

"And what? I did my job . . . for Dylan."

Jacob stands before replying, "You lied . . . for Dylan?"

"What? I didn't lie."

Jacob moves to the center of the room, "You lied! You didn't tell the truth. Lord, don't you even know the difference between the truth and a lie?"

"Of course I do." Adam walks toward the exit muttering "Just get off it. If you don't want to tell me, I can't make you." Then Adam stops as if he's thought of something new. He continues talking with his back to Jacob, "Listen . . . it's just that I can't get the look of Dylan . . . the last time I saw him . . . I can't get the look out of my head. He looked lost and . . . small. I've always wanted to know he's alright."

115

Adam turns back to Jacob taking several pleading steps. "Hey . . . if I did something to you, lied or something you say . . . let it go. I really don't know what it was, but . . . hell . . . I'll say I'm sorry if that's what you're after. I am you know."

Adam looks back toward the open door. "I really didn't mean to intrude and I don't think you owe me anything. It's just . . . Dylan's case wasn't my best work. There was something about him that really took me out of my game. I made mistakes but ..." Adam pauses then continues to Jacob. "I got him from a really bad place and gave him to you. If you're still his father, you must admit I made that connection. For that, if for nothing else, can't you give me just a couple of minutes of your time?"

"You really don't remember?"

"I don't," Adam states sincerely.

"I asked you flat out what was wrong . . . what was with Dylan. And what did you tell me?"

"I don't remember what I said . . . what?"

"Nothing."

"Nothing?"

"That's right." Jacob sneers, "You said nothing at all. You just repeated that he was a good boy."

"Then I didn't lie . . . I said nothing."

"You call that the truth?"

"I call that not lying."

Incredulous, Jacob explodes, "It was the heart of deception. Do you know what that not-lie cost us? What it cost Dylan? We'd no idea . . . were completely unprepared. At first he seemed to be okay, like you said . . . or . . ." adding exaggerated sarcasm "unlike what you didn't say. We didn't get the records for eight or nine months. By then, everything was a mess. We had to put the adoption on hold. Everything was screwed up because we didn't know what to expect. We didn't know what to do to make him stop."

"I admit I didn't tell you everything," Adam begins to defend himself.

"You didn't tell us everything?"

"That's right . . . not everything," Adam insists.

"Not his lack of toilet training and bed wetting?"

"Yes, not everything."

"Not his uncontrollable fits?"

"Yes, not that, too."

"Or . . . his language problems and learning disabilities? Or his outbursts of uncontrollable rage or his bouts of fear and then paralyzed states . . . his hiding in stores and breaking everything!" Jacob shakes his head, "Did it just slip your mind?"

"It wasn't as important as . . ." Adam starts to explain but Jacob doesn't let him finish.

"Unimportant, huh? All the times, I thought I'd see you again and be telling you what I thought, all the many times, I played this conversation out . . . And I never thought of that. Ha, not important . . . well, well . . . I'm speechless," Jacob sputters to silence.

"Listen," Adam says after a pause, "I wasn't trying to lie to you. You need to think where Dylan was that day, the day we met . . . you remember?" Adam pauses, looks around and sits on a nearby desk. With down turned hands, he motions Jacob to sit down, calm down. "Besides you agreed to take Dylan, forever.

You know I told you that much, I know I did. I told you it'd have to be forever, you couldn't take him for a little bit or go part way. He needed nothing less. You needed to be almost certain you'd go all the way before you met him, remember? And you agreed on the little knowledge you had to do that. . . no stopping . . . yes?"

"I remember. I remember." Jacob snorts.

"But you said you stopped the adoption? Are you telling me all the truth?"

Jacob glares.

Adam continues, "And you still don't get it, you don't understand where Dylan was that day, where he stood legally. At the brink! I can tell you that Dylan was on the precipice. One wrong slip and over he'd go. Yes, there were mistakes in his case. Yes, I said there were.

"So the only way . . . the only possible chance he had was to get a permanent family in a few days or go to hell! That was the choice for me . . . for him. A couple of days! Do you have any idea how difficult it is to place a five year old boy in an adoptive family? I'll tell you, it's damn hard . . . Oh, man!

"And more, his having specialized needs! You were it, don't you understand? You were it for Dylan, you or nothing else. That was the choice . . . so yes, I made a decision: You were better, whoever you were, better than the dead end the State had for him. You were it and I was going to make it happen. So, I didn't tell you everything. I couldn't take the chance." Adam concludes.

"If we were his only hope, why didn't you prepare us for what was to come?"

"I still wouldn't have taken the chance; it was his only one." Adam's lower lip protrudes slightly in resolve.

"Chance?" Jacob winces. "You took no chance. We're the ones who took a chance. Dylan had no choice, but we did. We chose to take him. We came to you with our eyes and arms

118

open. We were going to take him no matter what. How many problems he had didn't matter. We just needed to know what they were, so we could be ready. But we weren't ready . . . because of you . . . You never took a chance, who are you kidding?"

"How could I've known you'd still have taken him?" Adam states assured. "I admire you for your commitments and all but there are limits to everything."

"No," Jacob corrects in his most corrective teacher voice. "Not admire. You should've respected it and let us know what we were in for. You held back information that took away our choice."

"I couldn't let you know. No way . . ." to Adam it was a settled fact.

"You knew you were manipulating us!"

"I felt in his case that the ends justified it." Adam crosses his arms.

"That was your decision?" Jacob leans back.

"Yes, I made the call." Adam nods, satisfied.

"What gave you the right to move us around like pawns on a chessboard or troop flags on a map?" Jacob points to the wall farther left of Adam. "Who said you could do that?"

"Dylan gave me that right. I acted in his interest, not yours . . ." Adam meets Jacob's glare unwaveringly. "I was charged by the State to look out after him, not you. Sometimes the ends justify the getting there . . ."

"No," Jacob refutes flatly.

"I guess we'll want to agree to disagree. I've seen too much to believe otherwise." Belatedly, Adam looks to the wall left of him and then continues, "So, that was that. By my best estimate it was a gamble . . . for Dylan . . . but it must've paid off, huh?"

"Nothing personal . . . business, just business, huh? Is that it?" Jacob sits. "Did it ever occur to you that we became a family? We were joined when we adopted him . . . like a marriage; we became one . . . one family, not two. It doesn't get any more personal than that. You make a vow. It changes everything."

It was now Adam's turn to snort, "Vows? I was supposed to make this kind of decision on the basis of vows? People break vows all the time. Have you heard the stats on divorce lately?"

"We don't break ours." Jacob mutters.

"And I was supposed to know," Adam shakes his head. "Not on my job. There aren't questionnaires that can tell who's going to break a vow and who's not. This is my work; I've got to make decisions on the best information I have and the stuff people say about themselves is the most unreliable information there is." Adam states with self-assurance, "I'd never make an important decision based on what people say about themselves! No way . . ."

"But you didn't let us know!" Jacob repeats.

"I didn't tell you everything. I said that. You might've changed your mind. You said yourself you tried to stop the adoption."

"I said put it on hold."

"Dylan needed a permanent family ASAP. And you promised to take him forever. If you weren't going to keep a promise how could you be counted on for your vows?"

"We stalled because we weren't ready." Jacob insists "That's what I'm trying to tell you. Can't you hear me at all? We weren't prepared. We had to figure it out after the fact because you decided it was best not to tell us all the truth."

"I didn't lie," Adam repeats. "I stand by my decision."

Jacob shakes his head, still incredulous, "Can you imagine the trouble you could've saved us by knowing?"

"There are always transitional difficulties when families attach."

"Transitions? Transitions . . . that's what you say it was, a transition?"

"Yes, a time to acquire new attachments . . . you know, bond? Emotional attachments . . ." Adam begins a litany but Jacob cuts him off.

"A process?"

"Yes, a transition."

"You really have no idea..." Jacob laughs derisively.

"Sure I do." Adam spouts, his natural drive to defend himself rises quickly. "This is my profession. I've read the books . . . I took the classes and worked the cases. I know roughly what a family goes through when they adopt an at-risk child. Usually, there's a honeymoon at first, a period of relative peace where the adopted child seems to be making a smooth readjustment, then a period of testing follows, after which the child bonds with his new family. That's it in brief . . . if you stick around together long enough, it happens almost by itself. The specifics change but I've seen the same pattern work out a number of times," Adam concludes, articulating professionally.

"At-risk? Is that what you call them?"

"Yes."

"At risk for what?"

"For any number of things." Adam intends to list a few but Jacob goes in a different direction.

"In your professional judgment," Jacob puffs his eyebrows up when saying professional. "How long does this period of transition take . . . usually?"

"Well . . . depends . . ." Adam snipes a little taken back.

"Ballpark figure . . . you don't have to be that accurate," Jacob says, casually lifting his open hands into the air.

"Within a few months . . . several months."

"Several months . . ."

"Yes, that's right, several months."

"Not more than two years?" Jacob stares at Adam. Adam gets Jacob's inference.

Adam shakes his head, "No, never that long."

"Can't be never," Jacob stares with an undulating grin on his face.

"No . . . well . . . you must've made some big mistakes."

"Must've . . . You know, you're too smug. You know, I'm going to tell you Dylan's story, just to show you how wrong you are. You judge people too quickly and rely too heavily on your own imagination of facts. Someone needs to tell you what the results of your assumptions are," Jacob concludes more to himself.

"Yeah, well, stand in line. Telling me I'm wrong is becoming a national sport." Adam shrugs.

Jacob turns his attention back to Adam. "No, seriously, I changed my mind. You do need to hear Dylan's story. But first, to put things in context, I'm going to tell you a little about my dad. Dylan is now part of a family and that's something that goes back in a line. Its force, its direction is determined by an endless series, one generation back to another."

"Listen," Adam says impatiently. "I don't mean to be disrespecting your heritage but why are you telling me this? Tell me about Dylan."

"Just say it goes to motivation," Jacob continues unperturbed. "I need you to understand you were wrong about us. We wouldn't have given up on Dylan no matter what his problems. And for me, my dad is the reason why I couldn't give up on him. Dylan is part of a family. I learned about family from my dad. Dylan's story is nestled within the context of a family of stories. If you don't understand why I became a father how will you understand anything that follows? I'll tell you two quick things about my dad. And then I'll tell you what happened to Dylan. Are you willing to listen to it all? That's my deal." Jacob sits back.

"If that's the way you tell it," Adam supposes, "that's the way I'll hear it."

"First thing you need to know about my dad was that he was special to me because he could make something out of nothing. He always added the ingredient that made the extraordinary out of the ordinary. Take for instance the simple act of coming home from work. Most people sleep walk through it each day, not recognizing its potential. Not my Dad; he made it something that I'll never forget. He invented Nutsy-Coo-Coo Time and, to this day in my family, Nutsy-Coo-Coo Time is a proper noun. It was a ritualistic part of our early developing life.

"Every day, six days a week upon his return from work, my father performed a slow dance for our waiting eyes. In our PJ's, bathed and ready for bed, my six brothers and sisters and I waited down the hall and in the kitchen because no one was allowed into the living room until Dad came home. We waited in great anticipation for the headlight patterns that reflected through the bay window into the small living room that indicated Dad was in the driveway. Then the sound of his car door slammed and assured us he was coming up the walk. A moment later, the door handle jerked and jangled in just the right way: Daddy was home.

The door opened and a mountain of a man entered. Six foot four, 225lbs, clad in a knee length gray overcoat, dark, silent and brooding in the small four foot foyer, he removed his winter wear, shaking the rain off. Two shakes, then three, onto a hanger and put away. Fedora and wool gloves followed. Scarf folded and placed as we waited holding our mouths closed. Waiting, waiting so long . . . as, once again, my father stretched out the moment. It was a delicious agony. He removed and hung his sports jacket up, too, but kept his tie in place.

"Would he tonight? I'd think. Will he be too tired today? But he never abandoned his ritual.

"Slowly, he turned to the center of the living room, moved, deep in thought, not seeming to know we were there. Finally, he'd turn and go down to his knees, right in the middle of the living room carpet for no apparent reason, still not making eye contact with any of us. It looked for a moment like he might break out in a prayer; his expression was serious and focused elsewhere. Then, all of a sudden, he'd say, slowly pulling out each word in a low, loud and extended boom, It's NUTTSY-COO-COO TIME!

"Of course, there was an explosion from me and my sibs. It was like pushing the plunger down on a blasting cap; at that signal, all seven of us, nine and under, ran headlong, top speed and dove onto that holy mountain of a man, which moments ago had just settled onto our living room carpet.

"He erupted with a grin and repeated his call, It's . . . Nutsy-Coo-Coo Time. He'd stretch out his arms and we, seven small fast moving bodies, hurled into him from all sides. He articulated an exaggerated, Oomph, laughing as he fell to the carpet on his right side. We piled on like we were in a football game. We hit him with all our collected might because we knew we couldn't possibly hurt him and he'd never harm us. So we heaped on. Then up he'd rise onto his knees, lifting all who could hold on.

124

"The next twenty minutes passed as we pounded at him, grabbing him about his head and twisting his ear. Generally, we harassed him like puppies with a rag between them, while he growled and barked playfully at each of us in turn. He grabbed us and tossed each surely into the air. He spun us like pizza dough being stretched for sauce. Each of us clung to their piece of that gentle mountain, our paradise. Dad shook us until all the troubles of our day fled from us like dust beaten from old rugs. Eventually, we lay on the floor all played out, but before we drifted into a happy nap, Mom appeared and called us for dinner.

"My father knew how to make one-to-one connections with people, even when in a crowd. That was one of his special gifts. Sometimes all it took was the twinkling of his eye and his broad Irish grin. This was good because he couldn't spend a long time with any one of us. But he was good at finding the right moment and stretching it out. He could turn something inconsequential into something that could change life.

"When I was four and a half or five I had a bad dream. Now, I can't remember what it was. All I know is I panicked and screamed out. At once, my father appeared out of the dark beyond my door. He lifted me up without a word and took me straight out of the room, somehow leaving the bad dream behind. He carried me down the hall, his strong arms holding me secure and into the bathroom where he stood me on the counter by the sink.

"I looked into the mirror in front of me. When I saw my dad behind me, in the mirror, he was still taller. But only when I looked at him directly did I appreciate his real height. He smiled down and said, 'There now, you're okay. Hey Buddy, you know what you need is a good glass of cold water. Ah cold, Michigan Straits! Nothing better than a cold glass of water, to shake out the webs . . .'

"Now, I don't know if my father really liked cold water in the middle of a winter night. Perhaps, he just chose it as something nearby to focus on. But he busied himself getting a glass of water. After assuring I was standing safely on the counter, he found the open end of the Dixie cup dispenser and pulled one out. It popped into his hand. He turned on the cold water tap and

125

waited for a time. He told me a joke I don't remember. Although I laughed, I think I forgot it immediately.

"Feeling good to be near my Dad was all that mattered. His size, the warm strength within him and his soft, cotton flannel outside, all made me feel warm and safe. Just to be with him there in the bathroom waiting for the water to cool was enough.

"After he told his joke and squeezed me around my shoulders, Dad put on his best chemistry professor look and bent to test the temperature of the water now splattering out of the faucet. He stuck a large finger under its insistent splashing and held it there for yet another long minute. With the impatient expression of a person waiting for a late bus to arrive, he shook his head again, 'Where is that cold water?' he demanded.

"Then a bit later, 'Ah, there it is'. He shook himself with a loud 'Burr' and I laughed. He took his cup and filled it to the brim and said, 'Let's see about this'. He lifted it to his lips and took the contents of the waxed, paper cup into his mouth all in one big gulp. Holding it there like a mouthful of fine wine, he swooshed it around a time or two before letting it go down his throat with a single twitch of his Adam's apple.

"'Ah', he intoned and turned to me. He said, in exaggerated beatnik fashion, 'Cool, man, cool'. He pulled the words out into a smile. Then we laughed together; laughing at him, laughing at me, but most importantly, laughing at all bad dreams. We both knew it was extremely corny but I couldn't help but play along. He handed me my own cup. Down I gulped it and repeated to him, 'Cool man, coooooooool'.

"I don't remember anything else that night . . . just that! It may've only taken three minutes but to me it changed my life because that was the moment I fell in love, truly, deeply in love with my father.

"For many nights after that, I'd pretend a bad dream only to get my father to leave his warm bed for our quick nightly ritual. He, no doubt, was tired but it was the only exclusive time I had with him. He never declined or questioned me. Our time together was only a couple of minutes long and lasted for only a couple of weeks but after more than forty years, all we had to say to each other to know everything was alright was, 'Cool man, cooooool'. You see, I know my father was a man of hope not because his words were hopeful but because I was full of hope when I was with him."

"I'm still not sure why . . ." Adam interrupted impatiently.

"Don't you see?" Jacob implores, "I adopted Dylan because I had been gifted to be the son of a man who knew how to make things special. And just about thirteen years ago I felt an increasing pressure . . . like an obligation, inside me . . . to pass on what I'd been given, not to let it end with me.

"Being a father is like being a son of two dads: you must take your orders from both above and below. Being a father isn't like working in an agency. It's being connected. That's why my Dad called it a type of immortality. But it all becomes meaningless if you break the line. I was feeling this pressure to become a father, nothing more. I wasn't looking for a particular kind of kid. It wasn't about what I wanted but what I could do for someone else.

"My being a father was about me doing what I knew would make my father proud and was a necessity because a tired man once gave me a drink of cold water in the middle of the night. I wanted . . . no, needed . . . to honor him in that simple and awesome task."

After a silence, Adam begins, "How is he? How's Dylan? How's he doing?" Adam sits up eagerly on his desk.

"He's doing well . . . I suppose . . ." Jacob says distractedly, still inside a different thought.

"Tell me," Adam interrupts.

"How much time you got?"

"For this, enough . . ."

Jacob pauses, looking outside, "I guess we aren't going anywhere for a while."

"Guess not . . ."

"Well, let me think where to begin?" Jacob asks, not as a real question, but in a musing tone.

"What happened after you left Sharon's? Tell me it all!" Adam insists.

"Let me do this my way," Jacob snaps.

"That's right, it doesn't matter," Adam says and then consciously stops himself.

Jacob begins.

Book 2: One Son Rise (Jacob's Story)

Funny Looking Kid

My first impression of Dylan was that he was odd. When he moved, he was fast and when he stopped, he stopped abruptly. His eyes were bright and darted from place to place, his nose small and pointed. But it was his mouth that gave his overall appearance a most peculiar impression. His lips were held in a tight, perpetual line across his face, forming neither a smile nor a frown but a perfectly horizontal line. To me he was a funny looking kid, an FLK as some of the teachers around the high school say.

The day we met at the agency, he was trying to avoid us by bending over a sand table, a shallow wooden box with thin legs, in the corner. He was tracing a small design on the surface of the sand with a pinched forefinger and thumb. Scar tissue, like an old lava flow, undulated on the back of his drawing hand down to his fingertips. His big head was tilted forward to hide his face.

Our first visit at the Blanchard's house went well. We spent most of the time in their living room trying to play with Dylan. He didn't talk to us but at least he didn't run away either. Mostly, he played with Kyle and Nikki. We spent some time talking with Sharon and Dan, trying to get more information. Sharon, however, kept saying what a good little boy he was and how happy she was that he was being adopted by a family as nice as us. Then we took Dylan for a walk down to a small park in the neighborhood. It was Sharon's idea.

We walked across the street holding his hand. But I hadn't held enough small hands in my life to be certain I wouldn't crush his. I was a bit uncomfortable, wondering if I would hurt him. I held on lightly. When we reached the other side of the street, I didn't know if I should let go or keep holding on. As we stepped back on the sidewalk, Dylan suddenly grabbed our hands tightly and swung both his feet up into the air between Martha and me. I half expected he'd try to run away from us. But he played with us instead.

Martha was delighted. We laughed as he swung and swung all the way to the park. When we got there, I pushed him high on the real swing. He didn't talk to us that day but we played alongside.

The second time we visited Dylan we took him to Buckeye Bee's where kids ran everywhere. One of the huge rooms is filled with video and carnival games. The kids earn tickets by playing games for a couple of quarters apiece. Later they turn in their collection of hundreds of tickets for a few, cheap, plastic prizes.

Then there's a room filled from the floor to a second story height with play equipment: ball pits for tumbling, scooting slides, hidden tunnels and obstacles with thick ropes for climbing.

A third room is for dining ala child. There's a counter where you purchase cardboard pizza with catsup and other nearly revolting kid foods at repulsive adult prices. Numerous cafeteria tables are spread out in front of the food counter and there's a large stage where giant, furry robots sing and dance but mostly advertise that Buckeye Bee and all his friends were now available for purchase at the gift counter on your way out.

Buckeye's was a giant hit with Dylan. He ran and dove to his heart's content. I spent twenty dollars in quarters on games with him. For his efforts and my cash, he received a sticky, rubber hand on a rubber band string, a green and white plastic whistle that blew one forlorn note, eight tiny tootsies rolls, two washable tattoos and a diminutive super ball just about the right size to fill a small child's gullet. He was delighted with his treasures.

He dumped his loot into my out stretched hands and tore off into the play area where, at the end of a flying summersault, he disappeared under a sea of brightly colored plastic balls. I nearly ran to catch up but I didn't see him again until he emerged at the other end of the ball pit. He climbed up a large plastic tube that began near the ceiling and ended in the pit. From the sounds I heard over the din of white flour and sugar induced mania, I guessed Dylan had bumped into another child coming down the tube.

Martha came to me with a brown paper bag she found by the toy counter. It was just like her to notice I was having difficulty handling the mismatched collection of toys jumbled in my hands. She tends to find solutions for me before I fully understand I've a problem. "He's really enjoying himself." she noted. "We'll have to come back sometime."

"Sometime . . ." I said distractedly as I tried to find him again in the complex maze of plastic. "Some time in the distant future."

"It isn't that bad," she chuckled.

Dylan played hard. Just when I thought we'd lost him, his head popped up from some unexpected corner of the playroom. Over he'd trot to take a large swig of soda. He still didn't talk, but he was becoming noticeably more comfortable with us.

The next time we went out together, we went to see a movie, a film that'd become one of Dylan's all-time favorites, oddly enough about a foster boy and a whale. When over, we returned Dylan home where he told all about the movie, chattering as we hadn't heard yet.

The week after this, Martha stayed behind when I went to get him. This was the first night he stayed over at our place. After strapping him into his new safety seat, I headed the van north on Beck Road passing through the bright orange and yellow October scenery to our cinnamon colored ranch home in Commerce Township. Along the way, I talked to Dylan about anything I could think of. I guess I just wanted to let him hear the sound of my voice, perhaps even to reassure him. I don't know.

But after a while, tired of my monologue, I turned on the radio and listened to goodtime oldies the rest of the way.

Dylan and I entered the house by the side door, from where you could see most of the small home's living space. It was an efficient use of area, which defied its compact nature. The kitchen, the dining room and the living room formed a tight "L" delineated from each other only by floor coverings and an eight inch drop wall that hung from the ceiling between the living room and dining room. The carpet butted into the egg shell walls where intricate calligraphy and nature scenes were positioned and displayed. The furniture was modest and utilitarian, except for a huge, overstuffed, blue sectional couch and matching Lazy Boy lounger in the living room.

"Surprise!" Martha yelled as we stepped up to the table directly in front of us. On it, Martha had arranged a surprise party for Dylan. The table was overflowing with gifts in tinfoil wrappings and a red, white and blue tissue tablecloth sprinkled with sparkling cutout shapes of stars, moons and rocket ships. A brightly colored sheet cake decorated around its edges with sugar flowers was placed front and center. On the top stood a bright green Power Ranger, proudly surrounded by five lit candles, blue, red, yellow, black and pink. Overhead were balloons filled with helium, colored crepe paper, curled ribbon dangling and a long, wooden plaque that read FAMILIES ARE FOREVER. Tucked into the middle of this extravagant exhibit of good will and bright promises was a photo album.

Martha showed him the book first. She took it from the center of the table and opened it for him to see as she pulled out a chair and sat down to read it. He was reluctant but the picture of me, dressed in sweat-soaked gym clothes grabbing Martha to dance, and made him laugh. He especially liked her disgusted expression as she tried to pull away. He also laughed at the caption, which read, Jacob thinks he's a good dancer, yuk! Dylan crawled up onto her lap halfway through the pages to look more closely. I took in the sight of them together, an icon of mother and child. This was Martha at her best and I was fully in love with her.

We played with Dylan's new toys, watched a rented video and fell asleep together camped out in the living room on the couch and padded floor. We slept in and went out for a late breakfast before returning Dylan to the Blanchard's.

We tried to keep things pretty active and upbeat in those early days. Dylan wasn't required to do anything but enjoy himself when he was with us. We wanted him to feel okay, so we kept him busy, well-fed and amused.

He moved in with us three days before Halloween but this brought up a problem we hadn't anticipated back in September when we set the schedule. It was Halloween and at the Blanchard's everyone had been excited for weeks. Dan stirred up everyone every year. The family decorated the house and yard. They made costumes, spooked each other, baked cookies and talked about little else in the weeks leading up to the big event. Of course, these preparations got Dylan excited too. We decided we wouldn't disappoint him and agreed to go trick-or-treating at the Blanchard's.

I haven't been into Halloween since the sixth grade. That was the year my tinfoil armor peeled off my homemade Sir Lancelot costume. I had to run home in the shadows not to be seen in my long johns. As an adult, I'd never thought much of the holiday and during our time together Martha had given no indication or inclination for it either. So I was surprised to see how excited she got over trick or treating. Martha played like a kid.

At the Blanchard's, she helped Nikki put on witch make-up. And then, after I took the official picture, she led our ghoulish troop out into the street to ritualistically threaten the neighbors with "Trick or Treat." Dylan was dressed like a little Dracula, scary with his hair slicked to a point and his white and black make up smeared at the edges. He was most proud of his glow-in-the-dark plastic fangs and went about trying to bite people.

I stayed mainly in the middle of the street putting on my best hall-monitor demeanor, trying not to look completely out of place. But Martha did more than just join in. She wore a floral sheet with holes cut out for eyes and called herself an "optimistic ghost."

134

Her laughter got in your gut and tugged. Dylan looked surprised. Stooping down in hyperbolic good fun, Martha did an intentionally bad imitation of a child. She pretended to trip on the edges of her costume and stumbled up the driveway to the bright and opened front doors where she joined the children in their begging. She intentionally nudged them aside until they cried, "Hey, wait, you're not a kid."

When candy was dropped into her matching floral pillowcase, she'd scurry with her stolen treasures back to the street where she did an exaggerated victory dance, crying out, "Candy, candy, its mine, all mine!" The children clamored and protested after her trying to take her ill-gotten gain away. They hollered and ran around until we directed them to the next waiting door. Dancing in the street, clowning up and down the driveways, laughing and acting goofy, Martha entertained everyone that night, especially Dylan. After that night he began talking to us.

We had such a blast we agreed to visit back and forth; the Blanchard's would come see us at our house soon and we'd bring Dylan back to them on a regular basis. We agreed on this much for Dylan's sake but also because of the fun we had on Halloween night.

#

When Dylan moved in with us, we all had to learn new patterns. It was nice that Martha and I were able to take a two-week family leave from work, even if it was unpaid. It helped the transition. In the morning especially, it was odd to have this kid around all the time. I fixed breakfast and let Martha sleep in because she was tired. Dylan was up and still in his PJ's. I was in sweats and a t-shirt, so I decided to make pancakes mainly because it took up time and qualified as an activity. I didn't really know what to do with this little guy now that we had him home. I caught myself wondering, "When are his folks coming to get him?" I had to remind myself I was his folks and this was now home.

What happened to Dylan and how he turned out was my responsibility. I was overwhelmed by this little boy standing in the kitchen watching me make pancakes. I'd missed all the lessons you need to deal with a five-year-old son; namely, having a four-year-old son and a three-year-old and a toddler and a newborn. I heated the pan and the pan heated the batter until circles of it shone golden on both sides.

"Who's that?" Dylan asked, pointing to the postcard-sized image of Jesus in the little frame above the kitchen sink.

The postcard Dylan pointed to was meant to remind me of what my life was like before Jesus and Martha were part of it. "It's to remind me . . ." I began but didn't finish.

How should I have explained to this little stranger the connection Jesus and Martha had for me? Both had saved my life years before, Jesus first and then Martha. I always felt Martha was my reward for choosing to serve, because we met shortly after my baptism in a lake near Miami on a bright Easter morning. Love led me to love. And then that love led me to Dylan.

Difficult births were common in Martha's family and to be frank, she was afraid of the delivery. Being a father and a husband was more important to me than how I became one. I couldn't see pressuring Martha to bear children. There are always children who need what we were offering.

So this was how Dylan came to stand in my kitchen, watching me flip pancakes. I smiled at him and replied that the man in the picture was Jesus and he reminded us to be nice.

We were eating our pancakes when Martha joined us. I set a place for her and brought the raspberry jam she liked. We spent a time at the table that morning making our plans and getting ourselves together. Even though we'd two weeks off, we had a lot to do.

Dylan was really good that day; he sat at the table and listened to our whole conversation without fidgeting. Now that he'd moved in for good, he appeared to be calming down and adjusting to our house quickly. Several times I caught myself watching him, smiling and nodding affirmatively. I didn't understand that what we were seeing was the honeymoon period. We thought we were lucky to be his new parents and that this was how things would be for our family forever.

We did everything together those two weeks and laughter was our shared companion. I remembered how it was to play like a child. When I went back to work, I couldn't wait to get home each day to my new boy.

I'd wait at the mailboxes for Dylan's bus to arrive. I'd give him a hug and carry his backpack the rest of the way home, as we talked. Some days, we didn't make it to the front door before we fell to the ground in a pile of fallen leaves, rolling and rough housing to our hearts content. Dylan grabbed a two handed lump of leaf debris and with a pleased howl, thrust them into my face. Dead tree, dirt and grass never tasted so good. I'd growl and chase him around, never quite catching him although I really could have. He'd stick out his tongue, wag his fanny and run away quite triumphantly.

Afterwards, he'd be just as delightful indoors. He'd do what he was told and showed good manners at the dinner table. He'd join us in our conversations about the day and was quite well spoken for a boy with a lateral lisp. His adult-like comments were precious coming out in little boy sounding words.

One day, Martha surprised me when she told me she'd been thinking about things. "Dylan is going to need a lot of support," she started. "He's only in kindergarten. What is he going to do, stay half a day with another set of strangers in daycare? He needs to be cared for by his family or else he'll never understand that he belongs. We can't be just more strangers bossing him around," Martha said with determined knuckles curled into her hips. "We need to give him a foundation." She decided to take a personal leave until the end of the year. I was surprised to hear her say it.

I'd seen Martha teach and she was impressive. I'd never thought of her as a stay at home mom. In fact, I got the impression she needed to get out and have contact with peers. But Martha had a sixth sense about what children needed and I trusted her. I was proud of her self-sacrifice.

But I should've spoken up more for what was good for her as well as for Dylan and me. As her husband, I didn't do my job well that day. I should've saved more room in our family for her. But at the time, all we could think of was that Dylan came first. This became our battle cry as off we marched into parenthood, "Children first."

Martha spent every morning with Dylan before he went to afternoon kindergarten. They worked on fun projects together. I'm not sure of everything they did but I know a lot of brownie mix was involved. Every day Martha gave her full attention to Dylan and got him ready to have a good day at school. She dressed him in the morning. He'd lay on the couch completely relaxed and passive, allowing himself to be dressed by Martha's confident hands. "Be careful! Don't spoil him," I said as I scooted up to her side and gave her a kiss on the cheek. I had to get to work.

"He can do with a little spoiling right now." She pulled on his sock, tickled his foot and gave me a kiss in return.

#

Martha and I went to Dylan's school a few weeks later to celebrate Thanksgiving with the kindergarteners. It was a big affair with four classes coming together to have a traditional feast. Half of the children were dressed as pilgrims, half as Native Americans. Dylan was "our little savage."

Over the past several weeks, the children had spent time preparing for this feast by making costumes, place settings and room decorations using brown paper grocery bags, washable paints, beads and feathers. Some of the parents helped set out the food and moved our children through the line while video recorders and cameras documented the event as if it were an international treaty signing. I stood at the window, my camcorder in my right hand, having a blast in my new role as parent but secretly feeling like an imposter.

After things got going and a number of the children were sitting at their places, I saw that I needed to move to the other side of the room to get a shot of Dylan's face because his back was to me.

When I got to a place where I thought was generally in front of Dylan, I tried to find open space from which I could see my boy. Happily I looked to him. Gladly, the other parents were absorbed in watching their cheerful children. Everyone was happy but Dylan. He never knew I lowered my camera without taking his picture at all.

When I saw Dylan, he looked like a victim in shock. He was pale, his expression flat and his eyes unfocussed and far away. He appeared wretched as he watched the other children, looking as if he were observing an unfamiliar species. He was completely lost and couldn't have been more removed or forlorn sitting by himself at the South Pole.

In that moment, my heart went out to him. I tried to imagine what he must've felt like to be in another new school, in another new family, alone without friends or siblings. After the celebration, we took him home. He was exhausted so we put him to bed as if he were sick. We tried not to show disappointment but he seemed devastated, by what we couldn't imagine.

After that glum Thanksgiving Day feast, we set a more optimistic sight on Christmas. Martha and I decided it was time to celebrate big. Dylan needed it, hence we went hog wild, pulling out all the stops. It was our first Christmas as parents and we'd been saving up the urge to spoil someone for years.

But on Christmas morning, Dylan didn't bound out of bed to open his presents. We finally decided to wake him near lunch time. He came out to the living room and sat down, legs crossed, in front of the tree. He opened all his presents dutifully, one after the other, without changing his flat expression.

When he was done he gave no regard to anything we had bought him. He simply looked up and, as bland as can be, asked, "Can I go back to bed?" He slept like a dead man. He didn't move even when we went in to check on him and turned on the light in the middle of that night. He slept through the next day, got up briefly to eat little and go to the bathroom and then

139

he slept through the whole of Boxing Day and overnight again and then part of the following day, December 27th. We were trying to reach his doctor when he woke up.

Some Way Home

When Worlds Collide

For Dylan, the wild stirring began not in the spring but in the lifelessness of cold winter. In the darkest part of the night during the longest nights of the year, Dylan's fears began to rise and take over. At first, it was just his voice crying out down the hall. When we reached him, he'd be sleeping, but lost in some chaotic mental scene. We debated whether or not to wake him. I'd heard that dreams were worse for the dreamer if they were woken. As a result, we decided to let him be and stood like shadows in the corner. After a while, we went back to bed where we could still hear him. "Get him! Get that a-hole before he kills us!"

This was the first time we heard Dylan use profanity. Initially, it actually sounded cute. With his poor articulation he pronounced it without the "s" sound and all of "hole." Somehow it didn't seem that vulgar coming this way out of a five-year-olds' mouth. However, soon we were to find that he knew a lot more words that he could articulate all too well.

As new parents, Martha and I were like swimmers in over our heads who didn't yet know their predicament. For the next year and a half, we barely managed to react blindly to Dylan's mounting problems.

Dylan regressed emotionally. It was a backwards unraveling of his personality. That first winter we watched, not understanding what was happening. It was like his personality was a movie being played rapidly backwards. At first there were nightmares. The following day he was exhausted and edgy. But then the dreams occurred nightly. We were up every night with him, watching him trash the heck out of some dreamt "a-holes." But things didn't end there.

After he woke from his big sleep at Christmas, Dylan's demeanor changed. He was easy to anger and terribly stubborn. He began to refuse to do things around the house and started to yell, "No," often. We didn't react to this decisively because it caught us off guard. I don't know why, but I was completely taken aback by his flat refusal. I didn't think children did that. I knew kids would try to get out of hard things by whining or avoiding, but to simply refuse, I hadn't expected that.

The mornings were Dylan's most peaceful time of the day. In the afternoons, after school, he became more active, over-active. He'd want to play all the time and if Martha and I were busy, he'd charge out from some hideaway and head-butt us in the side. It wasn't just play; he'd really hit and kick us with his full force. He held no impulse back. We'd be walking with a load of fresh laundry or something and we'd get punched in the side or the back. To me it just hurt but on Martha it left real bruises.

After sleepless nights, action-filled afternoons and out-and-out warfare at bedtime, Martha and I were becoming dazed and confused. Martha began to have trouble focusing on what she was saying. Sometimes she'd just stop talking in the middle of a sentence. Sometimes she'd ramble on in a mumble.

Quickly we'd used up our collective bag of parenting tricks, most acquired during the few hours of training provided by the Crossings. We asked nicely. We spoke firmly. We gave him time-out. But after sitting on the piano bench for a second or so, he'd disappear and not be seen until he'd ambush us again.

Something had to be done. I talked to a friend at work and she suggested we "divide and conquer." One of us should do the chores while the other spends time with Dylan. He seemed to be seeking attention. Subsequently Martha and I decided what to do. Since Dylan needed to roughhouse to get it out of his system, we decided she'd go about the housework and I'd play with Dylan. At least she wouldn't be bruised.

143

I told Dylan I'd spend time playing with him after school if he agreed to two things: One, to do homework, and two; to stop attacking us. I created a play area in the basement by laying out a large square of padded shag carpet. Martha bought us large bean bags that we could fall on without getting hurt and a Batman blow-up figure we could knock over. Like us, every time you punched him, Batman would pop up again.

The first afternoon when we went down to the playroom to have what my dad called Nutsy-Coo-Coo time, I reminded Dylan there'd be no hitting or kicking anywhere else in the house. When I said go, a severe bout of wrestling and pummeling proceeded. Dylan hit with surprising force. In Dylan's words, I quickly morphed into an evil monster-robot whose name sounded like razors. It was Dylan's job, as the Green Power Ranger, to kill me. And kill me, he tried. I'm sure of it.

These Nutsy-Coo-Coo sessions became a regular part of our afternoons and seemed to reduce the initial, random parental abuse we suffered. Things seemed to get a little better between school and supper. But after dinner, Dylan was unmanageable. Instead of getting it out of his system, he became more hyperactive. In the evening it was next to impossible to get him to sit still or even pick up one tiny thing from the floor.

Like we were taught, I tried to ritualize bedtime but that was impossible. With difficulty, I could get him into the bathroom but it was a much different thing to get him to take a bath or brush his teeth. Often, I'd simply do it for him. I always began by asking but he'd flash his index fingers, fast draw style and snap, "No!" at me, "No, no, no, no!"

"Come on, Dylan, you know you have ta."

"No!" he'd reply and then add a vehement, "A-hole!"

"You know you have to." I turned on the tap, but before I had the chance to test the temperature, Dylan escaped through the open door. After a few times, I was more prepared and could catch him before he ran too far. But then I had have to readjust the water temp while keeping him next to me. He'd struggle, twist and squirm while I undressed him.

144

While Martha did evening chores, I'd make bedtime as positive as possible. After I'd get him through bath time, dried him off and get him dressed for bed, I'd move him in front of the sink. There we brushed our teeth. After a few minutes, I'd move him to his bedroom. As he bounced on his bed, I looked for a book to read from the extensive library Martha had collected from garage sales and second-hand stores.

After searching Dylan's bookshelves, I selected a book with the picture of a "mile high pie" on its cover. I held it up for Dylan's approval. He nodded an okay, while continuing to jump. I read the book to calm him. It was about a pie that saved a town by passing happiness from one person to another until everyone glowed in brilliant smiles and good works. Since he was still wide awake, I read him another story.

When I tried to leave after finishing the second book, he begged me to stay and grabbed onto my shirt. Since I thought he wouldn't stay in bed unless I did, I turned off the light and lay down beside him. Both of us looked up at the blank ceiling. Typically, about two hours after we'd brushed our teeth, he'd finally go to sleep. Then carefully, softly, silently, with utter attention and intense control, I slipped off the bed. I was willing to take such care because if I woke him, the whole process would start again.

By the time I'd removed myself, I was bone tired and went straight to bed. I gave Martha a peck on the cheek as a quick goodnight on the way. She'd stop her chores long enough to ask, "How'd it go?"

"He's asleep," I replied, "Let's hope he stays that way." But he didn't. Like clockwork, two hours later he began yelling. He'd either fall off the bed or bang himself against the wall hard enough to wake up, he'd sit in his bed and shake, eyes wide and wild. When approached, he'd pull back and cower in the corner between his headboard and the side wall.

If we reached out for him, he'd scream and flail wildly. Only if we lay down with our backs to him, pretending to ignore him, he'd slide over and lay against us, his back to ours. He'd stay like that for a time, whimpering softly. I wanted to hold him, to put my arm around him and tell him it was okay and that no one would hurt him anymore, but if I moved or said anything it'd send him back into a convulsive panic. It was best just to lay there, rigid back to rigid back, until he fell asleep.

That winter, this process repeated itself two or three times a night. By the time the alarm clock woke us in the morning, we were more exhausted than the night before. We took turns every shift of the night to spell each other, but neither got much rest. Sloppy and frayed, we'd stumble through our work day. Martha said Dylan appeared troubled. She said his expression was flat and she could no longer get him to laugh and play. He didn't remember the dreams he'd had, or at least he said he didn't.

Just about then his teacher sent a note home and asked if he was getting enough rest. She suggested we "establish an earlier bed time" so he could participate better at school. One day, my boss took me aside and said much the same thing to me. Martha and I were dead on our feet, but when Dylan came home from school at 3:25pm he seemed to be even more energized. He'd tear through the house jumping wildly, diving and tumbling over furniture. When he moved in with us, he seemed to know exactly three games: fight, flight and hide.

When I tried to do flashcards with him, he'd put up a fuss, run away or hide. He hated the cards and the instant I brought them out he became uncontrollable. He'd shout, bending forward at the waist, "No, no, no, no!" His eyes were fierce with defiance. And then he'd tear off. I'd chase after him but he was too quick to catch once he had a head start.

Martha looked at me as I ran after him and shook her head. Dylan was near impossible to find in the basement. About the only way I could really get him to come out was when I stopped looking for him, gave up on homework and went to the basement shouting, "It's Nutsy-Coo-Coo-Time." Then he'd appear, ready to beat the hell out of the monster on the brown carpet.

I tried to get him to fight the blowup Batman but I guess beating me was more fun than hitting the plastic superhero. Gradually, I'd let him beat me down until I lay prone on the rug, trying to protect my vitals while letting his anger take its course and play itself out.

But this was the wrong approach, as his rage seemed bottomless. After a while, he'd shout, "Bad Daddy! Bad Daddy!" as he beat me. I supposed he was hurting someone from the past.

When he was through, I'd limp to dinner much slower than he. At the table, his manners evaporated. He'd eat with his hands, belch and spit out food he didn't like. When told to use his manners, he'd pick up a wad of mashed potatoes and smear it across the tablecloth. I'd look to Martha, but she was as unprepared to react as I. I'd send him away from the table to give me a minute alone with Martha. In those moments we just sat in shocked silence.

I tried putting him in timeout on the piano bench but he wouldn't stay unless I held him down by force. He'd kick and scream until Martha couldn't stand it. She hated hearing a child crying in distress. I'd see the panic on her face. When he was desperate, she was too.

When he'd raise too much a fuss on the piano bench, I'd take him to his room and shut him in. He'd try to open the door but I stood outside in the hall and held the handle. He'd go completely wild and trash the room. He'd scream at the top of his lungs and cursed obscenely. One night, he screamed through the closed door, "I'm going to cut your cock off and shove it down your throat!" This was the vilest expression I'd ever heard. It sent a chill through me as he seemed to understand what he was saying. His intonation was full of violence and conviction. It echoed an adult voice. Where had he learned such things? My head swam with the possibilities.

Dylan rushed at the closed door with all his force. He'd pounded the door, the floor, the walls and then I heard things bounce off the ceiling. He was breaking what he could. He pulled the vertical blinds off the window entirely. When I heard it crash, I rushed into the room to find him tangled with the hardware in a pile by the foot of his bed. But he didn't stay down. The moment he saw me, he jumped out of the mess and rushed at me, head

147

forward, bent at the waist with both hands shaking in front of him, "No, no, no, no!" he screamed, "A-hole! Basser!" he shouted.

Out of surprise and from the oddity of it, I caught myself beginning to laugh at his pronunciation. But that was a mistake. It infuriated him even more. He began to kick me. I grabbed him by the shoulders and pushed him to arm's length as he flailed in wrath.

After a minute, I pushed him harder than I should've onto the edge of his bed and tried to leave the room. But when I backed away his expression switched from rage to desperation. When he realized I was leaving, he threw himself at me catching me around the leg, pleading like he was doomed. He begged for his life and shouted, "No, don't leave! Please don't go! I'll do anything. I'll be good!"

It broke my heart to see him this way and his promise seemed sincere. I stopped moving and said, "It's okay Dylan, I won't go." But before I could finish, he switched back, "You mother fucker, get out of here!" He jumped up shouting and swinging. I blocked a book's flapping pages before it hit me in the face. And seeing me flinch only fueled his fire. He came at me once more in fury.

I didn't know whether to go forward or to peel him off, toss him aside and escape the madness. Clearly, unless I did, I wasn't going to get away. I stood there in shock. He circled me, hurtling insults and anything he could lift. The room was a disaster. All the nice things Martha had bought lay about torn, broken and battered. Most were beyond recovery. It was bizarre. I felt like I was in someone else's nightmare. I felt like I was stuck in the mud up to my waist.

I stood there unable to move until Martha opened the door. She wanted to see what was going on. I turned to her but saw something hard fly over my shoulder in her direction. It crashed against the wall, barely missing her cheek. She disappeared from the doorway. While Dylan wasn't watching, I slipped through the door, slamming it behind me. He screamed like a person falling off a cliff. The sound pierced through the wood between us. I lowered my head against the door jam, hunched my shoulders as if to cover my ears and held tightly to the knob.

When I looked up, Martha was looking alarmed. "What happened?" she managed.

"I don't know," I replied. "He just went crazy. I couldn't control him."

A long time later, after he exhausted himself, I opened the door and put him to bed.

#

From that night on, this was our 24-7 routine: up most of the night with nightmares and screams, to work in the morning with dull and fuzzy heads; ; fights over homework in the afternoon, maybe some play time and, from dinner until a multiple hour bedtime, scuffles over manners, following orders, anything and everything. This pattern repeated itself with exhausting regularity, time and time again. Soon Martha and I were all played out; we'd no energy to continue. But to stop wasn't an option. So, we trudged blindly on.

Any time we were out in public, Dylan took the opportunity to humiliate us for our lack of control. At the store, he acted like a power crazed despot. I always feared the candy that hung near the checkout. My choice was to either buy him candy, which I resented because of the powerlessness it implied, or to face a tidal wave of screams that shocked even the most understanding parent.

Most people believe a child couldn't act that bad naturally, thus it was natural for them to blame us. Strangers looked at us like we were the scum of the earth. Their faces clearly said what they thought—we were horrendous, most likely crack heads or drunks.

I wanted to shout back, "No wait, you don't understand: he's not my natural child . . . I mean . . . I didn't do it to him. He came to us this way!" But, of course, I couldn't. To denounce him

149

publicly would've been too cruel. Even if he were acting a total tyrant, I couldn't do that to him. It would've ruined any chance at a good relationship. Martha and I bit our tongues more than once. I'd clenched my jaw and think, "You're wrong about us. You don't have a clue." And under my breath, I'd hiss at the strangers, "You pompous fool" and wait for Dylan to stop.

Church was no better; it seemed like Dylan knew instinctively when it'd be the most embarrassing for us to have a fit and then he'd let go. Right when Mass was at its most sacred, the pinnacle of solemnity, he'd shout out, "Give me that back" or something similar. If we tried to hush him, he'd scream, "Give it back a-hole," louder. When I'd take him out of the pew, he'd fight me tooth and nail. From the looks of my fellow parishioners, I was clearly condemned to perdition for defiling their worship.

All of this made Martha and me feel isolated, helpless and alone. We didn't have extended family support because we were older. My parents had retired and moved to Phoenix. Martha's dad passed away a long time ago and her mother was near eighty. Our brothers and sisters were scattered around the country, from New Jersey to San Diego, from Minnesota to Florida. We were in this by ourselves. Dylan's behavior in public increased our sense of separation. Shame became our constant companion at worship, shopping or anywhere in public.

Dylan's moods were unanticipated. At times, his behavior elicited from us strong feelings of pity. And other times, he was playful, even endearing. Psychologically, just when we felt a certain way about him, he'd suddenly change for no apparent reason, drastically, profoundly and immediately. This caused us to feel a constant anxiety.

Then Dylan regressed even further. He lost control of his bladder at night and now, in addition to being woken to the sounds of screams, we were intermittently roused by Dylan's small voice at the side of our bed, saying "Wet, all wet." We'd soak the spot with vinegar water and pat it dry with towels. While we did this, Dylan stood back against the closet looking guilty and humiliated.

His language also began to revert. His words, never articulated clearly, grew softer until unintelligible. I often found myself asking, "What?" Then I pretended to understand him and guessed like crazy.

Every day he seemed to be losing some skill he'd possessed the day before. At one point, we were retraining him in everything. How to clean himself and wash his hands, how to take off his day clothes and put on pajamas, how to eat, how to talk, how to wash his face, even how to wipe his behind after defecating, how to rip, fold and hold the toilet paper; all these skills had to be retrained. And his needs seemed impossible to meet because he wouldn't take any instruction. It was Catch 22.

Clearly, his favorite word was "No!" He said it over and over. If there was ever a mantra that brought him inner peace, it was this, "No, no, no, no!" Over and over, he repeated it like it was the key to his salvation. "No, no, no, no!" I heard it echo through my short bouts of sleep. I tried saying the opposite of what I wanted so he'd contradict me by habit and agree to what I really wanted. But that didn't work for long because, to Dylan, "No, no, no, no!" covered everything; it trumped a double negative by quadrupling it.

He was a two year old in a five year old body. Then he retreated into infancy. He needed to be fed and clothed, washed and dried, put to bed and gotten up again in the morning. How he managed at school I'll never know. At home, we needed to talk for him. He demonstrated with actions and gestures.

The only skills he didn't lose were his gross motor ones. He always retained his extraordinary abilities to run, dive and move silently. This wasn't necessarily a good thing as we had to spend an inordinate amount of time trying to find and corral him to where we needed him to be.

In the end, the regressive process came down to this: there was no trust in him on any level. All that remained of his emotional state was either a flat, zombie-like affect or a fit of utter rage. In the morning, he was like the walking dead. In the afternoon, he rampaged until late night when he fell into an exhausted and fitful sleep.

151

We just responded to these extremes. We didn't know how to change them. We set our sights much lower, namely, we tried to contain him and keep him from bodily harm, which we weren't always able to do. Once that winter, while running from me, he dove into the living room, somersaulted across the carpet and got back up to his feet all at a stunning pace. Unfortunately, he misjudged the distance to an end table and came up hitting his face on the sharp oak corner.

For a moment, I thought he'd put out an eye. I heard the crunch of his face against the wood and saw blood spurt from under his eyebrow. He was shocked and let me gather him up with a clean towel thrown on his face and rush him to the emergency room at the nearby hospital. There he screamed and fought so much four attendants had to hold him down.

The doctor put six stitches into the soft tissue above his left eye and said he'd never seen such strength in a five year old before. He asked that I stay at the gurney's side, hoping that I, as his father, would have a calming effect on him. Accordingly, I witnessed the whole gruesome thing, up close and personal.

Pain didn't seem to bother him however. He'd so many bruises from all his running and diving around the house his teachers began questioning him as to what we were doing to him at home. I found it ironic that we, passive and paralyzed at that time, would be suspected of abusing him. The sad fact was that for lack of training we were incompetent in our efforts to keep him from hurting himself.

Then his personality dissolved entirely. All that was left was pure infantile rage, out of control hate, mixed with fear and mitigated only by the understanding of an infant.

At that point, he'd only two emotional states, "on" and "off", and they were infinitely apart. When he was "on," it was a total arousal; no part of him was left unengaged in the passion which swept through him and our home. Then he was like a destructive force of nature, a bad storm or a tornado.

But when he wasn't aroused, he displayed no affect at all, just a straight, horizontal line across his face. Dylan was all or

152

nothing. As much as I hated to see him forlorn and despondent, I began to wish for his emotionless states. Martha and I both tried not to do the things that set him off. We tried not to offend with what we said or did. Our home was a mine field and we didn't know where the bombs were hidden.

To tell the truth, in the next month or so, I don't think we escaped a night in ten without an explosion. Vile and intense, his rage flowed over our possessions and property like a tsunami. Each day we lost a part of ourselves, of our previous lives. Every time he put a hole in the wall or knocked a closet door off its bracket, broke a lamp, a vase, a plate or any other movable object, a part of us went with it. Shattered pieces of our hopes, shards of our illusions, jagged fragments of belief that we could make a difference were all swept up and tossed into the wake of Dylan's anger. We had to face our own worst fear; we were complete and utter failures in making any real difference. In the end, we were left with only a clear picture of our own incompetence.

So, I'd no illusions left when one evening Dylan cursed me, adding his usual litany of no's. I needed to do something; I couldn't do nothing anymore. Somehow I had to stop this. I chased him down the hall. "That's it, young man, you go to time out!" I hollered as I ran.

"No, no, no, no!" he responded.

"Yes, yes, yes, yes," I rejoined and grabbed him around the wrist. He kicked me squarely in the shin. He had pinpoint aim and real power but I ignored the pain and dragged him back down the hallway to the waiting piano bench. I picked him up and placed him down stiffly on the blue rectangular cushion tied to the brown wooden bench. "Stay!" I said firmly and pointed. I turned and took a step away, but he got to his feet and ripped the cushion from the ties holding it to the bench. When I turned back, he was shaking it at me.

"No, no, no, no!" he screamed and threw the cushion.

"Yes!" I yelled and jumped forward catching him off-guard. He cowered for a moment but when I grabbed and lifted him around the waist, he cried out. I headed down the hall toward his room, the usual next timeout spot. I walked with certitude into his room and threw him down on the bed. His small form bounced off the mattress and landed on the floor. Again a startled expression spread across his face. He paused.

I turned to see if Martha was behind me. I didn't want her to see the rough treatment. She wasn't around, so some of my guilt fled. "Stay here and don't break anything," I demanded and headed for the door. I slammed it behind me and held the knob. Martha came from the kitchen to the living room and looked down the hall at me.

"Is everything alright?" she asked with a half dazed expression, dull in her eyes. How long had her twinkle been gone? All that was left on her face was a lost and pleading look, begging me to make it stop.

"Everything's okay," I replied without much conviction. In her full faculties, she'd never have believed me but I think now she needed to believe. She went about her chores, picking up broken pieces of our lives, as if nothing unusual were happening.

Just then the expected pounding began inside the room. Evidently, Dylan was stomping the floor with his feet. As the rhythmic pounding grew louder, he began to accentuate its beat with curses at me. Then as sudden as it had started, the pounding stopped.

After a minute of silence, I felt him trying to turn the door knob from the other side. I held tight and frustrated his attempt but cursed to myself because he knew I was still there, a captive audience.

Another minute passed in silence and then suddenly something substantial and hard slammed against the hollow core door. Damn! I said to myself and jerked my head back. I shook it off quickly as another flurry of activity began inside the room. He startled me and now my adrenaline was flowing. I felt it flush my face and set my resolve.

I opened the door and stepped rapidly to the center of the messy room. At first, I didn't see him. Then I felt a blow across my shoulders. It stung. I turned to my left and saw Dylan holding a long metal curtain rod. I'd no idea where he'd gotten it but, at the moment, it didn't matter. I was sure if I did a quick inventory of the windows in the house and garage I'd have no trouble finding one missing their curtains.

He swung at me again but I blocked it with my left forearm. "No you don't," I said and grabbed his wrist removing the rod from his hand. "I'll have no more of that. You'll learn how to behave." I articulated crisply, full of bluster and dragged him from his room. Walking rapidly down the hallway, not wanting to give him a chance to grab onto anything, out we spilled into the living room.

I paused a moment to look around for an open corner. The only one available was by the front door. It was good because there was nothing on the wall he could grab and rip down. I moved in that direction pulling him behind. "You're going to behave. I've had enough of this." I said in a surprisingly calm tone, sounding like someone else. "You'll stand here until you stop," I added, grabbing his shoulders and standing him face first in the corner.

He turned around and we faced each other like two gun fighters in a showdown. We squared off hips and shoulders. It must've made an absurd picture, a grown man and small child, head to head, face to face in an obvious battle of the wills. "No!" he drew first.

"Yes!" I quickly shot back, determined I'd win this fight, no matter what it took. If I didn't win this battle of the wills, all was literally lost. We could go no farther from this corner, at least not as a family, unless I finally won one battle.

I set my will against his. I was going to oppose him for as long as I needed. I was determined to prevail, no matter the cost or collateral damage. Hell, everything was falling apart or getting broken anyway. We were desperate.

I placed my hands on his shoulders and began to turn him around. But before I could spin him around he collapsed and began thrashing about on the floor. I reached down and thrust my hands under his arms from the back and lifted him with his face toward the corner. He screamed like an eaglet being attacked. He recognized his situation and curled his knees toward his stomach and then placed his feet on the wall on either side of the corner. He pushed throwing his head backwards, banging the back of his skull into my face.

Luckily, I reacted quick enough to duck my head just an inch or two. I took most of the blow on the side of my forehead and not on the tip of my nose. I steadied my feet and pushed back. But his feet pushed against the wall and kept me from getting him farther in. I pulled back quickly. With nothing to hold them up, his legs fell. Then I reversed the motion and pushed him in the direction of the wall before he could pull them up again.

Realizing he was trapped, he let out another blood curdling scream and flailed about. He banged his head against the plasterboard several times before I could readjust my grip and pull his head back an inch or two out of reach of the wall. But when I did, I unknowingly gave him the opportunity to stomp on my toes, which he took full advantage of. I almost lost him as the pain shot up my right leg. He twisted about in my grip and nearly got away to my right. But I grabbed him in time and pulled back harder than I wanted, banging his left elbow against the door with a loud thump.

I was now down on one knee and had my left arm wrapped around his waist and his right forearm held with my right hand tightly below his elbow but this didn't stop his left hand from whipping around and, with his nails, raking my right cheek just below my eye. I threw my head back and to the left while I let go of his waist with my left arm and reached around under his arm to grab his right hand. I let go with my right hand and grabbed his left hand, which was still clawing for my face. Luckily I snatched it before he could scratch me a second time.

Even though I now held both his hands I didn't hold tightly, trying not to hurt him. He turned his face to mine. Not more than an inch in front of me he spat a wad of something warm and wet into my eyes and screamed, "Let me go, you mother-fucker!"

With my arms wrapped around him from the back, each holding onto his opposite wrist, I pulled hard and tightened him into a position much like a straight jacket. This forced his face away from me.

Again, he tried to bang me with the back of his head but I was quicker this time and he hit nothing, just snapped his neck against thin air. But he managed to unbalance me and I fell back onto my butt still holding him tight to my chest. I'm sure he thought this some success as he tried to head butt again. I just held on tight.

He screamed, "Fuck you, mother-fucker!" and began to kick the wall and bang my shins with the back of his heels. I threw my legs out to both sides, spread eagle and held him so his heels couldn't reach my shins. I was concentrating on and holding him with all my might. He was strong, but I'd no choice. I felt like a cowboy holding onto a bull; I didn't think I could hold on but letting go wasn't an option.

Wrapped in my arms, immobile from waist to shoulders, Dylan continued to scream and yell and slam his feet against the wall. He kicked hard enough to imprint the sheetrock to the shape of his right foot. Not wanting a larger hole, I slid back half a foot and pulled him to me again. Unable to reach the wall with his feet he began to bang on the floor. In response, I threw my legs over his and wrapped his legs with mine. To do this I had to lie down completely.

And there we were, all wrapped up on the floor. I had him completely immobile except for his head and mouth with which he beat about, hollering obscenities at the top of his lungs. Now that I'd a moment to think, I realized I was holding his wrists too hard. Remembering his teacher's inquiries, I loosened my grip as much as I could without letting him go. It was difficult to hold him and not hurt him at the same time. But I did my best.

We were sweating profusely which made it even harder to hold his wet arms with my wet hands. I forced myself to breathe smoothly because I didn't want him to know how tired I really was. I could do nothing more than hold and take the brunt of his outrage. There was nothing as pure as his wrath. I remember thinking that someday he was going to grow up and kill me.

After a while his ferocity waned. Tentatively, I said, "It's alright, Dylan." This, of course, only aroused his ire again but I held on tight through the next squall as well. When it began to diminish, I said, "It's okay Dylan, everything's going to be alright," trying to make my voice smooth and reassuring.

"Let me go, you bassar," he shrieked back.

"When you're calm, I can let you go," I repeated and held tight.

I heard Martha behind us, walking back and forth from the kitchen down the hall to our room and back again. She went downstairs and then returned.

I took a quick glance at her over my shoulder as she passed. Seeing her expression, I shook inside. The sparkle was gone. She was pale and unfocused. She may've been muttering something to herself. It looked like the edge of madness was playing on her features. What had I done to her? I realized, perhaps for the first time, that I couldn't save us. I'd always had an optimistic nature, some might say arrogant, but I was now in a situation which I couldn't fix. It was all coming apart and I could do nothing to keep it together except to hold on and repeat my lie, "It's alright, Dylan. Everything will be okay."

Much later Dylan said, "Dad, I'm thirsty" and asked for a drink of water.

"No," I said, "not until you spend a quiet minute in the corner." Then I repeated affirmations in his ear "If you can't control yourself, someone else will" and "when you stop, I'll let you go." On and on.

Finally, he said okay. And when he did I let him up. He stood, with his hands behind his back, quietly for a minute.

After that, I brought him the water. He drank it and we went to bed. That night, as I lay next to him, I couldn't help but feel I'd won something. I'd finally gotten him to do what I said, for the first time he obeyed me even though he didn't want to. It was at a price but it had been a victory none-the-less.

The War to Save the Union

I didn't win what I thought I had that night. Dylan's story isn't a tale of a one-time miracle worker or the kind you can tell in a two hour parent training seminar. It resembles more a story about trench warfare and attrition.

Looking back, I see that the immediate effect of confronting Dylan wasn't as much of a breakthrough as of a stabilizer. It affected a difference like the one between accidentally falling off a high canyon bridge and sky diving. In both cases you're hurtling through space, rushing, en route to doom. The difference is that, in the latter, you think you've a plan to escape. At that point, any victory with Dylan was a parachute and suggested there was a way to survive.

The day after I won my showdown in the corner, our lives fell back into much the same, now old, new pattern. But with this variation, its ending was different. It changed in that instead of concluding in the bathroom, struggling over dirty clothes before a bath, we finished the day wrestling in the corner until Dylan gave in and said, "Okay, I will."

Now, instead of with a book and a hug, the night was completed with a glass of water and a wordless march down the hall to a silent bed. There we waited bitterly for exhaustion to take its course. In fact, the only abiding thing that changed was that Dylan began to act out more with Martha when I wasn't around. That's the problem with punishment; it's only effective while the punisher is present.

One time Martha took Dylan out of school for the day to go to lunch with her and celebrate Grandma's birthday. The three went out to eat at Mom's favorite restaurant, a fancy establishment which had a French Imperial décor and cuisine. It was silver service dining only. Halfway through the appetizers, Dylan decided to abandon his restaurant manners and revert to barbarian home style.

Impulsively, he lifted a bowl of onion soup placed recently near him by a waiter's formal hand. He slurped from its side, burning his lower lip and tongue. The heat was hiding under melted cheese. He slammed his bowl. It landed with a thud, spilling dark broth across white linen.

Martha went to cleaning.

Unconcerned by the havoc he was creating, Dylan knocked over a glass of water as he grabbed a roll from the basket. He tore it in half with such gusto, crumbs scattered everywhere. That night there were bits in everyone's hair.

Dylan was a success in making chaos of Grandma's birthday. Martha grew increasingly anxious as she unsuccessfully tried to keep up with his messes. She laughed nervously, frantically blotting up dark brown and clear fluids with cloth napkins. Apprehensively, she glanced around at nearby diners. Most of them looked back at her with expressions that contained multiple layers of annoyance, anger and disgust. As she set up a glass and righted the overturned bread basket, Martha saw her mother's face and turned pale.

"No, Dylan," she said at last. "Don't make such a mess. Stop that right now!"

"No, no, no, no!" he snapped back and continued his frenzy.

I don't know all the details but at one point, he held on tightly to the table's leg as Martha pulled on him and the waiters steadied skidding silverware. But by that time, Martha was determined and just tugged at him until he let go. His behavior continued to escalate until, in final desperation and panic, Martha brought peace to the state room by yanking Dylan and carrying him from the restaurant as he thrashed and blared to the air. "A-holes!" He intoned at the top of his lungs. "A-holes," he proclaimed shaking a defiant fist above them all.

Although Martha is still mortified by the thought of it, I should admit I giggled when I heard the story. The image of Dylan screeching as he was removed from the pretentious dining room, made me laugh. I've never really liked eating in stuffy restaurants and now Mom will never want to go again.

But I found the joke was on me when, during our next family visit to Lansing, Mom took me aside and wagged her ancient German finger at me, saying, "That boy has a fire in him. You better put it out." Her shaking finger in my face reminded me of the hands of old nuns who taught me with the back side of a ruler. With a touch of bravado I replied, "I don't want to put it out; I'd rather use it to make steel." But that was all audacity. I didn't believe a word.

#

That was before we began sleeping with a madman. You see, sometime, I don't remember exactly when, Dylan began to sleep with us in a new king-sized bed. Martha and I bought it thinking that since we'd such little uninterrupted sleep, we should enjoy all we had. Consequently, we selected the top of the line. Hoping to make up for quantity with quality, we spoiled ourselves and bought a big down cover that fluffed all over, plume light. Then, while we feathered our nest, we'd another thought. If we were as tired and fatigued as we were, perhaps Dylan was exhausted, too. We realized he needed some better rest, too. Perhaps if he got more sleep he'd calm down.

Hadn't he slept so long at Christmas? Didn't that mean he was tired and fatigued by all the change in his life? Think of how hard it must be for a child to have a new, now fifth, home. His sleep was haunted by nightmares. Could they be the fodder fueling his fire? Yes, everything bad began with the nightmares. It all began with lack of sleep and bad dreams then, didn't it? Perhaps, if he got some peace, he might not be as agitated the next day. And besides, the new bed was much larger than the old double, there was plenty of room. Or so I thought.

We changed our entire bedtime routine. When we talked to Dylan, he admitted he was afraid of sleeping alone. We told him we were going to have a pajama party. We got fun books, music and a video at the store. We bought snacks and treats and flashlights for three. We stuck glow in the dark green stars on both bedroom ceilings. Then we all changed into our PJ's and came together in our new king bed.

We told Dylan we'd thought of a way to make his dreams be good ones. "Because dreams begin in the imagination," we said. "It's okay to let our imaginations get rid of them." We presented him with a little dream catcher Martha had brought home from a trip she took before we were married. It was small and made from one long twig, bent and bound around a wide weaving of strings. Tangled in the twine, here and there, were a feather and two red beads. We told Dylan to imagine the bad dreams getting tangled and caught in the web. We told him if he imagined really well, they'd come no closer to him.

More importantly, we explained we were a family and that families are forever. Martha pointed to the plaque she'd bought the day he first came to stay. She'd moved it to the bedroom earlier that day. She told him that, as a family, we'd get through everything together. "So, until the nightmares are all gone, we're going to sleep together in this big bed," she said and patted the comforter around her. Dylan was delighted.

Martha looked relaxed and settled into the softness about her as we had our party. Dylan and I stayed up late and watched a video and played games with the flashlights on the ceiling. That night was the quietest at the house in a long time. Frankly, I was surprised at how happy Dylan was. And, at the same time, his happiness didn't excite but calmed him. He drifted off to sleep and we, as a family, got our first good night's sleep. In the morning, we all slept in.

When I awoke, Dylan was watching TV in the living room. I left Martha alone and went to join him for morning cartoons. As I lay on the living room floor, he seemed calmer than he had since

I'd known him. I was happy for him and happy for me. We watched "Recess" together, finding out how the fourth graders were able to take the playground back from the kindergarteners. After a little while, we played unstructured games.

During "Recess" that morning, Dylan and I had a laughing contest. I don't know how it began. I think he started it by rolling over to me, turning his face toward mine and laughing loudly in my ear. His moist breaths made me wince, which caused him to laugh even harder. As a final resort I laughed back but in kind of an intentionally high pitched giggling tone that had a touch of mockery and challenge. In response to my response, he jumped up on me, straddling my chest and laughed in my face, bent over almost nose to nose.

We spent the better part of ten minutes laughing like that, back and forth, eye-to-eye until it broke down into a tickling, wrestling and then pinching contest, which eventually woke Martha up.

But all this had the same effect on our lives as the showdown in the corner had. On the surface, everything seemed unchanged. Our days still had the same pattern. The morning with Martha and Dylan was sour. She said he wouldn't do what she asked and added, "You can never let your guard down." He seemed full with mistrust of everything, "Adults are an enemy to him," she said one day. "That's why he has to fight everything."

In the afternoon, he went to school where no news was still good news. Occasionally, I tried to do his word cards with him when he got home. It was always with less than positive results. His anxiety increased in the afternoons and peaked most every night with a rage episode. The closer it got to bedtime, the more agitated he became. I was fighting to hold him down in the corner almost every night for two or more hours. When he was done he'd get a glass of cool water and we'd go to bed and sure enough, two hours later the nightmares came back. The dream catcher didn't snag them.

We were sleeping with a madman as his astral battles were beaten out in this world by flailing against pillows, mattresses and sleeping parental bodies. Often we didn't awake to the sound of screams, but first to a blind blow. I'll never forget the time I was raised from a dead sleep by his elbow across the bridge of my nose. I sputtered and blinked for five minutes while he thrashed the bed.

It wasn't the best sleep we ever got but it was better than before. It was an improvement at the time. At least, we didn't need to take that long walk down the hall. All we had to do was turn over and cover our vitals. At worst, sleeping with Dylan was like sleeping through a battle. Bad nights were spent sopping our mattress with vinegar water and pat drying with fresh towels, only to lie down on a damp spot, just to be beaten awake again. Those nights, I wrestled with a madman angel, doing battle merely to wake up with a limp the next day.

On the whole, this was still better. We never sent Dylan away. When we let him sleep through his nightmares next to us, it was less traumatic for us all, better for him.

And still, we wore down. Martha started to slip from bed to the living room couch after Dylan's first nightly go-round of elbows, knees and maledictions. Eventually, she fell asleep on the couch and, in the end, stayed there for over a year.

In the afternoons, Dylan was the most hyperactive and impulsive kid I'd ever known. To tell the truth, this combined with his speed and lack of fear did more damage to the physical plant than his explosive, angry episodes in the evening. Those mostly sapped our wills. He broke so many things. Busted pieces of our lives settled around us like dust in a stirred and abandoned room. And no matter how hard we tried to clean it up, we couldn't get ahead of it; the disorder of our house grew day by day.

But Dylan's evening episodes of rage seemed less horrific by now; they felt somewhat more rote, like a weary ritual. They became stereotyped. Their regularity gave us the advantage of knowing where we were going. We'd already survived this. These bouts now had a defined beginning and ending. They were contained to the time between the two. In other words, they were just one appointment a day.

At their beginning, they were like the turning on of a light switch. That's how fast Dylan could switch moods. Faster than a quick click, he'd jump from one side of infinity to the other: Dylan okay, Dylan not: "No, no, no, no!"

#

Every week during this period, in addition to our regular routine, something big happened. It was odd because it seemed to pace itself, just about once a week something happened. The first time, Dylan snuck into a neighbor's empty house and left a large pile of things in the living room. He made the pile from stuff he found around the house: furniture, small appliances, pictures, a statue, etc. Some of it was broken, some wasn't, but it was all mixed together forming a mound on an old rug. In comparison to later events, not too much was damaged this first time. But it was embarrassing working things out with our neighbor.

Dylan caused more costly property damage the next week when he stoned a classic truck. It was painted in the original fiery red, was in cherry condition, and parked in the alley out back. I swear Dylan wasn't out of my sight for more than a few minutes. But the facts said differently because he managed to damage three sides, both headlights and the windshield with nicks, cracks and various sized divots. He had to be throwing stones for a while.

This continued through late summer. During some free playtime in the back yard, he stained the Peterson's two-story white house with purple berries found growing in a nearby stand of bushes. The house had to be re-painted to hide the purple stains. One evening, around the Fourth of July, he took some white stones from a flower bed and was teaching the young children of our guests to throw them at cars passing on a nearby street. In another neighbor's yard, he kicked off the tops of the foot lamps that lined the front walk from the driveway around the garage and up to the front door. All of this brought us into conflict and negotiation with our neighbors.

An unusual but good thing about Dylan was he never seemed to make the same mistake twice. Having gotten into trouble with each neighbor and having had to work things out with them seemed to give that neighbor immunity with Dylan from any further damage. Dylan kept his word. So, in a backhanded way, I thought we were making some progress as we only had a limited number of neighbors. While it was time consuming and expensive, I felt that through the resolutions of these conflicts by peaceable means, we helped Dylan learn that quarrels needn't be lethal.

#

One day that summer, Martha and I were having coffee on the deck at the back of the house. Dylan was occupied inside cleaning his room. Unknown to us, he went into our bedroom and took Martha's jewelry box, the big, cherry wooden one and carried it out to the driveway.

Then he got a hammer from the garage. He worked the wooden box over so thoroughly, later I couldn't tell whether he'd emptied the jewelry first, smashing it piece by piece into gravel before turning to the velvet lined box or whether he simply destroyed the whole thing all at once, indiscriminately and brutally. We heard the hammer pounding but I thought it was a workman down the street.

This was a disaster. Most of Martha's precious memories were shattered that day. The baby ring her mother gave her, one for graduation, presents from suitors and friends from years, everything I'd bought her, including her "camping" wedding ring; none of this was salvageable, most of it unrecognizable.

When I asked why he did it, Dylan said he wanted to have crystals like the Power Rangers. Then he got mad. Everything special in Martha's past was left smashed and strewn across the drive so Dylan could become a Power Ranger. This was an extraordinary blow to her and she took it personally. It felt like a physical attack on her, and for the next two or three days she walked through the house a little bent forward at the waist and tense all around her sides, up and across her back, neck and shoulders.

I really lost it with him that day. I couldn't bear to see Martha hurt so. I yelled at him for five minutes and made him clean the black driveway for an hour and a half in the hot sun while I consoled Martha inside. I made him gather everything in a brown bag and then search for missing pieces. It became a hotter day outside than I'd expected and after a while Dylan asked for a glass of water. I said, "No" and made him pace the sizzling asphalt for a half hour more. That was an awfully long day for us all.

I made Dylan work outside the next several weeks. It was summer and I wanted to give Martha some room. Since I was off work for break, I let her sleep in the mornings. When Dylan awoke, I took him outside to work in the yard until she joined us hours later. We were all on edge and ready to blow; little was said between the three of us.

I'd set Dylan to work in a spot, cleaning and weeding. Then I'd move around the house and work nearly out of sight. At least when he was outside the house he was away from our valuables inside. I got away by myself for periods of time to try to calm down and think things out. But I still kept him under covert surveillance. He understood enough to know he was in trouble and stayed pretty much where I put him. It was like one big time-out for us all.

But it didn't keep him from exploding in violent confrontations at other times. He hated getting his hands in things that were wet or gooey. One time I told him to clean a flower bed in front of the garage, which had a mixture of wet newspaper, plastic, dead leaves, broken sticks and mud mixed all along the wooden fence at the back of the flower bed. Seeing it was wet and slimy, he refused. I wasn't in the mood to be said "No, no, no, no" to anymore. I took a chair and sat it in the large empty field beyond the fence and north of the garage and made him sit there until he'd do what he was told. He went ballistic and raised a huge racket but he stayed there and didn't take off. For my concerns, if he didn't wake Martha, I didn't care if he made a spectacle of himself before God and country.

So I placed the chair in a spot far from the houses but near traffic. He just made a fool of himself and I let him scream it out like a two-year old. I went around the corner and pretended to do something else. When Martha came out later, she'd wonder what we'd been doing all morning. That's when I got mad. I know

168

she'd been through a lot, I'd gone through it too but she wasn't bouncing back. This was surprising and annoyed me.

One day, I think a Thursday, Martha came out and announced, "We're putting the adoption on hold."

I was shocked. "What do you mean?"

"We're putting the adoption on hold," she repeated to me. "We're taking a break from it."

I felt like the naive spouse who'd just been told that a trial separation would do us both good. I didn't know what to say.

"I made the call to the Crossings just now. The decision's been made," she said without blinking.

"You never told me . . ." is all I managed to stammer.

She looked straight at me and interrupted, "This has got to stop. Unless things change, I can't . . . I can't do this." She shook her head and, going back inside, turned away from me as if for the first time.

I stood between Martha in the house and Dylan in the yard. I don't remember everything I thought but I do remember brooding over everything we'd built as it was all falling apart.

It was obvious I didn't have the power to stop it. I was hopeless. We were all moving in different directions and I couldn't do anything except keep working around the yard, wondering what my father would've thought of me that day. If we weren't going to be a family, there seemed little purpose in yard improvements so this became an empty and bitter task. But if for no other reason than to keep Martha and Dylan apart, I kept going with the wheelbarrow and rake.

She wanted to stop the adoption, for "awhile." But I felt if we stopped at all, we'd never start again. This, our "forever family", was about to bust up and apart and no one was certain just where or how to stop it. That was the road we were on. I could see the signs clearly.

In the next few days, I worked pointlessly but finally came to a clear understanding of where we stood. We were three separate people living on the same small ground. And right then, we wanted little more from each other, other than to be left alone. We were barely polite strangers who knew too much about each other and only cared in theory. As a family, we were utterly desperate, each of us bleak, each at a crossroads.

I saw it clearly. Like rolling a boulder up a hill, we all had a heavy decision to move and no one could push for the others. We each had to make it over that hill or give up. This was our only chance. Each could veto the whole group. For us to become a family, a real family, we all had to agree, without hesitation or compunction, that families are truly forever.

That week, I moved things around aimlessly until a moment when I stopped in the front garden. Dylan was sitting on the chair in the yard north of the garage. Martha was inside. And I realized just how exhausted I was.

I sat on the small stone wall that edged the flower bed, breathing rapidly and too shallow, when suddenly something shifted in my mind. It felt like waking up startled. My perception unexpectedly changed and the bright day appeared suddenly washed out. The landscape dulled by several degrees of contrast and intensity. It felt like something wrong had just happened but I didn't know what it was yet, as if its consequence was coming at me fast but from a long way off.

I didn't know what I was feeling and not knowing frightened the hell out of me. I began to panic. Confusing ideas, like broken pieces of pictured disasters, suddenly filled my head. But they weren't memories or scenes from movies I'd seen. They were all the disasters possible from that particular moment in time and place. They had reality and rushed through me, too fast to comprehend or control. I looked around and saw nothing but fear everywhere.

170

That's when a completely odd thing occurred. It's hard to explain, even now it sounds kooky hearing it out loud but I felt it intensely. Everything around me appeared less substantial, like all creation was being drained of substance or life force. That sounds silly, I know. But sometimes when a person is pushed to their limit, when all their efforts have failed, when they've no more good to give, panic can turn, in a flash, to insight.

Instantly, I realized that everything in this world was flipped upside down and backwards, in an odd but literal way. If I tried to explain it sequentially, you wouldn't understand a word. But I saw that our failure was linked to a greater failure, an echo of a primal disaster when this world was created as the result of some horrible mistake. I can't describe it in detail but in that moment in my garden, I saw our problem in an entirely new way. And I learned I had to do the opposite of what was natural for me.

This insight broke abruptly through my panic: I saw the failure in the world. I recognized a flaw programmed inside of everything. Something in nature was wrong, something in the way it was made. It wasn't me, my intentions or decisions that were incompetent and pushing us towards disaster. It wasn't Martha's fault and, certainly, not Dylan's. I realized then that the fault was something more global, an error in the foundation of the world.

Everything worked out the opposite of what we planned. Everything we wanted to put together fell apart. The virtues we possessed were sin; victory was failure, and good intention did indeed pave us a path to hell. Everything was upside down and backwards.

That was my revelation. Call it the "Apocalypse of Jacob" and laugh if you like. I'm sure of it still and no sneer will make it false. As I was baptized into the Kingdom in a lake on a bright Easter morning, I was baptized into Spirit that day with fear and fire. The world and everything it contained was upside down. I mean that literally: upside down! Success is a failure and only through failure can success rise again. That is the nature and gravity of our world.

171

David & Barbara Kenney

I looked up from my stone seat in the garden and saw the clouds like glaciered mountains reflecting sunlight. Normally during my daydreams of escape, my thoughts rested there on those hills of mist. But on that day in the front yard, my mind traveled further out. It pierced the clouds and moved up and out of the atmosphere. And when my perception left the local and distorting effect of the earth's gravity, achieving orbit, I realized that I was no longer ascending but falling. Classical physicists define orbit as falling and endlessly missing the ground. Accordingly, once my focus left the atmosphere, I felt like I was going over the first hill on a roller coaster and descending rapidly. I looked down into space and saw the great outer darkness of infinite nothing. I saw then that I was falling into a bottomless pit. In that instant, my spatial orientation flipped inside me and my body felt like I was physically falling off the ground! I actually flinched and grabbed onto the edge of the flower bed.

I'd touched the unthinkable enormity of space. And inside I felt, for the first time, the Fear of God. I'd never understood that phrase before but at that instant knew it directly and solidly. No longer did I live in a world with fluffy white clouds billowing over my head. I looked down from an unimaginable height above the bottomless pit with only wisps of vapor below to hold me up. I felt the terror of my mortality and knew then just how fragile life was.

This was the vision I had that day, born out of panic but true: that everyone who lives in this world has a twisted sense of reality, a distorted perception. Everyone feels like the earth is pulling us down and, therefore, it becomes the center of our universe. But this is not true. The earth pulls us close, no doubt, and we struggle against it from day one. All our lives we push away from the ground. Our ego is born in that constant push away from the dirt, this struggle to be separate, which we call "our life". I push away from the earth and gain individuality. I am good, consequently, I am up. As the opposite then, the world is down, is bad, and needs subjugation. And with it, all it contains.

This distortion in perception allows us to function in our daily lives. We feel safe, that the garden that we live in is the rule and not the exception. This is, however, not supported by the facts. Because of our flip-flopped sense of reality, we have the courage to walk down the street and to look across the room at our office.

172

But this distortion causes us to be earth-centered in our biases and completely provincial in our sensibilities.

If you measure the physical universe and tally it up into two sides: places where life can exist and spaces where it cannot, you'd find that without a doubt life is the rarest thing in the universe. All life is currently so insignificant as to be meaningless to the greater emptiness of space and time. Life is scarce, hence, it is sacred.

Don't believe me and my vision. Do the math yourself.

But the real bad news is that not only is the dead, by far and in great excess, the norm here but all living things are egocentrically programmed to eat one another. When in balance, the cycle spins like a bike wheel but imbalance occurs easily when one part consumes more than it needs, as we currently do. We don't merely feed, we feast on each other. And because we are trapped in the distortions of our ego and don't see enough of ourselves in the life around us, we don't realize that we are threatening the entire cycle with our insatiable hunger. We feed off the rest of the living in order to give birth only to ourselves, our "kind", even though we could never survive alone.

I was horrified by the consequences of my vision and realized that the crimes for which I should be seeking forgiveness were not as petty as I'd thought. I was naked at sunset in my garden and experiencing the truth of original sin.

It all tumbles together in my mind and is hard to put into words.

Like Dylan, I was acting in direct opposition to my own benefit and not knowing it. I was traveling down an easy, wide slope, well-populated with other drunken travelers. I needed to look down and stop calling it up. In my perverted perspective, bent by gravity, I'd thought only in terms of "I", my good, my desire, my son and my work. How could I possibly act for the good of my family when I couldn't even perceive them correctly?

Martha and I always tried to make peace with Dylan, ourselves, and this world. We thought that was love. But I understood now that love isn't always pretty. Sometimes it's ugly and repulsive, more like war. Our natural and distorted instincts led us to attempt peace. We thought that was the way to build a family. But we were wrong. I thought to myself, "If in trying to create harmony with Dylan, we only increased the battle, perhaps making war was the only way to find peace."

I decided right then that what we needed was war. I declared it being determined to use any means necessary to heal our lives through holy battle. What else could justify Dylan's harm? I'd never seen such a pitiful piece of life, struggling to survive, in constant danger of being lost again and again. Could anything less than total war justify what had happened to Dylan? And by what other means could we make it right again?

So from that time on, personalities no longer mattered. The only thing that was important was life itself and in general, not a special form.

I've always been a sucker for the lure of the lost cause. The courage exhibited by those who fight futile battles in dignity fascinated me. This is what led me to study history in the first place.

I'd learned about generals, battles and why wars were fought. I studied the organization and conduct of war. If our family was to be my lost cause, not Dylan, not Martha, not any one individual, but our family as a whole, I'd better use what I knew. War was hell but hell was the only hope left us. So I came out of my garden ready to raise it.

I waged a systematic fight like the North against the South. I decided to grab hold of all resources, control all means of production, blockade all ports, restrict all access to vital retreat and squeeze the opposition like a giant snake. I had to be willing to cross any frontier to gain victory. And I had to insist on unconditional surrender alone.

But the fight I needed couldn't be one of brute force alone. We couldn't win the battle by only inflicting pain, not with Dylan;

174

his will was too strong and by now had become accustomed to most of it. If I tried to fight on the level of fists and fangs alone, I'd surely lose. Dylan would eventually be bigger and stronger and have a lot more stamina than me. Eventually he'd win a brawl.

Anger and violence were clearly not the only answer. On the other hand, no tactic or intervention could be summarily dismissed without consideration. Our war room had to take under consideration all possible routes to victory. And, although it isn't a panacea, brute force can solve some problems in short order. The day after I came out of the garden, I spanked Dylan for the first time.

It happened during our nightly go-round, throw down in the corner. Dylan was doing his best impression of World Wide Wrestling. Martha was working. And I was repeating, in monotone, "Control yourself or someone will control you" into Dylan's right ear. By now, I could hold onto his wrists and wrap my legs over him keeping him immobile without hurting or having to think much about it. I became a human cage that surrounded him almost without touching. He could pound against me but not get away. Although he still struggled and screamed, this posture allowed me time to think. On this night, I was thinking about strategy.

Sometimes battles are won by impulsive, brave attacks. But more often, wars are won by good defenses, another lesson from the Civil War. Accordingly, I was thinking about defenses. What were they? Did we have any in place at all? What were our rights? I needed to be clear about this, not out of a sense of self-preservation but to be completely impartial to individuals, I needed to protect all our rights equally. I had to think only of the family as a whole and not the individual members separately. We all had the right to self-defense; this is a human right and we didn't waive it to join this family.

Violence in self-defense is okay, right? Dylan had made his need everyone's necessity. We all required protection, so I established our union's Department of Defense.

Over my right shoulder, Martha walked back and forth with empty hands. Her face remained ghostly and far off. She was lost deep inside but continued to move physically on. In the end, it was her appearance that moved me to stop thinking and to act. I may've acted impulsively but it was for all our protection.

Abruptly, I got up from the floor and looked down at Dylan. I reached down and grabbed him by the shoulders, lifting him easily to his feet. I looked him in the eyes and said, "Dylan, this isn't going to work this way anymore. We need to make it right. You need to know it's my job to protect everyone in this family. I mean everyone! We'll all be respected. Do you understand?" He said nothing but his green eyes were on fire. "I expect an answer, young man."

"I hate you," he replied. "I'm gonna kill you."

"Maybe someday, but not today," I said with finality.

He pulled back his foot and kicked me in the middle side of my left thigh. I ignored the Charlie-horse and continued, "This is your only warning. Listen to me carefully," I grabbed him by the shoulders, straightened and directed him to look in my face. I let go with my right hand to point a finger. "Listen to me; if you hit me again, I'm going to hit back as hard as I can. That's my right!"

I knew he heard and understood because his expression made three changes. It went from shocked to indignant and then to determined. He reached forward, fisted his hand in my face and then tapped me lightly on the outside of my left arm. He didn't hit me hard this time. He was only testing my resolve, finding the line. Bad choice, because now I was as determined as he.

I grabbed him again and turned him around counter clockwise till he faced the corner. As he spun, I pulled back my right arm and planted my feet; when he stopped, I hit him with all my might, my hand connecting with his behind like hitting a tennis ball in the sweet spot of a racquet.

Not prepared for this blow, Dylan was thrown forward. He hit his forehead, with a deep thud, on the door two to three inches

176

left of the middle hinge. For a second, I feared he'd hurt himself. But when he turned around, he'd an odd expression on his face.

He looked at me startled. He was pale except for the spot on his forehead which was turning red rapidly. But he didn't cry. He just straightened himself, shaking out his wrinkles and turned to the corner to do his one minute of quiet. He made no fuss the rest of the night and followed all directions straight away. Later when it was time, he went to Martha and gave her a sideways hug before proceeding to bed.

While he was doing his minute in the corner, I turned around and saw that Martha had watched the whole thing. She was standing in the dining room with empty hands. The light from the hanging glass lamp over the table glowed on her cheek. She wasn't happy.

It's hard to describe Martha's expression as it consisted of a number of feelings in a combination I'd never seen before. In part, there was worry about Dylan's head injury, surprise at his abrupt compliance and betrayal by my violence all mixed with a bunch of other feelings I really didn't know how to interpret. All I was sure about was that she wasn't okay with Dylan getting hit at all.

Before I followed Dylan to bed, I went to talk to her. I told her we had the right to defend ourselves. I told her that I hadn't meant to hit him that hard and next time I wouldn't, but I would continue to protect the whole family. "Like you said, this has to stop."

"That way . . . Is that what you're doing?" Martha shook her head.

"It's got to stop by any means necessary."

"It isn't right. I don't want to see that again," She said seriously, as if she were re-drawing a line she'd unwittingly crossed but wouldn't cross again.

"Okay," I said, thinking how he'd stopped fighting immediately when he was hit, "I'll let you know when I'm going to spank him. I'll warn you and I'll take him to his room. But I'm committed to stop his destructive behavior. Without this family, Dylan has nothing and neither do I. The family is everything; he just doesn't know it yet."

"And me?" she asked directly. "Do you mean me, too?"

"I mean the family is all there is. We passed just you and me a while ago and don't think we can go back." Her expression changed, troubled as if I'd just laid out a scenario she hadn't thought of. "This family survives or it doesn't."

"Oh, I see," she said, turned and went downstairs.

The conversation didn't end; we just stopped talking about it for a while. I headed for the bedroom. After reading Dylan a book, I told him a story. It was the first I ever told him without a book. It was awkward and embarrassing but I thought it that important. The story was about two tigers and a lost cub. It was lame but it did what I wanted it to. It explained why I'd hit him. Dylan listened with his back to me and sometime later fell asleep. I'm not sure how much he'd heard. But after that I took a vow. I said it out loud.

"Everything and everybody has given up on you." I said with all my heart. "No one has stayed. But I make a promise I'm not going to give up. I'm staying here no matter what." He was my family from that point on. I'd made my decision. "I won't leave. If I've nothing when this is all over, no matter what I lose, I won't leave you behind." I lay there for a while, feeling more alone than ever. Later, I got up and went to the living room where Martha was sitting.

She said, "If things are so bad that you have to hit him, we should consider hospitalization. Perhaps professionals can better help him."

"No!" I said. "We can't send him away. If we do, we'll lose him forever. Hospitalization is out of the question. If I must, I'll make a hospital here."

178

Baptism: When Down is Up

Dylan was a giant and obscure crossword puzzle, a scatter of empty spaces in interwoven rows and columns, matched with vague clues referencing facts uncertain or unknown. He'd been with us for nearly ten months but we were basically clueless as to what would fill in his blanks.

We couldn't simply construe him as we presumed because he was already a matrix of wants needing to be met. We had to discover definite answers. Only by the precise pattern of specific responses could he be made whole again. He was full of things hidden in shadows, wrapped in inscrutability and shot through with enigmas. Unlike other parents, we needed to do less imprinting and more revealing. What was Dylan? What could we help him become? How could we help him put all the pieces together again? These were the questions we needed to answer. We had to uncover Dylan, not invent him.

However, in my view, one thing was certain; Dylan didn't need a hospital. He wasn't sick. He required self-restraint, not to be restrained by others. Because he lacked behavior control didn't mean he needed to be someone's experiment in pharmacology. He had to understand life to learn the command of himself, his behavior and fear. The world had to be recognizable and regular, not intoxicated. So, we set out to teach him what he didn't know through force of will and battle, when necessary. Strong teachers were essential, not hospital attendants.

In getting to know Dylan, in analyzing his behavior, I'd noticed he'd only three kinds of play. He knew only three games—tag, hide-and-seek and beat the monster. He'd three play skills: run, hide and fight. After being literally beat over the head with this fact, I finally noticed these reflected the three possible reactions to fear, namely, fight, flight and freeze.

Dylan was always reacting to the fear he felt inside; this was all he knew how to do. He was already a fighter. I decided to emphasize his best and teach him to be a noble combatant. If he was already a warrior, it was best to make him a holy one.

My job, then, was to teach him how, why and when to fight. I took full control of his schedule and started a new program. He was awakened early each day and was given regular exercise. While Martha was sleeping, Dylan and I hit the road early for training. We began with long walks through the neighborhood. We ran wind sprints between mailboxes and would always tie. Later when he learned how, we rode bikes through the neighborhood and in parks. This became a very good way to start our day.

When we got back from our morning road work, we ate breakfast and began chores around the house and yard, always starting with the dishes. We now worked side-by-side, doing every job together. He was, as I said, "on my crew." He needed to learn to follow orders and this wasn't easy for him. But he had to learn to get by in life, so I taught him the best I could. On many occasions, in demanding his compliance to orders, I went toe to toe and face to face with him.

Then we did school work at the breakfast table before going outside to work in the yard. With five minutes break every half hour, this became Summer School or Dad's Boot Camp depending on his mood. After that, we'd spend the morning working together; everything I did, he did. We had a lunch break at noon. After lunch, we went back to work. At about two each day, we'd transition into enrichment activities; Martha often joined us for these family outings, including sports in the park, field-trips to museums, plays and community activities. Dylan needed to learn about the world around him. These activities were often strong on entertainment but still educational. After dinner, about six or seven, we'd wind down with games and sports until dusk and then go inside for stories and bedtime.

We applied structure to his life around the clock and gave him no free time of his own. I took it all away. Later he could earn it back. Time is a resource and, to win with Dylan, I needed to control and utilize all resources and power available to me as his father. We cleaned out his room and put all his toys and play things into large, black garbage bags, which we moved to the garage. If he earned free time, he could choose one item from the bags to play with and then return it when the time was up. I moved all his books down to a bookcase in the basement. I took everything out of his room that wasn't necessary. Nothing was left that could be broken or thrown.

His room became ground zero. Any conflict that proceeded passed civility was resolved wholly and solely in his room. It became something of an isolation room, a padded place when all control broke down. It became the only place I allowed him to throw a fit and even there, there were limits as to what was allowed.

No matter where we were or what we were doing, if Dylan had one of his fits, we'd turn abruptly around and go straight home. Once at the start of Mass, I took him by the ear and pulled him from a pew of parishioners. I marched him back to the car and home without a word. It was a quick and focused maneuver so I caught him by surprise. And while I held his ear, he was completely under my control. He never made a fuss in church again.

Once, at the market, we had two overflowing grocery carts and Dylan started hollering over a piece of refused candy at the checkout line. Martha and I looked at each other. We left all our selected items, half in the baskets, half on the conveyer belt, swept him up and returned to the car. We went straight home.

After we started back, we never stopped, said a word or changed our minds. We always went straight to his room and to the ultimate confrontation in using the shortest possible path, holding him if needed. This procedure drastically reduced the number of scenes Dylan was willing to have in public.

182

Martha was still exceedingly opposed to corporal punishment and abstained from the issue entirely, typically by leaving the house to do errands. Consequently, it came down to me, by default, to establish the rules of engagement for the family.

Once I read a quotation that went something like this: "Before I was married, I had six theories about bringing up children. Now I have six children and no theories." I think Lord Rochester said it. Well, before I was married, I'd been opposed to spanking. But now I found it made many tired hours disappear with the swipe of my palm.

As the representative of the family in this matter, it was better for the whole group that I go against my prejudice and spank the child. It stopped our final daily trauma. It made the transition to bedtime successful and smooth. This helped Martha particularly, as she had indicated that Dylan's combative behavior alarmed her and caused her tension and actual physical pain. Dylan was more at peace with himself after I spanked him. He slept better. I didn't see how I, as "father," could hold back. So I spanked.

But if I was to carry through, I needed to have rules. I needed a policy. Dylan's room was already in place as the Judgment Seat. I thought out the rules I'd go by and told Martha to get her opinion. She gave a conditional acceptance of them as best policy 'if' spanking was to be done. This is what was agreed on:

- Dylan would be allowed to scream in anger, only in his room, nowhere else.

- Dylan was spanked for two reasons:
   a). Insubordination or direct defiance
   b). Destruction of property in anger, not by accident

- Three strokes were the maximum and he was hit only on the buttocks.

- He would be only spanked in his room

183

after Martha had the opportunity to leave the house.

   - In his room before spanking, a discussion was held concerning the reasons for the spanking and Dylan was given the opportunity to clarify and change his mind by giving in.

These were the rules and I habitually abided by them as if they were a religious obligation. The difference between punishment and abuse is that the first is done in a calculated and reasonable manner to obtain a goal and the latter done in frustration for revenge.

It became my policy to give Dylan a clear signal at the last moment before he was spanked. He could retract if he chose. I took to using the Magic 1, 2, 3 procedure and, at the declaration of three, spanking began. Later this became an extraordinarily good warning system in any setting as I was able to shorten it to only two. All I had to do was say the word two and immediately he'd straighten up.

Most people train for a career and are parents by accident but Martha and I trained to become Dylan's folks. I learned to parent him through confrontation and compromise. I met his force of will, attacking his behavior, redefining his mind one piece at a time. Slowly, I was helping him acquire the skills and knowledge he needed to interact appropriately with the world.

I didn't start from a point of perfection; flawlessness was never our family's standard. I started where he was and learned to take every opportunity to teach him something new.

For instance, we discovered Dylan was afraid of sharks when we took him to the Science Museum downtown. The nature film about the carnivorous fish was projected onto the planetarium's ceiling. Two minutes into it, he freaked out and screamed like he was being torn apart. I had to walk him outside until the movie was done. At home, Martha and I decided that he was afraid because of his lack of understanding. Ignorance leads to mistrust and then fear. We taught him so he didn't need to stay frightened.

We discussed sharks. We explained the difference between salt and fresh water and showed him on a globe how far we were from the oceans. We read him stories about the life and behavior of sharks. We drew pictures of ourselves on a raft in the water with sharks and then drew things that could save us; a bigger boat, an island, a long spear gun, etc. We even went so far as to construct an eight-foot tiger shark of cardboard and paste, painted in silver, white and black. The whole family helped with it during enrichment time. It came out really good, realistic, thick and durable. We hung up the effigy in the dining room and shot rubber bands at it until it no longer scared any of us.

#

At about that time, we went back to school and I realized if I didn't wrestle with Dylan every day or so, he'd tighten up. I literally mean all his muscles, especially in the back, neck and head, would constrict. After two or three days he was a flying board. He needed to play fight and be roughed up with laughter and loud cries; it reduced his tension and his boiling point considerably. Therefore, I resurrected Nutsy-Coo-Coo Time. But this time, I began to change it from being about beating the monster or bad daddy to a more imaginative play. I insisted we team up against Batman this time. He hated it at first but I insisted.

I'd pretend to hold Batman, while in reality I animated the plastic blow up character from behind. I made the big puppet fight back. He liked this. Then I'd start a storyline. We had to go on a mission to save some beloved character, say Santa Claus or an angel, from the monsters. It didn't really matter who. We'd climb around the basement, over high furniture and through piles of boxes and laundry. Martha didn't like that part. But eventually we'd rescue our friends together.

We made forts for ourselves with tables and chairs all draped with blankets and sheets. One time, we built a fort three stories high, up to the basement's open rafters. All the while, we did a liberal bit of roughhousing. After that, he'd calm down. It was as if I had to shake him loose like a wrinkled rug to expel the irritating grit at his nape.

When Dylan was able to really relax, when his muscles were loose, he looked different. He wasn't an FLK at all. He was quite a good-looking boy with bright eyes and a quick, easy smile. Typically, he slept better after a Nutsy-Coo-Coo-time adventure.

There were only two rules during these adventures. The first was when playtime was over, we had to calm down and act normal or we couldn't play the next day. And two, whenever I said "Stop" during our play, we had to immediately freeze and then sit down. After we sat still long enough to take a few slow breaths I'd say "Go." The longer it took to gain control, the longer we waited. This was a good principle. Dylan really liked the fun. So, while he was playing, he was seldom oppositional. It was a relief for us to spend time on safari.

Through these games we practiced self-control and team work. Later we began to shoot rubber bands around at the bad guys. Then we switched to soft foam rubber toys. It eventually came back to shooting at each other but by then Dylan had learned the lesson.

By using imagination while we played, I taught him stories, precursors to both reading and writing and through play, I found that Dylan had a knack for narrative. His rote memory was pitiable but his long-term memory for anecdote was just the opposite. So at night, I began to tell him stories and not simply read books.

Bedtime became more like a campfire under the stars as I repeated all the fables and tall tales I'd ever heard, read, knew or could make up. I'd a strong minor in literature at college. I knew a lot of the epic tales from the past and I told him all I remembered. I recited Greek mythology, King Arthur and then legends of today, the tales of modern history. I'll confess to trying to make them all lively, filled with action and quite dramatic. I started to wake up early in the morning to read so I could tell him accounts of the things I learned.

When I ran out of the yarns I knew, I started to make them up. Even though I thought they were awkward and stupid at first, Dylan didn't seem to notice. He lay still and listened, occasionally asking a good question. He started asking me to call the main character Dylan.

It was remarkable how much he learned through stories. Sometime when he asked questions, he'd reference a scene from a tale I'd told him months before. He could retell it in detail.

Dylan was still enamored with the Power Rangers. His favorite was still Tommy, the green one, because Tommy had a special weapon, a magic green flute dagger. Under great pressure, I helped him make one. We had several initial attempts that didn't come out too good. But Dylan was happy. He played with his handmade green dagger much longer than I remember him playing with any store bought toy.

I was proud of that. But when he started talking about power crystals again, I didn't say anything to Martha. But we collected rocks. We'd crack them outside, looking for sparkles; this led to talking about the earth's crust, rocks and minerals, reading books and exploring the outdoors, again fun and enriching.

It was important with Dylan that Martha and I trained ourselves to say only what we meant. There are many expressions we use on a daily basis but don't really mean. Saying only what we meant was necessary because trust was such an issue for Dylan. He was always testing what we said. One time I asked him, "When will you stop testing me?"

"Never," he replied.

I guess I knew that, I thought and laughed a short snort.

I don't think Martha had made up her mind yet, about the family, that is. She still seemed to be sitting on the fence. She was aloof. In truth, she was holding back and a little above us. The fact she left the house often to shop made her less relevant. One day, I found a letter she'd been writing to Dylan and me. It was lying on the coffee table next to her chair in the living room. It was an accident that I found it. It was unfinished but went like this:

187

#

Dear Dylan and Jacob,

I'm writing to tell you of the damage I think Dylan's behavior has done in a collective way to me over the past year. I was excited to help him initially, but now there is irreparable harm. When he is defiant, confrontational and possibly combative, it alarms me, which is reflected in my reaction to him and is a physical response inside. I'm afraid there will be a heart attack, stroke or loss to one of us if this continues.

I recommended mental health intervention, perhaps even a residential placement for a period of time. Jacob, I feel badly that the extreme confrontational behavior has caused this much stress to you, myself and our marriage. I'm upset that two well-intended people can be so hurt by a young child and that we have to live in such a sad environment. To me, I believe if this behavior continues, Dylan will be in a correctional facility someday and we'll die of heart attacks and all of us will be cheated out of a possibly beautiful life.

It is extremely offensive behavior that pushes me away from any family feelings or attachment. I feel sorry and would like Dylan to have some insight into this. He is single-handedly destroying about twenty-five years of my investment into what could've been a nice, peaceful life, something I believe is now lost. I don't want him to destroy the marriage, but that too is taxed. I feel that I'm stuck in a dilemma. We cannot afford to live in separate houses, since I'm not working and I cannot be further exposed to this garbage behavior or yelling anymore. We cannot be continually stressed out. Perhaps we should set up the camper somewhere, even just around the corner at the state park, to get away somewhere quiet."

#

To say the least, I was shocked. And for a moment, I felt it still reflected the day Dylan had destroyed her jewelry. I sat on the edge of the couch while Dylan ran in and out of the room searching high and low for a toy we'd lost.

To me, the letter read like a breakup note from a high school girl. It had all the intensity of passion and the feeling of loss. I felt in her words lost opportunities, good intentions, hopes and dreams. It was a miserable letter. It indicted me for my trespasses without a word written to specify them. She blamed Dylan's behavior out loud but I could feel a greater, unspoken complaint about me hidden there.

Out loud, we'd always said our relationship was fifty-fifty. We promised we'd work together to build a good peaceful life. In that vein, we both promised to help the other without becoming dependent. However, I suppose, there were unspoken promises that while unarticulated offered unconditional sanctuary in the other's strengths. In afterglow, through touch, we'd promised each other salvation. But that was far away and long ago.

The marriage was taxed. This was true and had been for a while, but to read the words in black and white pained me. Even though we had little time together for months and even fewer opportunities to have a complete talk, I always thought I was connected to Martha. But the words of her letter made me feel like I was eavesdropping on the conversation of a stranger.

I'd always assumed, even though we were having rough times, we were going to come out of them together. I knew consciously that divorce was a possibility; you can't miss that today. But it never really felt that way to me, until I read her letter. Martha might leave us.

I thought she'd every right to . . . but what was I to do? I'd made, for me, as strong a vow to Dylan as I had to Martha.

189

Although I spoke my vow to Martha in a cathedral so that many people heard and made mine to Dylan in a small bedroom so that only I knew, I'd meant both equally. I took the quiet one as serious as the one aloud. I couldn't forsake my promise to Dylan. I wouldn't forsake the one to Martha either. But how could I keep both? Martha had every right to leave and I'd help her in any way I could if she chose this. But I couldn't leave her any more than I could leave Dylan. I vowed to both.

Later that night, after Dylan was asleep, I crept out of bed and found Martha reading. I told her I'd seen her letter. We had the worst "fight" we've ever had. It's not that we shouted or cursed at each other. We never really even accused or blamed aloud but, in the end, it was clear we were as far apart as two strangers on a street corner at midnight.

She repeated what she wrote in the letter. And I said I understood her feelings and I'd support whatever decision she made but I'd already chosen. In my mind the family couldn't be subdivided. I wouldn't pick between them.

If she really couldn't take anymore, I'd help her set up her own home. If that's what she wanted, I'd do my best. But, to get by, Dylan needed more. I told her that because of the inequality of their needs, Dylan would be given the majority of my attention and resources.

"Besides," I threw at her, knowing it hurt, "I thought we'd promised to both be fully functioning individuals, you know, fifty-fifty. You're the adult; you need to stop blaming the child for your life."

What I said wasn't completely fair.

#

I went over the line with Dylan too. Looking back I must admit that I hurt them both because I was mad and not because it was the best. To be true to Dylan's story, I must admit that I went beyond what was needed of me in my role as husband and father.

190

One night soon after I had the fight with Martha, Dylan was angry at Martha for not washing some favorite T-shirt for school the next day. He looked her in the face and, in a calm and clear voice, called her a "fucking bitch." He'd cursed me out before but this was the first time he'd ever talked to Martha like that.

Her expression turned to stone as she sat at the dining room table. She bent forward and covered her face. I stopped in the kitchen and turned around. Martha was shaking. From the side, I saw a smirk on Dylan's face. It was clear he enjoyed hurting her. This angered and scared me.

I put down the plate in my hand, took two steps and grabbed Dylan by the back of his neck, uptight, right under his ears and skull. Without a word, I marched him down to his room. I was so quick he just started to panic as we got to the door. But it was too late and I was too angry. In we went. I closed the door.

"What did you say?" I began in a confrontational way. "Stand here and tell me what you said. If you're so tough, little man, stand here and say it to my face." I pointed to the center of the room. We stood toe-to-toe and nose-to-nose.

"Fuck you, who cares about you," he rejoined and stood in front of me.

"Tell me what you called her. If you're so tough, tell me here," I shot back.

"A fucking bitch," he spat back. But I was ready. The moment the words hit the air I slapped him in the face with my right hand. I hit him hard and fast. He didn't see it coming. I don't think I did either; it was a direct, emotional response.

How could you, I thought, after all she's given up to try to help you. How could you, you little . . . ingrate!

Dylan was both shocked and hurt. I saw it in his eyes. He'd been feeling pretty confident that night after having had a good afternoon. But he went way too far. He was way out of line and I felt I had to do something to keep this from happening again. I hit

191

him the first time out of pure emotion and with little reason, but that's not to say reason didn't follow.

He'd no right to talk that way! We were already teetering on the brink of disaster and this family wouldn't survive unless I did something dramatic to stop Dylan from hurting Martha. She couldn't take it on top of everything else. It would send her away from us for certain. After all she'd given him, he'd no right. This couldn't be excused by immaturity or past trauma. This was a personal attack.

Dylan tried to turn away but I shouted, "No! You get back here." And he did. He turned back with his hands at his sides and his face upturned to mine, with his eyes downcast. "What did you say?" I roared.

"A fucking bitch," he repeated quietly without the earlier intensity. As soon as he started I slapped him with my left hand. He was expecting it from my right. I hit him squarely on his cheek.

"Ow!" he grunted and blinked.

"What did you say?" I asked again.

"No," he said and started to shed tears. He squeezed them tight until they stopped.

"Once you say something, you can't take it back," I insisted. "What did you call your mother?"

"A fucking bi . . ." but before he could finish I hit him a third time. Even though he knew it was coming, I was still faster than him. He fell to the edge of his bed kneeling on the floor.

"Stand up!" I said. "We aren't done." He did slowly. I said nothing until he was standing in front of me again with a red, wet and trembling face. "You've no right to ever talk to your mother like that again. Do you understand me?" I leaned my face into his and continued without waiting for an answer. "If you ever talk to your mother like that again, you'll regret it. Do you understand? Do you? Answer me!"

"Yes," was all he said.

I turned and left the room. This time I didn't slam the door. I stood in the hall and started to shake, then cry. With Martha in the dining room, Dylan in his room and me in the hall, it was a real house of tears that night. I was wrong to hit him like that but it was out of pure desperation and a true desire to protect Martha.

I never told Martha what I did. I never told anyone. But Dylan never called her that name again.

This, however, wasn't the only time I went over the line. Once when he was giving me a difficult time in his room, I grabbed the sides of his face and pulled him to me. I placed my head in contact with his, forehead to forehead, until his two eyes became one big one. "Why are you so stubborn?" I asked him point blank. "Why are you always butting heads with me?" I restated in exasperation and then banged our heads together, not enough to bleed but hard enough to hurt.

"Why are you always butting heads with me?" Then I butted him again "Is this what you want? You want to knock heads all the time? Okay, if that's what you want, then I'm done trying to reason with you," and bumped again. "We'll just bang each other until you're all grown up. Is that what you want?" I said a last time for emphasis.

"No," he said again submissively. I left him alone. He took a long nap.

The last way I crossed the line was by getting addicted to spanking. Do you know what I mean? Just as an alcoholic has to drink increasingly more to get the same high, I began to spank increasingly more to achieve my goals. Near the end, it was almost every day. But he was better off; we all were. Spanking was a short cut and effective; it was an easy answer. So, in the end, I used it more than I should have.

193

I don't remember exactly when, but I started to use a paddle, only one stroke at first, but more later. Until one day as I was swinging the paddle and he flinched and took the blow on his back, upper leg. I know it hurt like hell but he didn't cry. He just turned to me, looked steady with a passive face and said, "You can't hurt me anymore. I know how to stop the pain. You can't hurt me." Again, I was afraid.

The next day, he showed me the bruise I'd made. It made me sick to see what I'd done. I promised myself to never hit him again and I've kept that promise. I didn't say anything to him at the time though. I couldn't think of anything satisfactory to say. In the sight of that bruise, I couldn't defend myself. Dylan had won; he'd beaten me.

I went beyond the line at least three times and rubbed up against it many more, sometime with words. Intentionally, I went where I shouldn't have and wept while going. Fighting gets dirty. I was never perfect, I only felt like it before Dylan. He was my test.

Parents are the shores their children break against. Whether we're rough or smooth, we contain our children, giving them form. Our resistance shapes them.

#

Just before Christmas that year, both Dylan and Martha got sick with strep throat. Martha was the sickest and came down with it first. I took her to the doctor and he gave her a shot with a gigantic needle. She was out of it by then with her high fever; she doesn't remember the jab. When I brought her home, she went to bed for three days straight. That's the longest she'd ever been sick. She hated staying in bed. On the fourth day she got up, walked around the house once, complaining about the mess, then went back to bed for two more days.

Dylan got a fever two days after her. The doctor said Dylan had the same thing as Martha. He was burning up. His muscle tone matched that of an over-cooked noodle. His face was bright red and his hair matted wet. At one point, he cried out he was cold even though his skin was quite hot to the touch.

194

I called the doctor every hour. I gave Dylan cold baths that he mildly struggled through. Mostly he was zonked out, oblivious. I put a cold, wet compress on his forehead, then I changed it every fifteen minutes. Between this, feeding, medicating and checking both he and Martha, I was up for most of three days and nights. Once Dylan's fever came down a little and antibiotics were taken, he began to rest well.

Even though I was tired, it was kind of calming to be the only one awake. Dylan didn't stay that way as long as Martha, but while he did, he seemed peaceful. I watched him quietly for long periods of time. There were no wrinkles in his face. He wasn't animated or defended or angry or defiant. He was just a sick little boy asleep. I listened to his regular breathing, with no huffing or puffing; it was just calm and regular. I saw him as he was meant to be, not as he had been twisted by life but as he would've been if he'd been our child from birth. For the first time, I recognized the Dylan that God had meant. He was just there, so small, helpless and beautiful, without a wrinkle on his face.

I fell in love with him at that moment. I remember it happened at a distinct point in time as he slept, needing to be cared for. I was overwhelmed with it. I couldn't look at him enough. As of then, he was my little boy.

Both Martha and Dylan got better before Christmas. We had a small celebration that year, in part because they'd been sick and in part because of our experience the year before. But it was pleasant, low keyed and without too much trouble.

#

After New Year's, we went back to school and passed through the dead of winter without much difficulty. We were all still tired and stressing to some extent but were content to make it day by day. Dylan was having difficulty with his work in first grade and was tested by the psychologist. It was found he had a reading and writing disability due to auditory, perceptual and memory problems. I think it means his brain didn't hear things right even though his ears registered them fine. He got extra support at school and, at home, I found out I could get him to do school work if I didn't try to teach him anything. He'd do drill sheets and work independently but I couldn't correct his work or try to teach him anything. If I did, he was still sure to raise a fit.

Speaking of fits, he was having less of them in these days, maybe two or three a week; that's all. They weren't as intense and always played out in his room with the door closed. Since I was no longer spanking him, if he went over-the-line I restrained him, holding him down again, but now I'd hold him down on his bed instead of in the corner by the front door. After a couple of times with restraint, he pretty much stopped trying to hurt me or break things. He was still vocal and vile when angered but no longer completely out of control. I saw this as an improvement. Martha was less impressed.

One day that winter, while playing in the basement, I got hit in the eye with the end of a belt. It was an accident. I wasn't looking as Dylan whipped a belt at Batman. As I turned around, I took it in the open eye. The blow brought water immediately. I turned and covered up with my palms. I bent forward and took two steps away. Behind me I heard Dylan scream, as if he were the one hit.

I was confused and turned back to see him scamper into the back of the basement. I went after him but by the time I got to the storage room, I couldn't see him. After checking, I found him hiding on the back shelf behind a big box of Christmas decorations, way back in the corner. I didn't go in after him but just sat there so I tried to talk him out.

He was afraid I was going to hurt him. But I wasn't. I kept saying, "It's alright, Dylan. I'm not mad. I'm okay. Don't be upset, Dylan. It's alright. It was just an accident." After a while, I tried to tell him a joke but that didn't work. So I said again, "It's alright, Dylan, I'm not mad." He stayed there for a long time. I stayed with him, intermittently talking and sitting quietly. When he came out he looked sheepish so I showed him my eye between blinks. "You see, it's okay. I can see."

He looked at me suspiciously and I looked back, inquisitive, when he said, "Why do you always call me Dylan?"

"Well . . . that's your name, silly." I stumbled wondering what this was all about.

"You make me call you Dad."

"Well," I began uncertain, "that's because I am and want you to know that I always will be."

"Well, won't I always be your son?" he replied and watched me steady.

"Yes, of course," I replied.

"Then why don't you call me son?" he asked with a tone of finality.

"I don't know," I stuttered. "I'll . . . from now on, I'll call you son." And I did.

Not long after, Martha relented and finally decided to commit fully to her relationship with Dylan. She still didn't agree with my approach completely but could see the improvement we'd made. She made some attempts at reviving her earlier relationship with him and received positive responses. This prompted her to try more and eventually the adoption was set to go forward. We finalized it by going into court. When done, we had a small party at home with just the three of us.

#

That spring, Dylan and I were invited by a friend to go on a canoe trip down a nearby river. It was an annual event by the Lions Club, I think. Fathers and sons went down the river and cleaned-up whatever garbage they could fit in a black and brown plastic bag. After the cleanup, there was to be a bonfire and some cocoa and treats for all the guys. It sounded like fun and we had a free day that Saturday. I decided we would go.

We met early at the boat launch and signed a waiver. But by the time we were in the water, a number of pairs of dads and sons were already paddling downstream in a line. I'm a heavy guy and Dylan was light. Our craft didn't balance well. The boat tilted down strongly in my direction, that is, toward the back. This caused the small vessel to stick its nose up high, the tip clearing the water.

But the river was flat at that point and we headed out, looking for trash to snag. The river stayed shallow for a stretch. I told Dylan we could take off our lifejackets. They were doing nothing, just getting in the way and making me sweat. After a short time, it was obvious Dylan was more interested in catching a glimpse at a turtle or a snake than he was in old pieces of plastic and paper. We didn't manage to collect much trash. We collected more mud and water in the bottom of our craft than anything else. But we were having a good time for free.

Downstream a way, the river opened into a lake. I noticed across its expanse clouds were gathering in the west and the wind was picking up. I decided to stay close to the left shore, which was fine with Dylan, whose eyes darted among the underbrush looking for life. He was ready with his net. The intensity of his expression made me smile.

As we hugged the coast and dawdled, the sky turned dark and the thunderclouds grew fierce. I noticed the disappearance of Dylan's shadow on the water next to the boat. Then lightning flashed. I looked over to the west and then back to Dylan who was apprehensively searching my face.

I didn't want him to panic so I decided to cut directly across the lake to the opening of the river downstream and its protective cover. I cut sharply into the lake to my right. But I hurried too fast as things went from bad to worse. The storm would hit us any minute. Dylan turned to check with me again.

"It's okay son," I said. "We're only rejoining the group." Another bolt burst from another thunder cloud. But as I neared the boats mid-lake the wind caught the nose of the canoe and started to lift it into the air.

For a moment, Dylan hung in mid-air, a foot or two above the water's surface. It was a long moment. I saw the back of the canoe begin to sink. We were about to take on water at my end. I knew immediately that if the water started to flow over the edge of the boat we'd go down rapidly. I looked back to Dylan who continued to hang in the air uttering, "Uh-oh" aloud.

He doesn't have a life jacket on! It came to my mind suddenly. In my rush to avoid trouble, I'd forgotten to stop and put on our life jackets before we entered the deep part of the lake. I hadn't noticed until Dylan hung there in the air. If we go down, Dylan might drown, I heard someone else think. If we go down in the storm, he could die. He wouldn't have time to swim to the shore before the rain hit. He was a good swimmer for six and a half but I wasn't really sure how far he could swim on a stormy lake. I couldn't take that chance.

But there wasn't much I could do to stop the progress of the tilting boat. The wind continued to balance the boat and inch the front higher. If I dug in to push my weight forward I'd only hasten the back end's rush down into the dark. Could I save him if we were both in the water? Or would he in panic drag us both down?

The solution came to me with certainty. There was only one way to keep Dylan in the boat and to keep the boat above water at the same time. That was to equalize the weight! Dylan's weight was a lot closer to zero than to mine. It was clear; I needed to leave the boat as fast as I could. There was no time. I had to act at once and couldn't warn him. So, I pushed with both my feet and straightened my back. I threw my head backward and arched my spine so that I'd clear the edge of the craft as smoothly as possible. My hands were at my sides. I'd no idea of what was behind me under the water. It could've been a rock or a tangle of weeds. I didn't know what I would land on. I simply knew that to save my boy, I had to get away from that canoe ASAP.

I remember being in midair for an odd moment. It's like a snapshot in my mind I can always see. I was prone in the air and falling back, head first into the water. I saw Dylan in the front of the small vessel grasping to the two edges with tight, white hands. Dylan and I were no longer connected; we were heading in different directions free from each other. He was safe and going forward. He'd be alright. I watched Dylan glide away with the boat on the lake's surface.

Then I relaxed into the fall. I remember I still had time to wonder if I'd crack my head on a stone, be impaled on the end of a broken tree branch or be entangled by the tough cords of the rope-like weeds below.

The water was hard and cold when I hit it and shocked the hell out of me. But I stayed still as I sank into deep murkiness. But Dylan was okay, so I was alright. I let the cold in and embraced it; my muscles stiffened and began to shake. I lay back into the descent and let God have his way. I was okay with whatever; my boy was alright.

For a moment, I hung in the dark, motionless as if God were wondering. Then I felt myself begin to rise. My face broke the surface of the water with a pop. I heard myself breathe and saw myself huff out steaming air. I heard the world about me.

I looked for Dylan. He was in the canoe and calling out but staying still. The boat was steady enough in the brisk wind and on the choppy surface. Two other canoes noticed what had happened, one to the right and the other from behind on the left. They were heading in Dylan's direction. The one that was closer to him, the one from the right was yelling something at him but I couldn't hear what they said.

Dylan was calling to the other canoe, calling for help I supposed. The first word I understood him to say was "Daddy." I'd never heard him call me that before. Was he calling for my help?

"I'm coming, son. It's okay," I shouted the best I could as I tread in place. It sounded dim to me in the heavy wind but evidently was loud enough because Dylan turned in my direction. He searched the water frantically. The boat tipped a bit when he turned around. "No, son, stay there, I'm coming to help you. Stay there!" I spat.

I saw him turn again and cry to the other boat, "He's over there. Get my Daddy!" I'd been wrong, he wasn't calling me for help—he was calling to get help for me. That hit home. He wasn't frightened. He was as worried for me as I'd been for him. This realization was beautiful and will stay with me forever, as long as I've memory. I was sunk up to the neck in the cold lake. I felt the twinge of a cramp in my left calf. The storm was coming and would hit before I could get out but Dylan and I were both alright and looking out for each other. So it was one of the best moments in my life.

I felt spirit lift within my chest.

I called out, "I'm okay, son. Don't worry, buddy, I'm alright." Clumsy in my soaked clothing, I swam to him, getting there just as the first canoe reached him. The man in the canoe grabbed on to steady Dylan in the water. I grabbed onto the opposite edge of the craft up near the front where Dylan was and let my legs dangle. "It's okay, son, everything will be alright." He leaned over and looked at me face-to-face, a foot away.

"Daddy, you were gone . . ." He still looked startled.

"It's alright, buddy. I just went for a little swim." I laughed, ostensibly attempting to cheer him but really expressing the happiness I felt so intensely.

The rain began to splash on my face but it couldn't slap my joy away. I squinted up into the ribbon of water that snapped at my eyes but I didn't stop laughing. I saw the canoeists, now on both sides of Dylan, hunch down and forward against the downpour but I didn't stop. I laughed harder when I saw the man to Dylan's right shake his head wondering and then, even harder when Dylan grinned back at me.

In his smile, I knew that all my sins were forgiven.

Cool, Man, Cool!

That summer we went to visit Martha's second cousin, Mary, to join in celebrating the graduation of her eldest of eight children. We drove the mini-van down the highway to a neighboring state through a thousand Midwest fields, all growing countless, rich, green stalks.

On the way, Dylan and I played Calafoobu. It's a car game he taught me. Dylan said he made it up and played it on the bus to school. I don't know. It doesn't matter. It's a deceptively simple game. You look for any car, truck or motorcycle that is yellow. If you see one, you shout, "Calafoobu!" If you're the first to finish the cry and you can show the Calafoobu to others, you get a point.

At first, it seems easy but later you realize this is just a small part of the game. You see, the actual competition is debating over what "the meaning of the word 'is' is," and what counts as an authentic Calafoobu. I didn't know, but found out a Calafoobu becomes fake when parked in someone's driveway or on a car lot, but real when parked on the street. Industrial machines don't count. Yellow lines on the sides of trucks painted a different color do tally but solely on trucks and not if they are only a line of yellow lights. Big yellow letters don't count unless they're really big, which is bigger than any I found.

After a while when all of us were sufficiently annoyed by the bickering and changing rules, we decided not to play anymore.

202

Dylan proclaimed victory and two minutes later asked if I wanted to play again. I said no and suggested we sing a song. Dylan said, "No way!" Martha suggested we compromise on a good time oldies station. We listened to the best of the sixties and seventies. I sang along softly as we rolled through the sunny fields, ever changing, always remaining the same. Dylan fell asleep from boredom. I yawned sympathetically while Martha studied a publication she'd got from the state's tourist board.

At the party that followed our arrival, I remember sitting with the other adults and thinking how odd it felt to be normal. Just to visit with relatives, reminiscing and joking, felt both absolutely right and completely odd. I was relieved Dylan was occupied with two of Mary's boys but, even so, I was constantly worried about what trouble he might be getting into. But he didn't; we got only good reports back about him.

Watching Dylan was now such a habit it was difficult to focus on the party. At first, Martha and I took turns going to check on him. He didn't look any different than any of the other kids. This relaxed Martha and she visited with relatives for hours uninterrupted. It had a different effect on me. Although in theory, I appreciated the freedom of not having to watch Dylan at every moment, I was simultaneously drawn away from the adults, time and again, to watch him play. I wanted to be near him. I'd an urge to join his play but was constrained by the situation. I stood back and watched.

Earlier that school year, Dylan's teacher had sent a note home which was positive and said he was coming out of his shell. In fact, she'd written, he's becoming quite the social butterfly. We'd no evidence of this at home, so we didn't know what to make of it. But at this family gathering, I saw. He was completely pleased with his brand-new friends and acted as if they were long lost buddies.

#

After our visit, we headed home. However, we ran into a strong storm in the northern part of the state. Since it was late and we were tired, we decided to stay the night in a motel along the freeway. Inside the lobby, Dylan dashed abruptly away

203

across the patterned carpet and jumped up on a padded chair. His dirty tennis shoes rubbed a dark brown onto the clean fabric. I called for him to get down but he only replied, "No, no, no, no" and raised a defiant fist in my direction.

I looked back to Martha and the overnight desk clerk. Martha's look was anxious. The clerk was annoyed, his expression disgruntled.

"Now, Dylan . . ." I began but didn't finish as he leapt from his perch and tore off down a long corridor to the right.

Everything had been great on the trip until now. I shook my head, held up a feeble hand to reassure Martha and the clerk and headed out after Dylan. As I scurried down the corridor, it occurred to me that this was Dylan's first night staying in a motel. As I passed the entrance to the hotel's pool and glanced in on the still water reflecting blue, it hit me he might be afraid. There'd always been a correlation between his fear and hyperactivity.

I stopped chasing after him and turning to look at the pool some more, said only, "Wow!" I did nothing else.

After a minute I felt Dylan side up to me. Evidently in his rush the first time by, he hadn't seen the pool because now he looked intently. It was evident from his expression he no longer was afraid; his fear was replaced by the anticipation of pleasure. Even though he was still over-active, it was easy to get him to the room and changed into his swimsuit before returning.

Once on the pool deck, he dove in without hesitation. Near the edge of the shallow, he splashed the blue water as he called me to join. I put on my goggles and hastily tossed my towel to a white, lounge chair, waiting nearby. Shortly, I cannon-balled into the deep end. He was favorably impressed with my wave and paddled toward me.

He grabbed my wrist with both hands and pushed both his feet against my ribs. He twisted to his right, hung there a moment slanted and smiled at me wickedly. Treading water one-handed, I couldn't keep my head above water for long with his weight pulling me down. I took a deep breath and upended myself in the direction he was twisting, pretending he'd spun me over.

When he let go, I swam toward the bottom of the pool, reaching out my left hand and touching the drain. Upside-down, I looked up by tilting my head down and saw Dylan treading water above me, below my feet. I flipped right side up and pushed off the bottom, grabbing his feet with both hands.

When I felt him stiffen against my grip, I kicked twice and with an extension of my arms, pushed Dylan out of the water completely. As my head broke the surface, I heard him laugh just before hitting the water again. While he was occupied, I swam to the shallow end where I could plant my feet.

After a rapid bend and twist at his waist, he broke the surface of the water in an impressive freestyle stroke, heading directly toward me. He threw several play curses my way as he came, all the while smiling maniacally.

I'd only moments to get my balance. When he came within striking distance, I sprang forward placing one of my arms under his mid-section. I lifted him as my other hand held the back of his head to stabilize him. Then, when he was completely airborne, I spun him about my left arm like a paddle wheel. As he spun, I lifted my left arm rapidly, directing his spinning figure back into the middle of the deep end.

He hit the water on his feet and then fell forward extending his arms to reenter the water smoothly and touch the bottom by the drain in imitation of my earlier maneuver.

We had the pool to ourselves that night, therefore we played wild games. Most of these had to do with me, four or five times his size, throwing him about. The harder and farther I threw him, the more he liked it and the quicker he came back for more, shouting, "Do it again, do it again."

Martha read her book, watched us and smiled nervously from the deck as we played Torpedoes and Shark's in the Middle. Next, we tested our ability to lie on the pool bottom near the drain. We tossed a penny and watched it spin under water, flashing like a lure. Pretending it was a doomsday bomb, we tried to catch it before it hit cement. When we did, we saved the world.

We played a game I called Yo-yo Boy where I pretended to be a sea dragon and catch him. "You can't get away from me," I shouted in his face.

He laughed as though I were tickling him.

"You're my prisoner! You can't get away." Then I'd laugh and turn away. Of course, he took that opportunity to swim toward the far edge of the pool. But I didn't let him get far.

Just when he thought he'd gotten away, I reached out and grabbed him around the ankle, yanking him back to me with a quick jerk. He'd shoot through the water swiftly on his return to my waiting arms. Dylan felt like a yo-yo returning to palm. That's why I called him the Yo-yo Boy. I held him in the air, shaking water this way and that. I let him fall and bounce off my chest. Then I wrapped him around with my arms and squeezed, roaring.

He laughed when he could catch his breath.

"Thought you'd get away, did you?" I hollered and rubbed my forehead into the side of his head. "You'll never get away from me, ha!" I bellowed as he continued giggling.

"I will," he snarled back and twisted in my arms. "You can't keep me." He roared like Simba in imitation of me and then kicked me in the chin.

With an exaggerated hoot of "Oomph," I threw my hands out and back and lunged away from him, pretending to be knocked out. But I didn't stay down for long, for just as he thought he was away from me, I came at him from behind and grabbed him up in the air with his legs still thrashing. I held him above my head with both hands and walked back to the center of the pool.

As I reached the quick slope of the deep end, he placed his feet on my shoulders and stood, hollering and waving to Martha. After seeing she was watching, he bent his knees and sprang from my shoulders, entering the water like an arrow hitting its bulls-eye.

We played for hours. When finally we were tired, we lounged in the spa. Martha joined us there. With the hot bubbles massaging us, we floated in silence. Occasionally, we giggled at a memory and shared a story with Martha, laughing when she shook her head.

After a long time, Dylan turned to me and said with a completely straight face, "You may be fun but I won't ever love you . . . just know I won't." His expression was completely straight with no hint of tease. His eyes stayed in steady contact with mine. He was neither angry nor upset. He simply stated it like one would recite any common fact. It was as if he was saying, Gravity holds us to the earth, as if it was a law that couldn't be questioned or broken. He was simply stating a fact. I don't love you and I won't. Then he looked up to the ceiling in a completely relaxed manner.

I didn't know what to do but, luckily, I didn't react too quickly. We floated in the bubbles, still silent for a time. Martha and I tried to converse with our expressions while Dylan looked nowhere in particular. Finally, I asked Dylan calmly, "Why won't you love me? What did I do to you?" I forced my voice to be monotone, passionless like a stranger inquiring about the weather, while inside my head spun.

"Because you stole me," he replied without hesitation. "You and her," he said and nodded toward Martha.

"Stole you? We didn't steal you," I said with a questioning inflection.

"Yes, you did," he replied in a convinced tone. "You took me from Sharon. You remember. She told me."

"Sharon who . . . what?" I stumbled momentarily trying to put this in some kind of context.

"Sharon. You know Sharon. You took me from her and made me live with you. You were the two bad turtles. I can't forget that. I won't."

I was shocked and said nothing more, just went blank. Martha said nothing either; we just looked at one another. Later, we dried and left the empty pool still echoing lost play. Martha suggested we get ice cream as a way to let Dylan know we weren't mad. I didn't eat my ice cream as much as dutifully kept it from melting over my knuckles. Later, when Dylan was asleep, Martha and I talked about what was said. She was as surprised and disturbed as I. "What should we do?"

"Call Sharon, I guess and find out what this is all about," I said and said no more.

#

We hadn't heard from Sharon and Dan for a while. When Dylan first moved in, we visited back and forth every couple of weeks but as time went on, we stopped seeing them on a regular basis. The last time they were over, the kids swam in the pool, Dan and I played chess on the back porch and Martha and Sharon grilled dinner. We had fun but since then our visits had faded.

Martha made the call the next day telling Sharon what Dylan had said. At first, Sharon was just as surprised as us. But after some conversation, Sharon's memory was jogged by his comment about us being "two bad turtles."

She recalled a story she'd told him about two turtles searching for a special little boy to love and call their own. She told Martha the story was supposed to help him make the transition. It wasn't intended to give him the idea that he was being stolen.

208

But as my grandmother used to say about the path to hell and good intentions, things don't always work out the way we expect. It was clear Dylan didn't hear her story the way she'd meant it.

After they talked, they scheduled a get together to clear things up. Sharon and Dan came over on Wednesday, without their kids. When they arrived, we took time to gather in the living room, sit down and get to the point. Dan sat on the Lazy Boy but didn't recline while Martha and Sharon were on the sectional couch. I brought a chair from the dining room and sat in front of the TV. Dylan knelt on the carpet in front of me.

As we moved to our places, all eyes settled on him. There was an odd silence waiting to see how this'd turn out. No one was sure where to begin. Finally, deciding to be surgical, I said, "Dylan, Sharon and Dan didn't come to visit today and they left the kids at home because we wanted to talk to you about something important." I trailed off as his attention wavered.

Dylan didn't know why we were meeting but this scene made him squirm in place. I thought we'd lose him if we didn't move soon, so I sped up and talked rapidly. "Do you remember the other day at the pool you said we'd stolen you? Well, you need to know that isn't what happened . . . And Sharon and Dan agreed to come and tell us what really happened and why you are with us and not them . . ." I trailed off, losing my impetus and then I nodded over to Dan and then Sharon to go ahead. Dylan stopped moving and looked up at Sharon. She fumbled, clearly wondering how to tell him what needed to be said.

Dylan, babe, I told you a story when you were going to move away but you may've misunderstood the way I meant it," she started in an uncertain tone. "I never meant they stole you . . . we weren't able . . . we weren't going to . . . we couldn't . . ." Her voice wavered and her throat tightened as she looked to Dan. As was their way, Dan stepped in for her and spoke up.

"Dylan, we weren't going to adopt you. We couldn't do it," he said. "It was my decision; I was the one who did it, not Sharon." Dylan was pale and we all froze for an uncounted moment. "You were too much," Dan continued "we couldn't handle you. Martha and Jacob came to your rescue . . . not to take you away." Dan ended his speech sounding like a convict's allocution. Everyone there heard the truth; it both seared and cauterized simultaneously.

Dylan faced away from me, so I couldn't see his expression but in the stiffening of his back I felt Dan's words hit him like a thump on the chest. From my vantage he seemed like he'd gotten the wind knocked out of him. He was hurt again. It seemed a deep, painful wound. But this was the only thing capable of giving Dylan some chance at normality; it was the final procedure needed in the grafting of Dylan to our tree.

The truth had been applied; I could see no reason to extend the torment. I sat up in my chair and said, "We're sorry, son . . . you're hurt . . . but we all needed to hear the truth together. We love you and want the best . . . We're going . . . your mom and I, to go downstairs . . . so you and Sharon and Dan can say what you need to alone. We'll be ready when you're done. There's no hurry . . . we love you . . . there's no hurry anymore."

Martha reached up and grabbed my hand as I stood near her seat. We went down to the basement to wait, talk and try to hear what was happening above us. We heard voices but couldn't quite make out what they were saying to each other. But they were talking.

When they were done, we were called to return by a voice from the dining room above us. When we went upstairs Dylan looked okay but sounded different. He looked alright; better than I thought he would. He was still hurt but something seemed settled in a new and final way. Was he being brave? I reassured him without talking, gave him a hug and we went back to the basement.

After that, he paid no more attention to Sharon and Dan and never asked about them again. We got together once or twice more, but things were never the same; Dylan treated them apathetically. He was never really mad at them, not really, but to him they no longer mattered; he acted indifferent.

#

We played that summer; it became the first summer of our fun. It was as if our property itself took a deep breath after years of rigid control. All of us began to inhale deeper. These fast days both exhausted and exhilarated us. We played soccer in the park; in the open field, Martha and I together couldn't keep up with Dylan. He was unstoppable and he loved beating us badly. At basketball, I still had the advantage of height, weight and experience, although he beat me in straight, speed and natural cleverness. And, of course, we continued to swim and play in our pool. All the times that weren't filled with enrichment were overflowing and splashing with fun.

The tone of everything changed in the most obvious and subtle ways. Accidents still occurred in multiplicity around the house, even on a daily basis, but they were almost always due to impulsive reactions or play and not out of frustration, anger or fear. Dylan was less resistant and more accepting. He tested less and seemed to understand we were on his side. He often tested the rules but now it was almost perfunctory, nothing personal, just business, you know. His rage seemed to subside over the sizzling days of summer. He relaxed and began to soak in his new life.

And as he let go, as he let down the heaviness he'd carried for so very long, he began to do something wonderful and marvelous—he began to grow. You could see it happen before your eyes. It was like a sped up movie of a bean sprout pushing away the dirt. But the development wasn't just physical. It was also emotional and spiritual. It was remarkable to watch and worth more than the cost of admission. To be part of the rapid growth of this child, denied a healthy family root, was an unbelievable thing. All the sacrifice now seemed like petty, overly dramatic play.

Health invaded his life. He started sleeping in his own bed. His nightmares became few and then disappeared altogether. His bedwetting stopped. He gained weight and height. His articulation improved to where he was almost always intelligible. His temper became easily managed with a brief time-out in his bedroom and was only occasionally a problem. Finally, quite overdue, a monarch butterfly was breaking free from confinement and spreading full color into life. It was a happy time and we celebrated it constantly.

211

One day turned over into the next as casually as rolling over on a beach blanket in the sun. The sense of hurry and the time for desperate solutions had passed.

From then on there were easy messes in the yard. Empty milk crates and wood boards made good ramps from which to jump his bicycle. He used whatever he could find in the garage to make obstacle courses or forts for himself and his friends—life jackets, skis, ladders, wheelbarrows and five gallon plastic buckets, folding tables; whatever he could find he'd use creatively.

On his bike, he'd love to skid and stop quickly, hitting the gravel with his whipping back tire. He'd watch the gravel scatter with a grin.

He joined a local soccer team and was next to the best kid on the team, even though most of the kids had been on teams before. He was terrible at following the drills during practice but on the field in the game he caught on to strategy quickly. But he especially liked to fall down in dramatic ways. Whenever the ball was taken from him, he'd flail with arms and legs and do three hundred and sixty degree flips falling forward onto the grass to lie on his face waiting for the ref to call a foul. One time, he got his free kick as reward for his unusually dramatic performance. He liked that.

He played on the same team in the fall and continued to do well. But as the days grew colder and Dylan ran more and more in the chilled air, he started to have trouble breathing. He'd one episode, a wheezing fit, the spring before when he and his class visited a petting farm. That night, after spending the day with hay and fur, we took him to the ER because he couldn't stop coughing. In the end, the doctors said it was a "mild allergic like reaction" to the hay. We didn't worry about it much. We just kept him away from hay.

But with the advent of the cold season that next fall, we started to notice him coughing after running outside in chilled air. However, we didn't know what we were dealing with until Christmas when we decorated the living room with a live, fir tree.

212

The one we bought must have been moldy because two days after getting it, Dylan began to cough.

Dylan, Martha and I decorated together. Dylan and I put on the lights and then we all placed candy canes, bright bulbs and other ornaments all over it. At last, we put an angel at its top. I lifted Dylan to let him place it at the highest spot, the branch pointing to heaven.

After that we played a game with the reflecting lights. We darkened the house and tried to find all the places where the tree lights reflected around the room. If you could look into any shiny surface, even the smallest spot and see the Christmas tree lights reflected there, you earned one point. Window glass, picture frames, the TV's face, the side of a glass by a chair, reading glasses, nick-knacks, each other's eyes; all these were places where we scored. Dylan was good. It was hard to stay quid pro quo with him.

After a while the game ran its course and we settled down. Dylan lay on the cream carpet up under the Christmas tree staring up into its center, in order, he said, to see all the lights all at once. He lay like that a long time over the next day and a half.

But then Dylan began to cough and soon was hacking so bad his thin ribs shook. We tried several things to help him breathe better, a camphor rub, a steam bath and I gave him a decongestant with an antihistamine but nothing eased his cough. In fact, it seemed to get worse.

Dylan was fearless and stayed quite calm during the whole event. He tried to ignore the coughing by staring at all the Christmas images around him. Regardless, his breath became a rattling spasm soon. When his head began to shake along with his chest, we decided it was time to visit the ER again.

Halfway there, his cough settled into a high-pitched wheeze as he suddenly was unable to draw in an unobstructed breath. His chest muscles strained against his ribs trying to pull a lung full of air, but he only succeeded in sucking a hiss.

213

At the hospital an indignant doctor snapped at us and pointed to the flesh between the bones of Dylan's neck and chest. It was like a balloon inflating inward "They call this refraction." His skin pulled in with every breath. "Whenever you see this, he needs to already be at the hospital. Do you understand? It's deadly! This is too late to bring him . . . next time, act don't wait." He brushed us out of his way and pushed the wheeled bed into its curtained cubicle. He started oxygen and spat, "Keep him calm, I'll be back." He disappeared to write orders.

Martha and I went to either side of Dylan's bed. I held onto the rails and bent down over him feeling guilty. I looked at what the doctor was talking about; the skin in the hollows of Dylan's throat was pulling in. When he tried to breathe, his soft tissues were literally collapsing into his airways.

His eyes were glazed but still calm and focused, not panicked at all. I was more frightened than he. I reminded myself I was supposed to be keeping him calm. I leaned way over and told him some lame joke, I don't remember what. Then I smiled in his face and rubbed him on the head as if nothing were wrong.

He reached up with his small right hand and grabbed hold of my grinning left cheek. He held on to it, squeezed and squeaked out, "Dad, I love the way God made you."

I searched his gaze to find a falsehood in his words but couldn't. His expression was completely without guile. As he tried to breathe again his lips froze, tight and straight, slit open and straining to pull in. But his eyes stayed calm and kept in steady touch with mine. He soothed me with his green eyes. I stuttered and then laughed out loud. "You'll be okay, huh? You're right; you're okay already!"

He nodded and smiled tightly.

Nurses came in and moved us out to give him treatments, take vitals and get blood samples to the lab. For a time that seemed too long, we waited in the large room next door, filled with couches, magazines and two large TV's blaring nothing.

Dylan had literally used what could've been his last breath to tell me he loved me. I was surprised and blown over as if by storm. It was both simple and elegant, striking home with me completely. It still amazes me how, after all that had happened, a few words could count for so much.

It changed everything for me; that moment cemented my love and committed me to him forever. Nothing can change that. With a few words, he reached across infinity and grabbed hold of my soul. From then on, I was his. And if we're ever across infinity from each other, we'll still be together. This is all the payback I'll ever need for everything I can give to him.

He remained in the hospital for four days. He was treated and Martha and I were educated on the signs and symptoms of asthma. We'd never make that mistake again.

We stayed with him around the clock. We took shifts, canceled our formal holiday with the in-laws and threw out the tree before the twenty-fifth. We were just happy he was okay. That year, Dylan was our baby Jesus as we stood by and watched peacefully.

#

Then the years flashed by. I remember Dylan at six, sharp and clear and then he was seven; I remember every detail plainly. But something happened between then and eight. Everything blasted off like a Fourth of July rocket.

Because the years flared like a sparkler writing circles against the dark, I can't recall all the different bright strands for you. All our good times are tangled together in my mind; I could never untie the threads and lay them out for you in sequence.

At all times, I keep pictures in mind of Easter egg hunts and St. Patrick's Day Leprechaun Traps, treasure tracks, splash fights, rubber band wars with Big Bertha and a trip to the edges of the Grand Canyon and down. These images and many more play in my memory constantly. When it's quiet in the morning or I'm out on a long walk, I can be there again in an easy instant.

215

But I'm afraid I can't take you with me as Dylan and I grew up together; I was simply too caught up to remain objective. Trips and adventures, playing in water everywhere we went . . . water alone was enough to celebrate and, in a pool, we worshipped like children on Christmas morning.

These were the good times and made beautiful memories for Martha, Dylan and me. My father once told me that the time when my brothers and sisters were young was the best time of his life. But, he mused, "I was too busy and didn't notice. I wish I'd paid more attention then." He was right. This time for us, Dylan, Martha and me was both tiring and exhilarating and went by in a flash, un-reflected and unfathomable.

Story time in Dylan's bedroom became the sweetest part of my best days. We'd lie down in his room under the florescent green stars on the ceiling. By this point, I'd stopped reading books and was telling him stories, which he still asked to be made into Dylan Stories.

So, I'd start with something that might've happened that day, a game, a fight with a friend, a teacher's reprimand, an accident at lunch, anything that was plausible would do. From this mundane chronicle of daily life, I'd spin off a tale of adventure and magic that would take him around the world and back again before another sleepy story hour had passed. Often Dylan chimed in with different directions and plot twists he wanted included. What a blast we had!

When the story was finished, we'd replay a ritual that'd developed over the years, one I'm sure that is familiar to many. After silence calmed the room, I'd stand and walk toward the door, slowly. Then Dylan would call out, "Dad" and when I'd hear his voice, I'd remember another voice coming down to me through many years, another cry in the dark echoing, "Dad . . ." and I couldn't move an inch farther. That time every day, I was at my son's command.

"Yes, son?"

"I love you," he'd say from some unperturbed place in his heart.

"Yeah, well," I'd reply with a tricky grin. "I love you more."

"Un-uh, no way . . ." He'd smile back competitively. "I love you all the way to (blank) . . ." then he'd fill in the blank with some place remote, somewhere different each night. It could've been some place he'd heard of in a story or at school. His look challenged me to think of a place even farther from which I could love him back.

In this way we'd go, back and forth, farther and farther away until we spun seven times around the world, down through the planets, our stellar system and galaxies until we'd reach out to infinity, then out farther and back again. Each night, in this playful ritual, we competed to proclaim our love from one infinity to another.

For me, this was all "cool, man, cool."

Creeping Back

Then he turned thirteen.

There was an odd phenomenon with Dylan. As things got better at home, they got worse outside. Until this point, we'd few bad reports about Dylan from school. This no news we took to be good news, which allowed us to put our focus where it needed to be, on our happy home.

Dylan became a teenager at the end of the summer before he started seventh grade. And, as if on cue, things took a turn for the worse.

That summer Dylan started playing with just one friend. In the summer, there were always times when fewer kids were available for play. Families go on vacation. Kids attend bible school or camps of different types. But in the past, Dylan had always maintained at least four or five friends even in the lean times, as many as fifty during the school year. But that summer he started playing exclusively with a friend named Howard. I didn't think much of this change at the time, but in retrospect I now see the pattern of a problem.

For a long time, Howard and Dylan played well together. They were both well-mannered and behaved at our house. We never heard anything bad about them from Howard's place either, so we let them play. With our free time, Martha and I started to take walks and ride bikes together again. Dylan kept spending more and more time over at Howard's.

Martha was concerned about all the time away from home but I remembered being in the seventh grade and having the freedom of my bike and my friends. I encouraged Martha to let him have more of his freedom. And, for a while, things seemed to be going well. Why should we worry because he was focusing on only one friend?

As we neared Halloween, Howard's mood turned dark and sour. I'm not sure why. He talked less and looked tired more often. He stopped laughing at my jokes; even rowdy music in the car didn't affect his mood as he withdrew. This change was, to a lesser extent, reflected in Dylan's behavior. Dylan and I weren't as close when Howard was around. Dylan gave me signals to back off when he was over. It was clear he didn't want me involved with his friend. He drew a bright line for me to keep behind.

Dylan was pulling away. He was continually distancing himself from us and I was beginning to feel somewhat like Sharon and Dan when he'd finished with them. Whenever I got too near him and his friend, he'd shut down and clam up. I'd try to say something but my comments sounded pretty lame when they were met with only silence and dull expressions. I'd fumble a bit until I'd stumble away, chagrined in this new outer darkness.

When his friends, especially Howard, were around I had to keep my distance. When we were alone at home, he was fine, just like normal, but with his friends, he was like some other kid.

A seventh grader is supposed to do that though, right? It's normal for them to want to be different than their parents and to move away, distancing them emotionally. That's what everyone, says . . . right? We'd worked hard to let Dylan be normal, was I wrong to regret it? Would I be the one to keep him from being ordinary now? I shivered inside, shook my head and accepted my new status in Dylan's life. I kept watch at a distance.

Okay, I'm sure a lot of people would say, "So what? That's just a normal teenage phase." Children simply grow away from their parents in middle school. And, generally, I'd agree. However, this was when Dylan began to have trouble with the law.

219

The first time, it was snowballs. One night when he was staying over, Dylan and Howard walked one street over from Howard's house and rolled up a big snowball like the bottom of a huge snowman. They made it as big as they could and then pushed it out into the street. They left it in the middle of the small, residential lane so when cars came by, they'd have to slow down to avoid it.

Then Howard and Dylan went back to the side of the road, hiding at the foot of some trees up a small embankment and made a supply of snowballs while waiting, giggling in shared anticipation. When the cars came, the boys burst from the underbrush flinging their frozen orbs at the slow moving windshields.

The woman who called 911 to report them was shook up. She was coming home from the store with her groceries and her toddler. The police found the large snowball when they arrived but not the boys. Unfortunately for the boys though, someone recognized them running away and directed the police to Howard's house.

Martha gasped audibly when she found the police on our front stoop after dark, her eyes wide like cornered prey. The young man was polite when we let him in and apologized for disturbing us. He told us he had Dylan in the back seat of his patrol car and explained what'd happened

As we approached the car, Dylan's face was ghostly white, haunted by fear and regret. His lips were held in the short, horizontal line I hadn't seen for a long time but still knew well.

The officer poked his thick finger into Dylan's chest as he chastised us in the driveway. Then he turned to Martha and said, "No charges are being filed . . . this time." He turned to Dylan and emphasized the last two words with another poke. Dylan was let off with this verbal warning. We were all relieved. Dylan was grounded for two weeks and had extra chores to do.

In two weeks, after much work and discussion, Dylan was allowed to go to Howard's house for two hours on a Friday night. He ran out of the house as if it were on fire. With his Cheshire

220

grin and hair curling wildly and bouncing as he ran, he seemed determined to get every last minute of fun he could before he was doomed to be back home again. We were surprised when he tumbled back through the front door, puffing, less than an hour later.

"Are you okay?" we asked simultaneously as we looked up from our books and coffee at Dylan standing on the small green mud-rug. Yes, he nodded apprehensively, he was okay. "What's wrong?" we asked. He gave a guilty glance to the floor and turned his head.

"Well," he stumbled "I think I'm in trouble."

He was. The police came about ten minutes later. We heard the story and made arrangements all before Dylan's original two-hour curfew was up.

Howard and Dylan had gone over to the elementary school and vandalized cars in the teacher's parking lot. As school had been out for many hours, the boys ended up busting the cars of the most dedicated teachers and one poor evening custodian. They broke all the mirrors on the cars, pulling some off the doors completely. They broke windows and scratched paint. This was serious. Dylan was now officially in trouble with the law.

With a summons and a policeman's business card in our hands, Martha and I were left shocked as the officer tramped down the three wood steps from our front porch. The hollow sound of each boot's fall echoes in my head. Nothing before in our lives had prepared us to deal with criminal law. Of course, all of Dylan's freedoms were suspended until we could think it all out the next day. We'd always taught him, "if you abuse your rights, you lose your rights."

We slept late in the morning. There was no hurry anyway; we needed, as always, to slow things down for Dylan. He was always fast to act, impulsive, what were we to do? How could we keep him safe and allow him a normal life at the same time? He'd been out of the house less than an hour and had committed a felony. He was grounded. What else could we do?

221

#

We got lucky. There was a good youth program in our county; they say the most progressive in the state. Dylan was given the opportunity to avoid going to court if he could work with a social worker to "heal" the community.

He was given the chance to participate in a reconciliation program. There, the community, especially the victims, confronted the offenders who were forced to explain their behavior and come to terms with suitable recompense to the aggrieved. If possible, a plan was submitted to the social worker, who followed through to make sure the offending parties fulfilled their agreements. If the plan wasn't completed, the child offender was then forced to go before the judge at juvenile court.

Like people eager to gain an inheritance, we signed our names rapidly to the agreement the county social worker handed us across her small desk in her cramped office. This was an opportunity to keep Dylan's record clean. It meant more time and effort on our part but it was worth it for Dylan's future. We dragged ourselves to several meetings at the worker's office on the third floor of a renovated high school building, to have our lives picked over by a stranger.

On the night of the big meeting with the aggrieved, we gathered on the second floor. We waited a long, uncomfortable time in a large classroom before everyone arrived.

I made Dylan sit down with Martha and me, although Howard was hanging out at the window. I got a dirty look for my effort and looked back unimpressed. Howard's dad saw what I was doing and called his son away from the window, too. We waited in silence in the semicircle of old desk chairs. The entire circle was large enough to fill the empty classroom. Our families, the offenders, took up one part of the circle. On the other side, the victims sat with their support people along with the school's principal and social worker we'd met earlier. These last two represented the larger community.

It took a while to get things going, for everyone to arrive and for the social worker to get all the papers she needed in their proper order. The boys squirmed in their seats expecting doom. Martha and I, who'd put Dylan in between us, sat quietly to increase the effect the wait had on him.

The social worker finally started with a fairly long and stiff explanation about what we were all doing, what role we'd play, the order in which we'd play it and the ground rules for the interaction. Her words droned on, grinding the boys' will to smudge. About then Dylan and Howard were coming out of their skins. Good, I thought, snakes molt to grow. If the boys were old enough to do real damage, they were old enough to face the consequences.

The teachers at Dylan's ex-elementary school went first. They knew us well and spoke in affable tones but their words and expressions let the boys know how betrayed they felt. They told the boys they'd been there late that Friday working on a special assembly for the children as a prize for the recent fund raising drive.

"Do you remember how much fun those assemblies were?" Dylan's fifth grade teacher leaned toward him, her eyebrows held high over the bridge of her nose, imploring. "I don't know if I can stay late anymore. I have to look out for myself as well. I no longer feel safe," she ended and settled back in her chair. Each teacher, in turn, said they were now frightened at this school that'd been a second home to them.

The principal, looking as disappointed as a house dog left behind, reminded the boys how well he knew them and said he believed they'd always been treated decently by him and the school. He wondered aloud why they'd do something so mean in return and said all the boys and girls in the neighborhood paid a price for this behavior.

"These good teachers . . ." his hand swept down the line of the three teachers and their spouses' sad and mad faces as he spoke "aren't required to stay at our school. They're wanted in many districts. If we lose them because of you, what will the children do?" he finished and cocked his head to the right, his shoulders rising to near his ear lobes.

The custodian lived close to the school but drove to work that night because it was cold. "But now," she said, "I'm cold all the time. I don't have the money to fix my window. We don't carry that type of insurance." Her husband, who was now clenching his teeth and glaring at the culprits, had taped a thin plastic over the opening but it snapped in her ear with the wind. It didn't work well. She agreed with the teachers that she no longer felt comfortable in her own neighborhood, all because of what the boys had done.

Then the boys were forced to confess publicly how it had happened and what they were thinking, which turned out to be nothing too much. They said, convincingly, they didn't have anything against anyone; in fact, they didn't even know or care about whose property they were destroying.

Then, after a pause long enough to ensure that the guilt settled in, it was the parents' turn. We were asked to speak, to say anything we felt appropriate. I looked to the other parents and it was clear we all felt put on the spot. Howard's mother's face was all scrunched and his dad was looking down at the floor. Martha looked expectantly at me. I began to talk.

"I need to say first that Dylan knows we don't approve of what he did. It isn't what we taught him." I looked to him and he looked away. "So, I don't know why he did this thing. He knew he was doing a wrong thing, no doubt, but I don't think he realized how he hurt you in particular. That's all I can think . . . he mustn't have really thought . . . I don't believe he had any grudge against the school or anything like that; he had good years there. He talks about you all positively.

"How could he have known who the cars belong to?" At this point my throat began to tighten but I needed to continue. I wanted to find something to say or do that'd make a difference for Dylan; I didn't want him to go on like this. How many times had we talked to the police that year? Was it three?

"As a father, I'm worried . . . so worried . . . about my son and so sad by what he's done . . ." I felt my chest spasm, my throat collapse and my breath evaporate. Will Dylan keep going like this? Keep getting into trouble? I realized I couldn't stop him. I couldn't keep him safe anymore . . . not from himself.

I began to cry. These tears were unexpected, messy, undignified and mortified Dylan completely. Dylan didn't ever cry. I'd seen him rage and roar like a tornado spawned off the heel of a war god, but I've never seen him cry like a little boy. Perhaps I did it for him because my eyes ran with water like they were trying to drain a reservoir of pent up distress.

It was only the second time he'd seen me cry. I really sobbed that night in front of the whole community. I was more surprised than Dylan at my public display of emotion, but when I saw the effect it had on him, it didn't bother me so much. In fact, I may've even turned it on a bit to drive my point home.

The blurred expression I saw when I looked at him was kind of a sick awe, with enough curiosity mixed in to keep him studying me. He heard me; he was really listening. "If you knew Dylan as I do, you'd know he's a good boy. We love him very much. And I don't want him to be in trouble anymore . . ." I ended with a weak wave of my hand and then wept profoundly as I looked at Dylan. I wasn't the only one visibly shaken that night. As a middle-schooler, it's tough to watch your father sob in public.

The rest of the meeting went well and ended soon. It seems that once I broke down, it opened things up for the other parents to speak. The boys looked vaporous by the time it was over. They seemed truly repentant, which was sufficient for the aggrieved parties to offer terms to settle the affair without intrusion from the courts.

Each boy and/or their families had to pay half the damages. The boys promised to compensate the school in the form of volunteering to clean the yard and help out in the neighborhood. There were some other legal requirements, too, that I forget, but all in all the boys were put through the mill and the grownups left feeling we made a collective difference.

In addition, there were many restrictions at home as well. Dylan and Howard were split up. They weren't allowed to play together anymore. It wasn't until all the community's conditions were met and the social worker sent off her final report to the court that all the restrictions were eased and Dylan was able to get back to his social life with normal supervision. We called it that, but what we called "normal" might be seen as excessive to others, I suppose.

For a while thereafter, Dylan was immersed again in his old social life. He played or "hung-out" with a ton of kids. It was like we were living in the middle of a lively pageant, new faces constantly laughing through our home. Eventually the problem Dylan had with the cars was almost forgotten.

At school, Dylan joined the swim team and seventh grade passed well. His grades were good along with all the teachers' reports. At home, everything was calm and went easily. There was time to enjoy each other again.

The fall of eighth grade was solid and uneventful. Dylan and a new friend, TJ, developed a fast friendship and were hardly ever seen apart. They enjoyed each other's' humor immensely. TJ wasn't as skilled as Dylan at the games they played but threw himself into the action with gusto and a lack of fear, which Dylan always respected. TJ always had a smart quip on his lips to make Dylan fall down laughing. That autumn, they worked hard at improving their skateboard tricks and I helped build some rails to grind on and ramps to jump off. Dylan allowed me to watch if I stood by the corner and made no comments.

As the weather grew cool, dark and damp, we saw no signs of problems on the red horizons; all was smooth sailing. The nights TJ spent over, the boys settled down early and we never really heard a peep from them. When they were at TJ's, we heard no news at all. Martha was concerned by the lower standard of supervision at TJ's but I thought we needed to trust the boys. They'd never done anything that even appeared wrong. If we didn't show Dylan trust, how could we teach it to him? Eventually, my arguments overrode her concerns and we let them be.

#

Sometime after this, we found out Dylan had been sneaking out at night. One night at three in the morning when we were asleep, we got a call from the police. Dylan was two miles from home in a police cruiser at the corner of Wixom Road near the strip mall and gas station. He was by himself. He'd been riding a bike to TJ's when he was stopped for violating curfew. He'd done nothing else wrong, consequently, he was simply turned over to me and we went home, went to bed and talked about it the next day. By this point, we both knew he'd be grounded for more than awhile. There was no hurry.

In the morning, I found a small screen pushed out and tossed aside by the little basement window on the south side of the house. Cigarette butts on the ground, smoked and smashed, lay dark and soggy in the grass. He admitted they were his. We were astonished that, with his asthma, he'd smoke. We vociferously reminded him that this was potentially lethal.

He was grounded. Grounding Dylan to the house became an easy solution for us and perhaps we relied upon it too much. Dylan didn't like it; he wanted to be with his friends. But after an initial outburst at being punished, he'd settle down and, in fact, was quite pleasant and cooperative.

When he was grounded, Dylan got a lot done, both in housework and schoolwork. He was developing skills when at home and he never got in trouble there. We knew he was safe. Also, perhaps out of boredom, Dylan played with me more. So we'd end up doing fun things like family outings, playing basketball or going to a movie. So with each infraction in the community, Dylan's groundings increased.

The next time he was off grounding, we decided he couldn't play with TJ. They were getting in too much trouble and were heading in the same direction as he and Howard the year before. He was grounded from TJ permanently.

The first weekend after this grounding ended, he went to the movies with a group of friends, both boys and girls. He'd always done well in large, mixed groups. But in the morning, we found Marijuana in his jacket pocket. Martha was retrieving a key she'd lent him when she found the little plastic bag. Dylan admitted smoking it more than once. In fact, he said he was only smoking cigarettes because they covered up the smell of weed; he didn't like them in themselves.

He was open about everything when we confronted him. In the garage, he showed us where he'd been making small pipes out of thimbles and hard plastic tubing. He used a small, disposable torch to burn a hole in the thick plastic to seat the thimble. He turned over a small decorated box he used to keep his "stash" in, hidden under the stairs in the basement.

We didn't know how long to ground him for . . . forever? We sent him to counseling and started regular, random drug testing. We knew he was clean for a long time after that. We talked to him and tried to get through this together. We spent a lot of time talking about all kinds of things involved in his decisions. We warned him and cajoled him, instructed and alerted him but it was only so many words. Dylan didn't have a fondness for too many words and, in the end, he only responded to everything with "I'm not like you; I'm different," accompanied by a blank stare.

Separate Lives

I learned a lot of things about my house in the next few months. I learned the fact that, if you count an unfinished garage and basement filled with storage, there are most likely tens of thousands of places to hide things.

I found myself getting up early in the morning, sometimes even as early as in the dead of night, to wander around trying to find spots where Dylan might hide something. It was kind of like the Christmas lights game we'd played at an earlier stage, but instead of looking with Dylan for bright colored reflections of joy, I was now solitarily searching darkness itself.

Did he hide something here in this corner, I'd think as I worked or under these things? It was a question that propelled me forward in fatigue, monotonously probing for things I couldn't find: mainly reassurance of Dylan's safety.

Has he hidden something here? I thought over and over again. I played numerous scenarios in my mind until finally I was certain I couldn't stop him from hiding things. Dylan was now of the age where, if he were determined, we couldn't stop him completely.

With great effort, we could slow him down but we couldn't force him to do what we thought was right. He was too persistent and downright sneaky. And Martha and I ran the risk of becoming jailors to our child. I wanted to be his father but he was making me his warden. I'd fought hard and endured much to be his father. How could I now allow myself to become his oppressor?

In those days, "What was Dylan doing? Who was he doing it with?" were the topics of nearly all conversation between Martha and me. And the only thing we ever really established was Dylan needed as much structure and oversight as possible. So, he was only allowed to attend organized and monitored school activities. As it was the only way for him to see his friends after school, he joined as many sports teams as he could. On the swimming team at school, he started to hang with a boy on the team named Sam. We and Sam's family took turns driving and picking up the boys. On the weekends Sam came over for the night but we didn't allow Dylan to go away from our property.

Again, things went basically smooth when Dylan was at home. He was bored but safe. Through the middle of eighth grade he attained his goals at school of C's or better. Because he was being good, Dylan gradually was able to spend short amounts of time at Sam's house. We held our breaths and let him have some tentative, supervised freedoms.

Sometime in the early spring when there was plenty of wet snow still on the ground, we let Dylan go to Sam's. The sun was out and a warm breeze was tumbling up from the southwest so the boys, who had cabin fever, went to play outside. They threw some snowballs and took a run through a nearby wood. After a bit of a walk, they came out onto the beach of a small local lake. They threw some stones into the frozen water to see if they could break the ice but it was still too thick. Sam wanted to walk farther out on the lake but Dylan thought there were too many puddles; he'd get too wet.

"Hey look, there's Manny's house. He lives over there." Sam pointed for Dylan.

"Yeah, really," Dylan replied. "So?"

"So let's go see if he wants to do something. We can test the ice in the shallow by his house and see if it'll crack with all three of us." Sam nodded down the beach in the direction of Manny's. Dylan nodded back and away they went slapping the

231

wet ground with their high-topped, cross trainers tied low and loosely.

They went to the front door but when no one answered, Sam said, "Let's go around back." He headed to the north side of the house and followed a path winding through some tall oaks around to the back. Dylan wondered where Sam was going but only for a moment. He followed, kicking snow and wet leaves along the way.

Around back, Dylan paused to watch the sun reflecting on the pools of water that spotted the ice but then he heard Sam say, "Come on . . ." He was at the back door, which was covered with blistered and peeling white paint. With his hand on the handle Sam said, "Come on, they never lock the back door." He turned and he pushed with his right shoulder, disappearing into the shadow inside.

Dylan paused only a second as he tended to react quickly to anything a friend did. He followed Sam inside. By the time Dylan went up the little step from the landing to the kitchen and took a few steps to the sink, Sam was already out of sight in the living room ahead. Sam knew the house better than Dylan and was evidently more comfortable walking about in the dim light filtering into the house.

"Hey, where're you going?" Dylan called to his friend and stopped to look out the kitchen window. He could see where he'd been moments ago and got an odd thrill from being inside the house where he didn't belong. It was a rush that made him simultaneously nervous and excited. "Sam," he whispered loudly to the darker living room, "what are you doing?"

Sam's head popped back into the doorway, "I'm going upstairs. His sister has this cool digital camera. Come on," he said and disappeared again. Dylan followed.

The brown carpet was worn and the walls were smudged going up the narrow stairs. It was lighter on the second floor. Two rooms and a bathroom were up there. "Sam!" Dylan called.

232

"In here," Sam's voice came from the room to the right. Dylan recognized it as Manny's sister's. Its decorations obviously said GIRL. Sam was digging in the closet. "Wait," he said and rummaged farther back. He drew something black from the darkness. He turned to Dylan and smiled. "Look, this is sweet . . . see?" He held out the camera case to his friend. "I want this so bad . . ." he said almost imploring. "You should see what it'll do. Sweet!" He repeated and drew a quick breath as Dylan, questioning, looked on. "Are you keeping it?" he asked.

"Well . . . I . . . hey, why don't you grab something too?"

"I don't want anything. Are you taking that?"

"What are you . . . afraid?"

"No!" Dylan snapped, "no way!"

"Then get the laptop. It's next door. Come on, we got to get out of here." Sam, with his quarry tucked up under his arm, slipped by Dylan out into the hall. When Dylan turned to follow, Sam was already halfway downstairs. "We got to go." Sam's voice trailed off.

Dylan went into the other room and saw the laptop on the bed. He grabbed it and followed Sam downstairs. When he got to the living room Sam was looking in a drawer. As Dylan approached, Sam looked up, closed it and went toward the garage and Dylan followed.

As rapid as that, Sam slipped out the side garage door and was into the woods in a few steps. Dylan stopped a moment. He was nervous and wanted to get away but he didn't want to take the computer. He left it on a workbench next to the door and scrambled out. He looked down the drive but no one was there. Swiftly, he ran into the trees where Sam had disappeared. When he caught up to his friend they were both out of breath. Sam was giggling, windless.

Dylan wasn't happy. He felt a sick feeling in the pit of his stomach. Later, he told me that he had this bad feeling they were

233

going to get caught. He just wanted to get away. When they got back to Sam's, Dylan immediately called home for a ride and waited outside for us to arrive.

But the police made it there before we did. Manny's neighbors had seen the boys and had called it in immediately. It wasn't hard for the police to follow the boys' footprints in the snow straight back to Sam's house. Sam's muddy shoes lay on a rug by the front door. When the police confronted Sam's mother, she demanded Sam bring "what you took, out now!" Her voice held enough threat to get him to produce the camera from his bedroom. Sam identified Dylan as the other boy and they apprehended him before we arrived.

This time we were headed for court. The digital camera was worth almost a grand; hence what Dylan had done with Sam was felonious. Things were straightforward with the police on the scene. No time was wasted with lectures or advice. We were sent home and grounded him indefinitely.

When you ground a child, you ground the family because more than one person must always be at home. And Dylan wasn't let outside of our sight for months. In fact, it ended up being seven months straight we watched each other. Dylan was perfect but we wouldn't let him go this time. We dug in our heels preparing to go nowhere fast and just held on.

#

We hired an attorney for our son, a task few parents enjoy. Her name was Susan. She had helped me at school on a unit about the justice system. She was bright, well researched and well written. She met with us to let us know what to expect.

There was a delay but by early June we'd been assigned to a case worker at the local county building. Her name was Ms. Moses and, according to Susan, she had a good reputation in the system. This was the good news. Dylan was also assigned to a hearing officer. Her name was Leigh Walters but Susan said down at court they called her "Hang 'em high, Leigh." This was the bad.

When we met with Ms. Moses at her office weeks after the burglary, we were somewhat more assured by what we found. We sat for a while in a large waiting room that the court offices share with the county health department. It gave the atmosphere of a large doctor's office until your name was called and you were summoned to the glass window at the north side of the big room. Then everyone knew you and your family were in trouble with the law. Walking across that room, you couldn't help but feel scared, guilty and aware of the looks from random citizens waiting for their flu shots and looking like they'd suddenly remembered seeing you on a recent episode of COPS. Their faces said they knew all about you and your child.

We were led through a long series of narrow corridors and small offices. At the end of this winding trail, on the left, was the office of Ms. Moses. We didn't enter her small space as it would've been too small for Ms. Moses, Martha, me, Dylan and Susan whom we still expected. Ms. Moses suggested that instead we go to the larger conference room next to her office at the end of the corridor.

Susan was late but we went in and sat around a large conference table without her. Martha, Dylan and I sat with our backs to a double window on the south wall. The afternoon light was bright and warmed us as we waited for Susan. In a while, Martha called Susan on her cell and found out that she'd gone to the wrong set of offices; she'd gone to the big ones at the county seat. We told her to forget it since we were already beginning to feel comfortable with Ms. Moses. We didn't want to irritate Ms. Moses because she held much power over Dylan's future. We decided to handle the meeting ourselves.

Dylan was asked to sit in an office with another caseworker while we were interviewed by Ms. Moses. She was a light-skinned African American woman who'd an air of knowledge and compassion about her. She was calm, reassuring and had light twinkling in her dark eyes. She was supportive and said we were to work together to help Dylan learn from his mistake. Our collective task was to get him back on the right track as soon as possible with the least disruption to the family and community. I know Martha liked her, consequently, we were at ease recounting our families' story in detail.

We assured her Dylan was well behaved and cooperative at home. We put together a plan. And if he did well with this new set of services and structure, he'd only go to court to have the whole incident removed from his record completely. It was called a Consent Decree and was the lightest punishment the court could give out in a situation like his.

Over the course of the next six months, Dylan needed to complete fifty hours of community service. He was required to have random drug and alcohol screenings. He needed to attend and cooperate with a substance abuse group conducted once a week at the county offices. And he needed to stay in his current therapy sessions with his current therapist. Both of these sessions were weekly. He needed to meet with Ms. Moses and one of us at least once a month. He was to have no contacts with the police. He had a strict curfew, although since he was already grounded, this didn't mean much. He was required to write a letter of apology to the family whose home he'd invaded. He had to attend school regularly and pass his courses. And he was to get a job on the weekend to help pay back court costs. If he did all these things at the end of his probation period, all charges would be dropped.

Ms. Moses sent for Dylan and she talked sternly to him with our silent hurrahs supporting her. It was time for Dylan to grow up a little more. If he was choosing to act as an adult, he needed to understand he was choosing to be treated like an adult, too. He was placing himself in the hands of others. We couldn't protect him from the State; we didn't have that kind of power. He had to learn to live in a world full of people. On the way to the car I told Dylan he was grounded until he was free from the State.

#

Dylan finished his requirements for the court early. He stayed out of trouble and did well at school, even though, initially as we expected, there was a rough transition into high school. But in spite of difficulties Dylan held it together and attended every day. He worked off his fifty hours of community service at a local Salvation Army Store. He wrote his letter and submitted it the next time he saw Ms. Moses. He attended group and individual therapy without absence and had several clean drug and alcohol screenings. Everything looked to be on the up and up.

But in mid-Autumn, Dylan became more bored than ever. He stopped talking to his friends on the computer and spent hours in front of the TV. He dropped out of basketball saying he'd too much to do. He stopped having friends over. He became quieter and quieter, saying only "whatever" or asking "does it matter?" He slept a lot. When we tried to cheer him by going out, he rejected family activities out of hand, "No, no, no . . ." His voice faded by the third repetition. In short, grounding was no longer working.

So by the time Halloween came, I was ready to relinquish. Halloween was Dylan's favorite holiday so I decided to let him go out 'treating' but said there'd be no 'tricking' that year. We were required to go to court in less than six weeks. The last thing we needed was more problems.

We said Dylan could go out for three hours. Dylan wanted to go with Nick, a boy whom he'd known over the years and played with on occasion. They'd never gotten in trouble together. We held our breath and let him go for what ended up being four hours in all. At the end of this short duration we picked him up. Everything was okay! Dylan got a huge amount of candy and no police were in sight. We hightailed back home and threw the dead bolt on the front door.

We slept late the next day. When I woke up, Martha was snoring loudly.

I stretched slowly enjoying each warm feeling as I did. Dylan was next. His mood was bright. He wore an "I told you so" grin as he said good morning.

I mussed-up his hair and asked, "So?" Nothing had gone wrong the night before. We smiled over hot bowls of cereal until he asked if he could spend overnight with Nick that night, Saturday.

He must've learned his lesson; it'd been long months. To be truthful, I hated to see the sulking and suffering more than his days of rage. He'd done well last night away from home. It was probably easier to get into trouble on Halloween than the next day.

I wasn't smart. In fact, I think I knew better at the time. But I just didn't have it in me to say "No" anymore and make it stand.

"Come on, Dad," he pleaded as he read my hesitation and suspected my weakness. "I've never gotten in trouble there. I'll come home early. And Nick's mom will be there all night long. Come on, huh? Just give me one more night and I can handle that lady at court. Come on, Dad." He covered all the bases. He'd thought it all out. So, after feeble resistance, I capitulated and let him go. He went back that afternoon over Martha's opposition. But at that point, she was easier to fight than Dylan. I was just exhausted with struggling. I gave up, sat down and refused to fight him anymore.

After I dropped Dylan off at Nick's I went home and went to bed alone. I rose early the next day because I couldn't sleep and I busied myself in my basement office. The call came at 4:37 a.m.

It was black and bitter cold when I got out of the car and crossed the deep parking lot behind the local substation of the county sheriff's office. Under-dressed and miserable, I was led to the back through a long wide corridor and passed a holding cell where I saw TJ with his mother. This was a dreadful sign; Dylan had been banned from TJ.

Dylan was in the next holding cell with that same look of guilt he had had on all the previous occasions. What good had it done? Just after I got there the deputy asked to see me in the hall. We stepped only a few feet from the outside of the cell, which struck me as odd because Dylan could clearly hear what we were saying.

"Yes sir, thanks for coming so quickly," he began in a polite manner. "We don't think your son is to blame in this. We believe he was just a witness to this boy stealing from parked cars. All

238

we need from your son is his statement and we can send him home and . . . if I were you, I'd watch your son's choice of friends." He handed me a clipboard with a consent form to sign.

"What's this for?" I asked confused.

"It's consent for us to take his statement. He's a minor. We need your permission."

Well, this was a dilemma. I was relieved for a moment when the officer said Dylan wasn't at fault. But when he said "consent," I had a problem. You see, when I'd hired Susan she'd set certain conditions. She agreed to take Dylan as a client, not us. She specified this clearly and she insisted that if he'd any further contacts with the police he should NOT give a statement without her being there. With this in mind, I didn't feel I could sign. Dylan might've gotten off, I'm not sure. It sounded like the deputy was offering a good deal. But then again, I didn't know the legal system and Susan did, so I was uncertain what to do. I looked at the police officer who was waiting for me. "Yes, well . . . I can't do that," I looked him in the eye but then shifted my focus to Dylan. "Under advice of his lawyer, I can't do that."

He looked surprised and replied, "I wouldn't lawyer up if I were you . . ." I couldn't believe it; he actually used the phrase I'd heard a dozen times on TV. "That'd be a big mistake. We just want him to tell us about this other one. He's already confessed."

"No, I can't. I'm supposed to protect his rights." I said, feeling like it was a mistake. "I'll bring him back with his counsel later. That's the best I can do."

"This is unbelievable." The man shook his head.

"I'll bring him back later."

"Sure." Just then another deputy stuck his head through the back doorway and hollered. "He's got something on his sheet. Felony Home Invasion."

"Oh," the man said with recognition.

239

"The action's pending in a couple weeks," I added quickly. "We think it'll be purged off his record. He's met all his conditions and we're just waiting for the judge to give the word." The words tumbled out as the man looked unimpressed.

'It's a mistake," he said in a disinterested tone.

"I just need to come back later with his lawyer. He'll make a statement. He's a good boy. He'll tell you then," I droned not even convincing myself.

"Uh . . . yeah," he muttered.

"Are you releasing him?" I said after a pause.

#

Dylan and I walked over the crisp snow to our waiting minivan. We drove in silence. I pulled into the garage, closed the door remotely and killed the engine before either of us said anything.

"Well," I finally broke the quiet. My tone reverberated inside the car before Dylan talked. He spoke softly with parts mumbled. I had to ask him to speak up, which always aggravated him but I didn't care.

He held his head forward and down, his face in a shadow, motionless as he told the story about what happened that night. His voice was detached, monotone. His thoughts were fatalistic as if his actions had been predetermined.

I thought going over to his friend's would lift his spirits but it hadn't. That was the big mistake; everything else was secondary. I'd given in and made Martha do the same. All this was the result of that—sitting in my garage on a slate gray pre-dawn and listening to my son tell how it was possible he'd gotten into trouble again. I knew I'd given up too easily the night before, let go too early and now Dylan was in real trouble. Dylan had been away from home for less than eighteen hours in seven months

240

and he was involved with the police again. With him, it seemed like a compulsion.

I listened to him passively not wanting to hurry before I had to go in, wake Martha and tell her what I'd done.

#

The last days before court are hard to remember except they went by painfully slow. A sense of guilt and dread hung about the house. We didn't do much except talk about it over and over again. In a long meeting on Monday before the day, we spoke about our options with Susan. We discussed the process at court and what the hearing officer may or may not do.

Eventually, court day came. Nobody went to school; we all called in sick. We dressed in dreary silence. Our mood was sullen at best as everyone seemed unwilling to mention what was ahead. When I saw Dylan putting his good clothes on, I thought for an instant he was dressing for a funeral. We ate a small breakfast that was hard to swallow and sat like lumpy oatmeal in our chairs. We went to the car, turned north out of the drive and headed for the county seat and the court house.

The road rambled through an area known as The Lakes, passing parks and nature trails. But they meant nothing that day. They passed by like ghosts left from a livelier time. Nothing looked the same, everything was foreign, a part of other people's fantasies. Then into the silence, into my morbid thinking, I heard Dylan say, "I'm sorry. I didn't mean to hurt you."

I adjusted the rear view mirror to see him. The face I saw was his. It was my Dylan's face with no angst or sullen wall of defense. He was tense and obviously afraid but he wasn't the tough guy he'd been playing for the last year. It was the face I knew well and longed for, the face from our now good old days. I looked him in the eyes and knew that what he said he felt. It wasn't said for effect. Then he cried. He squeezed the tears out strong and deep. I watched him and gave him quiet to dignify these rare gifts. When he stopped, I asked, "Why?"

241

He shook his head. "I don't know, I don't . . . I'm just not like you." Martha responded as if she thought he didn't want to say the real reason why. But I saw it differently. He sounded as if he really didn't know. Perhaps he didn't.

Or . . . perhaps . . . he'd already told us. That's right; he'd said it, didn't he? "I'm just not like you!" Was he saying that this, all of this court and police stuff, was just a way to tell us he wasn't like us, that he's different and our expectations weren't his and were too hard? Is this what he'd been really saying, what we were unable to hear?

"Dylan," I said. "It's normal for a teenager to want to be different than their parents. That's normal. The only thing we want for you is to be happy and have a good life. We don't care what it is . . . that's up to you. We just want to love you and see you happy, nothing else. But Dylan . . . son, you don't have to go to jail to prove you're different. Now, that would be abnormal!"

He looked up at me and snorted with a wry smile and wet eyes, "Yeah . . . right."

#

That Tuesday in court was one of the longest days I've ever had. If waiting with nothing to do but ruminate on fear and remorse is a form of punishment, then going to court is sentence enough. And the waiting room for the juvenile division was hell.

Tons of people were crammed into that large room. It was a big room but had a diminutive feel. Two-thirds of it was filled with racks of connected black seats like those in airport terminals or bus stations. And they were placed so close there was hardly room for two opposing people's knees in the middle of the aisle, let alone space, if someone wanted to walk through.

The last third of the waiting room doubled as an overflow area and a walkway into the courts themselves. This walkway is used by clerks, lawyers, families, people from the prosecutor's office, security, janitorial staff and anyone else who needed or wanted to pass. This made it both a bad place to stand and an even worse place to move through.

242

When court was in session, the black seats were occupied by people in dread and distress. They had wild looks in their eyes. Few made eye contact. They were scared bodies crammed together with the smell of sweat pervading the stale, institutional air. Here is where you waited and waited. First you waited for your lawyer. Then you waited for the court's. Then they talked, yours and theirs, and then reported back to them and you. Then you all waited for the hearing officer. The fates must've been set against us that day because we ended waiting nearly all day. Finally we were called into the hearing room at about 4pm. Ms. Moses wasn't there and the worker who replaced her was young.

In her court, Officer Walters sat at the far end of the narrow but long room. She hunkered behind a desk on a dais that dwarfed her gnarled body, draped in black robes with thick spectacles, worn down on her sharp nose. Her face was all roughed up and lifted to the left; she appeared older than her sixty-plus years. She looked uncomfortable and had an expression as if smelling something putrid.

When she was ready, she stopped moving papers about her desktop and looked up at us. She took her time eyeing us up and down. I got the impression she could only see well out of one eye.

In front of her large desk was a short wooden wall that extended from one side wall to the other. In front but to the side of this wall was stationed a court reporter. Between us and them was a long empty space of bare floor. A wooden rail divided the rest of the room into a small cramped gallery.

There were two tables set against the wooden rail with two chairs close to each other. Behind each table and its pair of chairs were two groups of three chairs each. Susan and Dylan were to sit in the two front chairs on the right side. Ms. Moses' replacement and a man from the prosecutor's office were assigned the two chairs behind the table on the left. Martha and I stood near the back wall of the room in the extreme right corner.

Hearing Officer Walters was reading, seemingly unaware of our presence. After what seemed awhile, she recognized our presence with a grunt and quick nod. "Be seated then," she spat at us without removing her eyes from the pages in front of her.

Then, as we settled down, she looked up. From a distance, perhaps it was too hard to really see, but I'm sure she looked directly at me with a fierce, piercing gaze, under-laid with a sour and disgusted feel.

Ms. Walters picked up the phone and dialed four digits. She said something quickly about "transport" into the receiver and then added, "Yes, now!" louder. Then she asked the A.D.A. to begin. He stood at his seat and announced the case and stated the charges. He continued by saying the D.A.'s office was ready to proceed in the matter but that he understood the defendant had a motion he wasn't adverse to. Susan had told us in the waiting room she planned to ask for a continuance due to Ms. Moses' absence. "Really," said Walters and turned to Susan. "What do you have to say?"

Susan stood and her voice began to quiver as she spoke. It wasn't too bad but it was obvious to everyone she was nervous. Walters sneered. Susan made her motion for postponement but Walters cut her off before she'd gotten far.

"Yes, the caseworker isn't here but her report is," Ms. Walters said and lifted the papers in front of her. "The court thinks highly of Ms. Moses and isn't in the mind to disregard her opinions."

"But, we're not ready to discuss the new issue until we've a chance for discovery . . ." Susan trailed off while Walters shook her head.

"Consent Decree was given on the basis of No Police Contact! I understand this young man has had another contact with the police?"

"Well, yes but . . ."

"Then we know all we need to know about this. There's your discovery. I'm placing him in lockup for the rest of the week. His parents can retrieve him on Sunday morning."

"But you haven't heard from the parents. They wanted to address the court." Susan stumbled. "Can't they at least address the court before this is done?"

"It's already done, counselor. I already called for the lockup," she said without blinking then looked at me and said "You've something to say?"

"It's already done?" I questioned feebly.

"Yes, it is. Do you or don't you have something to say? I know that people like you . . ." She stopped herself and decided to rephrase "people who aren't used to the courts think children with a past shouldn't be punished. I think that's naïve and I'm not impressed. Do you still wish to say something . . . well?"

I shook my head and said, "No, if it's done . . . it's done." I looked at Dylan. He looked away.

Just then the door to our left opened and two large county deputies strode into the room. They paused long enough to get a nod of direction from Walters and then proceeded straight to Dylan.

"Stand up," the second one said "Stand up and turn around." Dylan did.

"Take your coat off," the first one added. Dylan did this, too. He handed the coat to his lawyer, she passed it along to Martha, who clutched it tight with both arms in front of her.

In what seemed like no time, I saw handcuffs placed on Dylan's wrists held behind his back. He was locked in with a ratcheting sound.

245

"Don't I get to say goodbye?" Martha burst with panic from her corner.

"No, you do not," said Walters, matter of fact. And before anything else was said, Dylan was led from the room. He was gone in a flash, taken from us.

For the first time in ten years, we weren't in charge of Dylan. We couldn't feel him anymore. Martha squeezed his empty coat till it had no breath left. I turned to Martha and began to reach out for her but Susan imposed herself between us and said we must leave the room, quickly.

In this way, we were belched out into the hallway where Susan hollered to us, through the noise, that we should go wait in the outer room. She said she was going to go with Dylan and would check back with us before we left. We faltered back to the waiting room and stood in the middle of the walkway between the court and freedom, no longer aware of the flow of bodies about us. I held Martha. She held me back, tight in shock.

Susan came and told us we needed to go over to the Children's Village, the juvenile detention facility across Telegraph Road, to sign papers for Dylan's admission. She added she was leaving us to see if she could get a judge to override Walter's decision. She said she'd stop and see Dylan again before she left and call us later. We tried to ask her questions about what'd just happened but she said it was late. She had to go if she were going to do anything for Dylan. Accordingly, we let her leave and walked down the long corridor where we'd entered many hours before.

When we got outside, the sun was low in the sky and the shadows were growing longer. We shuffled to the car. I held the door for Martha then trembled as I rounded the back of the car as if suddenly chilled.

When I sat behind the wheel, I had to do everything sequentially, one step at a time. I looked down at the key in my hand. I looked at the ignition. I inserted the key. I took a breath as if I were already exhausted. I turned the key and listened for the revving engine. I buckled my belt. It seemed to take forever to readjust the already adjusted mirrors. I found it hard to go forward. Every action was a conscious decision taken with great effort of will.

We didn't know how to behave. Had we just lost our son? The van was empty in back; I really couldn't bear it. But step by slow step we made it across the street, out of the car and into the front administration building.

We had to wait before we were led through security. We were told to go through the doors to our right by a woman sitting behind a thick Plexiglas window. She pushed a button and the metal door buzzed. We shoved through, but only barely and walked down a short corridor, pushing through another set of metal doors as if in a hallucinogenic haze. We trudged to another window made of security grade plastic. A woman, dressed as a nurse, came to the window and then passed us some forms to fill out. I stared blankly at them in the stainless steel well, inches below the plastic.

Martha picked up the papers and moved to a counter on the left wall. I stood behind her but not close enough to read. I was off-center in the little white room; everything was a clean bright white, the tile, the walls, the ceiling where florescent bulbs hummed. My mind paled. I felt dizzy and nauseous for a minute then straightened myself consciously. What was happening? I couldn't really seem to make things out.

I asked Martha a vague question, which thankfully she ignored, being busy with the paperwork, head down, shoulders hunched uptight to her ears. I reached to touch her back but didn't make it, as just then a door opened out in the small hall we'd just left. A single file line of boys marched in from the north and shuffled south across the corridor to another door where they exited into another small room.

I went to get a better look at them as they passed and saw they were all in shackles on their wrists and around their ankles. I didn't see Dylan at first, but when I did, I turned to Martha and said, "He's here." I'm not sure she heard me as she grunted something inarticulate to the paper in front of her. I turned back to the door that now separated me from my boy. It was cold and

247

white and made of heavy metal with a large pane of chicken-wired glass in its middle.

The boys were made to stop and turn to someone who, out-of-sight, was evidently speaking to them. Every boy looked forward focused on the instructions. Two boys down from the end stood Dylan. As I saw him, all I wanted was to make it stop. I held my breath. This wasn't right; he doesn't belong here. We don't belong here!

Then Dylan looked away from the unseen speaker and turned his head directly to me, as if he'd known exactly where I was the entire time. He looked and I looked back but through confusion and shock it was hard to see him clearly. I was able to catch one sad expression distinctly before he turned away. It was a powerful look and demanded me to let go. It was as clear as if he shouted at me, "Let me go! I'm okay, let me go . . . now!" I staggered a half step then tried to rebalance myself.

"Okay, okay . . ." I mumbled, trying to gain my stability by looking at my feet and willing my legs to grow strong and steady. By the time I was moored to the floor the boys were turned again and filing out of the door farther on. I saw the side of Dylan's face. I saw the back of his head and the little spot in the back where his hair was always ruffled. And then he was gone. Martha and I were left in the cold, white room.

After Martha finished the papers, she talked to the nurse behind the window awhile. She asked several questions concerning Dylan's care and wanted to know exactly how he'd be getting his asthma inhaler and the other prescription medications he took. I didn't think this was necessary and just wanted to get out of there. He'd be alright, I thought, they'll take care of him that way. Missing his medication for a few days wouldn't be life-threatening. But Martha wouldn't leave until she was certain that all his needs   were met.

#

We went different ways that night. It was a mistake but for some reason being apart seemed rational. There was something I was supposed to do at church but I don't remember what it was.

248

Martha insisted on driving all the way home, getting Dylan's medicines and returning right away to the Village.

The last place I wanted to go was back to that place. I couldn't take it. I told Martha I was going to church and got away from her as soon as we got home. I went out to the car and headed for church but along the way I was seized with a pain in my chest that blinded me. I turned off at the next right, which was a short dirt road that led down to the edge of a small lake. I stopped the car and hugged my chest as if my arms were tied in a straitjacket. I couldn't breathe.

It was dark and when I turned off the car and lights, it seemed pitch black. I sat in the gloom, seized with pain, confusion and guilt.

I'd let go too early, I'd stopped fighting for Dylan. I said Yes when I should've continued to say, No, no, no, no!

And then I was silent when they took him away. I didn't stand and fight but let him be led away in chains, passive and dumb like a line of draft mules. By doing nothing, I betrayed him. My courage failed. So now, I sat shivering in the outer darkness, shedding bitter tears. I trembled as the cold pushed through the cracks of the car and rolled over me from inside the windshield. I was completely enclosed by bitter cold and utter darkness until it seeped within and I became it.

#

Martha later told me she left home and drove all the way back to The Village with shear, direct determination. Nothing turned her aside or caused her to hesitate but, as she finally approached the building where Dylan was being kept, she felt her courage break within her and flow away like water. As she attempted to walk the last, little distance to the door, she quickly emptied of resolve, stopping short of her goal.

She said she didn't make her goal. As all her strength rushed away, her lower gut shuddered way down deep in her loins. She felt a contraction, a great sharp spasm that took her

249

breath away. She bent forward and, at the same time, her knees collapsed. She caught herself in a crouch on the grass in front of The Village.

She said she held tight to her knees, squatting and gripping herself like some distant ancestor giving birth in an open field. Consumed by pain, she held on until it passed, eventually it would pass, like the skull of a baby. That night, alone and cold, Martha said she felt the pain of the birth she'd always feared, as a teenager was pulled from within her, kicking, clawing, turning her insides out and deeply raking her soul.

End of Book 2

<u>An Invincible Summer</u>

Dim light illuminates Jacob and Adam, sitting among the students' desks. They remain in the classroom hours after-hours. They are solitary figures even though they sit in proximity. Evidently, Jacob has been telling a story. The building is deserted as the rainstorm freezes outside. The sun has set and is forgotten.

Adam McDonnell was Dylan's case manager ten years ago. Jacob Ebonite is Dylan's father. Adam came to see Jacob from a long way off. Jacob sits turned slightly to the side, his gaze down.

The room is silent as Adam begins, "You promised to tell me everything. Don't say that's the end." He sits upright and gestures with open hands held toward Jacob.

"End?" Jacob wonders aloud.

"Yes, of Dylan's story. That can't be the end . . . of the story" Adam insists. "I need to know how he turned out . . . you remember our deal?"

"No, I'm not forgetting." Jacob looks at Adam a little annoyed.

"Well . . . you're not telling either. Remember you promised. So don't stop now," Adam blusters.

"There's really not much left to say." Jacob shakes his head and looks away. "That was just three nights ago." And looking outside, Jacob continues in a fading voice, "It seems dark since then."

"Don't keep even the smallest detail from me," Adam says disregarding Jacob's musings.

Jacob glares at Adam but continues, "Martha and I got home and that was as good as it got. I don't remember if we even turned the lights on bright enough to see that Dylan was not there. The next day we went back to court. We'd hoped we'd be heard by the judge but all I remember is unfocused despair while waiting more. But we wanted to fight and get Dylan back ASAP. For two days, we waited to be heard. But it never happened. Last night we visited him . . . at The Village . . ." Jacob trails off distractedly

"How is he?" Adam whispers.

"Susan had seen him the day before," Jacob continues not seeming to have heard Adam, "Wednesday night, and told us he was okay, he was just worried about what he'd put us through. She said he didn't want us to hate him too much."

"Ah-ya-yi!" Adam mutters.

Of course, we don't . . . we couldn't. We just want him back. We went to visit him as soon as we could." Jacob looks back to Adam.

"Inside, the Village looked more like a High School than a jail. The hall to the right of where we sat was set up like a school with classrooms and a gym at the end of the corridor.

"We waited for Dylan. He came out from a doorway down at the opposite hall from the gym, back past where we'd come in. He saw us right away but tried not to let it affect his cadence, posture or expression. He was playing it cool.

"I could go with that, but when he reached us, I didn't let it stop me. I grabbed him and squeezed. I'm still bigger than he is and sometimes it still matters. In fact, he gave Martha more of a problem when hugging him. He fussed, saying, 'Come on, mom!' He gave her a small push away and sat down red in the face. But I could see he got the message. His muscles relaxed. We were far enough away from everyone else that we couldn't be heard. So we talked freely.

"The actual words we said are unimportant and unremarkable. Just talking as if nothing unusual was happening was good. Mostly, we made simple, small talk. You know . . . newsy stuff. We were happy to pretend for a few minutes that nothing was wrong.

"Near the end of the hour, we said we missed him and told him what we'd done to get him out of there. He said we shouldn't worry; he'd be okay, even though he told us he bunked with a boy who was in for murder. During the visit he said, 'He's nice enough.' But Martha and I didn't buy it. The last few minutes, at the end of the hour, our talk was more serious. He was sorry about what'd happened, about what he'd done to us," Jacob concludes.

"So, you think he's learned his lesson?" Adam asks quickly with some trepidation in his voice.

Jacob looks at Adam's expression for a moment and wonders why is he worried? "Yes, I think so; perhaps . . ." Jacob shakes his head. "I don't really know. I'm hoping it's like all the trouble he got in before, like with the neighbors; he bothered each one once, got in trouble, made up and then never had any more trouble with them again. At school . . . his first year in a new school was always a year of testing and trouble and then he'd stop. I'm hoping it's the same with the law. He has to test everything; it's his compulsion. Ironic, huh? He still has so much fear within that he thinks he needs to get into trouble to know he'll be okay."

"Ironic, yes," Adam agrees.

"I think that's the most enduring scar," Jacob says flatly. "He has to test everything to feel safe. At other times I think Dylan is the test."

"What do you mean? That's outrageous," Adam croaks.

"Yeah, it's like he was sent to test us all, the system, everything. He tested me. He tested you." Jacob stares into Adam's dark eyes. "How did we do?" he asks bluntly. Adam doesn't answer. There's silence again for a bit.

"You think he'll be alright?" Adam finally asks. "He'll be okay in the end?"

Jacob momentarily recalled Dylan's cool eyes the night he was unable to breathe in the hospital when he was just a little boy. "I think he already is and we just don't know it yet." Jacob looks at Adam but really only sees Dylan smiling, which feels like an invincible summer in his heart. He looks at Adam with a wry smile, "In the end, he'll be like us all . . . dead." Jacob scoffs. "Oh, you're still wondering how he'll turn out? Don't you get it yet? That means nothing; it's more than absurd. People don't turn out."

"You know what I mean," Adam protests.

"No, I don't," he retorts. "How can he turn out? He's not a product. He's a process, a developing, learning, living process. How can you judge? What part of his life do you analyze to get that verdict? How would you evaluate a man who spends most of his life in prison and then at forty becomes a hero? Or what about the hidden pedophile priest, who on the outside looks to be a righteous man, a man of God, all while he lays in lethal wait to destroy children? How can you possibly judge how a person turns out?"

Showing anxiety, Adam pleads, "I just need to know he's going to be okay. This can't be a tragedy. It has to turn out differently. Don't say my mistakes have hurt him forever."

"You really think too much of yourself. You think you've been important to him?" Jacob scoffs.

"No . . . probably not, but he's been important to me." Adam's voice steadies. "He keeps me awake at night."

"I'm afraid I can't tell you more. This is where we are. From here we go forward, that's all. I won't make up things to ease your conscience," Jacob states with a note of finality.

"One last question," Adam implores. "Just one more!"

"If you ask me one, I'll ask you two."

"Okay, fair enough," Adam agrees after thinking a moment. He begins to talk rapidly but then slows himself to a moderate, steady pace. "Tell me, from your point of view, is it possible to heal a child as beaten as Dylan? Is it really possible for one person to save another?"

Without hesitation Jacob answers, "You can heal a wound but not a scar; scars only fade. You endure scars, forget them or explain them away.

"When I was a child I always wanted to save the birds with broken wings. But everyone told me it wasn't possible, therefore I never tried. Do I think it's possible to heal broken wings? Now, through Dylan, I have learned that we can heal the children with broken hearts. I know we can, as long as we catch them early enough and work hard enough. The heart has an enormous potential to heal but other aspects of personalities are more brittle and being brutalized, remain damaged for a longer time. All we can do then is hope and wait for the outward wreckage, the scars, to fade.

"You really need only one thing to heal a wounded child. It's simpler than you imagine. What you typically think of as necessary is irrelevant because all you really need is compassion. This, literally, means the willingness "to suffer with." You must be ready to suffer with them. Because the thing they need most is to know that they belong and are loved beyond circumstances. To lead them from their nightmare, you must learn with them, fear with them and rejoice together, too, whenever you can. To lead them from their nightmare, you must be truly with them and share a common vision, healed and complete. They need you with them no matter what. And you need them too. You must learn to give up what you thought was your way and attend them along a common path. It's simple but hard to do. And nothing less matters.

"That's how good families have always worked. And, no, it can't be reproduced by a system, especially one bureaucratic in nature, where C.Y.A is the order of the day. But you don't need some esoteric process or therapy; you just need committed love . . . a profound dedication, to be willing to give up what you thought you wanted for them. If you are able, you will realize that this is what you really wanted all along. And it doesn't matter what your family looks like to the world, whether you are judged to be good or bad, whether your efforts will be appraised as a success or a failure; all that counts is that you are going through all the changes this temporary life holds for us, together.

"Another thing while we're on the point, at one time I thought solving ALL Dylan's problems might be possible. We worked feverishly attempting to fill every want and need. This may work over the course of a short-term foster placement, but not over the long haul.

"During the good years, we became insatiable in our desire to make Dylan all better. And in our voracious lust to mend, we consumed a part of his possibilities, in the end, turning him off to the things we wished him to have most. I saw this most at church and school, in education and in faith. I think he rejected them because all he saw was our unfeasible, unending demands, which we called, love. You see, what we really needed was to give up some more of our dreams in order that he had a chance at getting his own. This is another kind of sacrifice but one we didn't know to make. In the end, I think we exhausted him. That was a mistake.

"So, go on and do all the things that parents do to make their children's lives rich. But find a balance in your work as you aren't responsible for everything. Let them make their own

257

mistakes, as they certainly will, and be there when they do. Don't stop and, simultaneously, don't lose your peace, your stillness within. Finally, when you can, look beyond your children . . . down into eternity."

"But is he healed or will he go the wrong way?" Adam questions again.

"How can I answer truthfully?" Jacob shakes his head and continues, "Only Dylan can know. We must wait for him. It's now a matter of his heart and not his history. But whatever he chooses, I know he'll carry one thing with him, a part of me. With all my faults and limitations, I did the one essential thing. And on that I'll rest, wait and watch for his conclusions."

"I'm afraid." Adam whispers.

"I'll always will be . . ." Jacob agrees. "There is eternity within me and infinity outside. For me, being Dylan's dad was the only thing that could've balanced both. By giving up what I thought I wanted, I ended up getting back more than I could've imagined. I got everything back better through the love that connects me to him. It doesn't matter what he chooses or does from now on. We're linked across infinity, as far away from circumstances as we can be. This is the invincible summer I found within myself. So, in the end, Dylan gave me more than anyone else ever has. Being Dylan's dad was the best thing I ever did."

"You'll be there for him . . . yes?"

"Still no faith?" Jacob chuckles. "Yes, we will be there . . . that's what we do. Dylan may leave us but we've nowhere else to go. For us, Families ARE Forever, no matter how they turn out."

After a long pause, Adam begins to conclude, "Well, I guess that's all . . ."

"Not before I get my answers," Jacob interrupts. "I need two answers from you."

"Alright, fair enough," Adam accepts.

"Do you remember earlier today when you said you'd acted as the State, with the power and authority of the State, to decide what to let us know and what to hold back? Do you remember that?"

"Yes . . ." Adam hisses hesitantly.

"Well, then answer me as the representative of the State. Will you take him away from us?"

Adam looks perplexed.

Jacob continues, "Now, after all we've done, after the burden we accepted from you with no guarantee and barely any backup, after the distance we've come, will you take him away from us? We need to know because if he goes down, so do we. So . . . will you?"

"I don't know . . . what could I do?" Adam stammers "I don't make those decisions . . ."

"I know that the local courts now have the power to make the decisions for Dylan. But no one person will accept responsibility for the decisions the system makes. Everyone says it's the system. But today, you said you acted 'as the State', so then, 'as the State', I'm asking you, will you lock him away from us?"

"I don't know. I can't answer you."

"Is that your best answer?" Jacob cross examines like a lawyer.

"It is . . . I don't know." Adam won't change his mind.

"Then," Jacob goes on, "the second thing I ask is this. I'm asking you for all adoptive parents that, in the least, you don't judge us. When you find us, as a commotion in the middle of the

259

grocery store or an obstruction at church, no doubt an impediment you breach on your way to the divine, could you please hold back your look of derision and supercilious contempt? We don't need it. It only gets in the way, distracting us from what's really important. And, frankly, you don't know enough to judge us, do you?"

"Is that all?" Adam asks flatly.

"Yes? That's all then," Jacob concludes dismissively.

"Okay . . . this is the end."

"No one finds out about the end, not in real life."

"Fine . . . Take care . . . of Dylan." The Farther and the Father conclude their dialogue.

Adam gathers his things and, without another goodbye, leaves. Jacob sits in the dim light for a time indeterminate. Eventually, he gets up and moves to the chair behind his desk. He closes his grade book and stacks the quizzes, putting them away for another day.

However, after straightening up his work area, Jacob doesn't go home. He opens a drawer and retrieves some lined paper and begins to write something for Dylan, something that explains them and their life, something that makes sense of all the troubles. Jacob only half believes that Dylan will ever read it. It takes the form of a myth, one you might tell at bedtime.

Much later, he goes home.

David & Barbara Kenney

Memoir's End: The Exultation of Normalcy

Riding in our worn minivan, Martha and I turned into the restaurant's looping drive off Maple Road. The faded blacktop and long shadows of late afternoon reflected the deep grey of the old car. Outside the winter air had a sharp bite but inside warmth enfolded us.

Easy words of daily trivia passed back and forth. There was surety in these words and in it I found relief. Talking to my two-decade partner; planning the days, weeks and hours; thinking about the love displayed in Martha's careful considerations; all these made me breathe deep and trouble-free. I untangled inside.

The van rolled into an open spot on the north side of the Downtown Pub & Grill. Its gearshift set smoothly into park. I turned and smiled to my Martha. Her well-tested features and busy brow made me smile even more as she finished reciting a list of chores she still needed to do before the end of the weekend. The next day the week began and she was quite busy that term. She needed to be ready as her work was important.

Martha returned to employment a few years before. However, she didn't go back to K-12 education. Instead, she instructed at a local college, teaching teachers to teach. She was very good at this and had risen swiftly in the community of educators.

262

Her smile had returned. Her twinkle had been misplaced not lost forever. People were again drawn to her, warmed by her sturdy and playful personality. Her steady sense of balance had revived. I was proud and inspired by her; she had come through well, much better than I. But I was proud of us both, of what we had accomplished as parents and of Dylan as well.

I still taught high school history. I'd gained weight and was out of shape. But I'd recently began to exercise again on a new elliptic trainer we'd set up in the basement.

I breathed fully before announcing the obvious, "We're here."

"Do you see his car?" asked Martha.

"No, maybe it's around back," I rejoined while opening my door. Before stepping out, I glanced down to look for ice. There was none, so I made it around the car at a good pace only slowed by some wet pavement behind the back bumper. I listened as Martha's door snapped and popped open.

Dylan had invited us to this "0-16" party. The Detroit Lions were about to make history by becoming the losing-est team in the National Football League. I thought it would be fun because the party theme was completely in opposition to the way I felt. I no longer felt like a loser. The empty, bad feelings I had when Dylan was in Children's Village had faded like soft vapor, leaving no scars behind.

As we entered the pub side of the restaurant we saw that the place was already crowded. The room was long, tall, and narrow. A convoluted bar oscillated on our left and meandered down the whole length of the room. Above the bar were twelve huge, liquid crystal televisions all tuned to different NFL games. On the right was a long row of four-top tables. A waist-to-ceiling, glass window made the far-side wall behind these.

I watched TV as I waited by an open table. Martha wanted to look further into the busy room for one with a better view.

263

After a minute, she turned and waved for me to join her. I left my sentinel's spot and wove through the mass of bodies between myself and my wife. When I got to her, Martha pointed to two open tables. I chose the seat with the best view. Martha was less interested in the TV's than in the crowd.

"Do you see him?" Martha asked with anticipation as I grabbed a menu. I looked up.

"No, he might not be here yet. He said he had to stop at a friend's first." I said after making a quick visual account of the room, then went back to the menu. "Looks good," I said with hunger in my eyes.

Dylan had invited us to come watch the game at his work. We were excited because we'd heard many good things about him there. For instance, on his third day the manager had asked him into his office before his shift. Two of the owners were there already. Dylan was nervous, wondering what he had done wrong, and thinking he might be fired. But they were not there to reprimand him.

All three bosses told him that they were impressed by his work ethic and gave him a 30% raise in pay before his third day! They said if he continued to work out they would train him for management or bartending, whichever he liked better. Over and over again, there were reports of how Dylan was natural with the customers, how hard he worked, and how responsible he was. Now, we would get to see firsthand.

While we waited we discussed diet, scheduled appointments and home improvements needed. After a time, a young girl came and took our order. I wondered how young? She didn't look old enough to work in a bar. Her attitude was all business, almost curt.

So this is where Dylan works, I thought as I tapped the table top, waiting.

After graduating from high school, Dylan had worked a series of entry level jobs in the food and construction industries. It had been years since he'd been in trouble with the law. He

264

seemed free from the strife, the wake of disasters that followed him through middle and high school.

Around the age of seventeen there was a big change in him. It happened quickly and without effort. One day he was just different, settled inside. It reminded me of the day he had let go of his foster parents. When he was done; it was just over.

Every day since that time, we were amazed by the changes we saw in him. He was no longer seeking out trouble; this compulsion had ended. Instead, he was goal-directed and confident and, for the first time since we knew him, he no longer needed to test the world. He finally believed he was not broken inside and the world was really his too. This was his life, his choice, and his responsibility. The lessons had finally settled in. He'd finally put his fears to rest. God, I was so proud of him.

"There he is."

Martha turned to look in the direction I nodded. Across the dance floor that began beyond the bar and extended back of it. Behind the wood floor, to the west of the bandstand, a door opened and bright, sunset colors spotlighted Dylan's entry from outside.

He moved easily. His actions had a certain grace and confidence as if he'd just entered into his own domain. He zigzagged through the people like an athlete on a ball court. He was of moderate height but with good, strong proportions.

People greeted him along the way. He nodded to each and stopped to say something to a man who began to laugh. Dylan patted him on the shoulder then moved on. He stopped again to help steady a heavy load of dirty dishes a woman in jeans was trying to lift. Apparently it was too much for her. He carried the large, overfilled tray, exiting behind the wall in back of the bar.

A moment later, he emerged again without the tray, smiled to a couple and headed directly to us, as if he knew where we were all along.

When he got there, he gave Martha a big hug and clasped my outstretched hand. We all smiled, looked around and then looked back as if to say, "We've come a long way."

"Indeed," I said out loud and they laughed.

"Gotta go in a couple," Dylan started. "Have you been served?" he looked around for a waitress.

"Yes," Martha replied "a pretty young girl, with brown hair, shoulder length."

"Oh, Sarah," Dylan thought aloud.

"Is she the one you told me about?" I butted in.

"What one?" Martha queried quickly.

"No," Dylan said definitively.

"Which one?" Martha repeated grinning and shook Dylan's right arm in jest.

Dylan smiled but didn't say.

"Oooh," Martha gave up.

"Think the Lions will make history?" I said trying to get Dylan's attention but a middle aged woman in wrinkled jeans and a Downtown Pub shirt interrupted.

"Thanks for the help," she said to Dylan.

"No big," Dylan replied. "Hey, I want you to meet some people. These are my parents," he continued and gestured "mom and dad."

"Oh, you're the parents," the woman injected with animation.

"Martha and Jacob Ebonite," I gestured and extended my hand.

"Oh, I can't tell you. We all love your son . . . You must be so proud," she said with sincere eye contact as if to say: it's true. She continued aloud, "I've never seen such a hard worker. He's always there just when you need help. And he helps everyone, laughs and works even harder than before, as if he were playing."

"He's a good guy," Martha agreed and squeezed Dylan's forearm.

"Yeah," I started then paused and then started again. "He's a good egg in the long run, that is, if you don't mind long, runny eggs." I laughed.

Martha shook her head. Dylan smiled wryly. And the lady tilted her head to the right but then she was distracted by some regular customers to her left. She was gone in a second. All the workers in the bar continually buzzed about.

"Are you on the clock?" Martha asked.

"Not for a minute," Dylan replied.

"Is she the one who gave you that trouble about your nametag?" Martha inquired.

"Yeah," Dylan laughed in a soft, choppy voice.

"Doesn't seem to be an issue anymore," I chimed in.

"No, no more," Dylan looked up when our waitress came back with drinks. "Can you get me a coke?" Dylan asked her.

"Sure," she said back warmly.

"I gotta get on in a second but these are my parents. Can you take good care of them?" he continued.

"Yeah," the girl perked up and looked at Martha and me as if for the first time. She grinned and her features softened. She looked back to Dylan, a kind of longing in her eyes. Then she left the table quickly, saying she'd "be right back."

Dylan smiled. As did Martha and me. An awkward moment passed (awkward for Dylan but fun for me.)

"Well, I guess I better go," Dylan sighed and said "Be by later. Love ya." He kissed Martha on her left check, nodded to me and moved away.

"Love you to," I called after him. He disappeared quickly into the crowd and was gone from our view.

I thought about him for a time after he left and smiled at Martha. I realized that I was sure that whatever would happen, whatever life would bring, it was clear that Dylan had found a way home, forever. And so had we.

Appendixes:

Appendix 1: Jacob's Gnostic's Tale

On the last night he met with Adam MacDonald, Jacob wrote a story for Dylan. He called it, "Buds in Heaven by Dad". He named it that because he wanted Dylan to know that their relationship went beyond the situations in this world. The bond they developed endured the harshest events because it was made immune before anything here existed. Jacob felt a connection of deep friendship and loyalty to Dylan that went beyond rational understanding. So he found it convenient to talk about them in the non-denominational language of mythology. The way Jacob felt was that they were friends a long time before time. The myth that came to him was like the stories told to little children about baby angels or angel boys playing in heaven, somewhat like Huck Finn and Tom Sawyer in paradise. This is how Jacob thought about it on the worst day of being Dylan's father:

Buds in Heaven by Dad

In a long ago time, before what is now known as "The Big Bang," there was paradise, which took the form of a holy mountain. Now paradise is divine and therefore can only be understood in spiritual terms. So those with two good ears had better listen.

At the top of the Mountain is the Living Temple, the dwelling of the most ancient of days, the great I AM. And there, there is never dark! The four sapphire walls of the Great Temple are inscribed with primordial ciphers representing the four ancient elements; earth, wind, fire and water. And from each wall flows a living river.

These four rivers meander down the sides of the holy mountain, carving the four faces of glory. They scratch out many sized valleys, which twist, convolute and branch out like arteries bringing life to flesh. They twist and diverge until the entire mountain is covered with life, animating all the kingdoms of heaven.

Now, along these rivers lived the children and the grandchildren of the great I AM and among the people lived the two happiest boys in all of paradise. Their names were Dill Finn and Jakelford, who liked to be called merely Jake. They were happy because Dill had won the right to dive bomb the elders with impunity.

As they tell the story, during his time away from lessons, Dill had taken to stalking the river banks through the soft underbrush that ran along the edges his neighborhood. Out past the stand of giant ponderosa pines, upstream from the elder's cottages, he'd wait. He moved through the woods apparently hunting something. After time and training, Dill learned how to pass noiselessly and to hide so no one could find him. Like a phantom from chaos, he became adept at stealth.

When fully confident in his skills, Dill started stalking the elders of the community, tracking their slow progress near the river. He'd wait till they sat, deep in some meditation. Then he'd creep up a nearby tree without busting a twig and with a huge shout of "Kowabunga," he'd jump out high over the river's bank, aiming for just short of the contemplating personage.

High in the air, he'd curl his body into the shape of an orbiting sphere and then splash down with one gigantic splatter. The reactive, living water of heaven sprayed higher and farther than the ordinary stuff we know. His impact sent a far-flung wave in all directions. But most importantly, it ran in the direction of the victim, the nearby, un-expecting elder. The water drenched and startled the prey into rising from their deliberations with a sputter and a vow on their lips.

271

"What do you think you're doing, young man?" they'd holler as Dill rose from the deep water, both cool and amused. He'd laugh to see their startled faces and then let himself be carried away by the current on his back until he was downstream and around the bend.

Well, this behavior didn't sit well with the elders, whose peace was being infringed upon, not only by the attacks themselves but even more by the threat of attack. This caused the Elders to lose their focus and kept them from their contemplations. In due course, this loss of meditation made their heads heavy, dizzy and wobbling from vertical until they staggered around the neighborhood like drunken sailors.

Feeling these behaviors undignified, the elders meant to stop it at once. With impassioned speeches expostulated in terms of public harmony, they expressed their concerns to the local council, who passed them along with their complaint to the Regional Board for Childhood Affairs. They requested intervention from the Office of Special Assistance to aid in restoring the community's previously stable tranquility level. Their complaint reached all the way to the lower courts of the Kingdom, but once there, their case was summarily dismissed for their lack of humor as basically being "all wet."

The boys laughed when they heard this and did a boogie-dance. They planned a party and went to their fort in the woods, down a path the elders couldn't find. There they played games and drank sweet drinks and told each other about adventures they'd have someday when they, at last, were allowed to join MiKahl's army at the edges of Chaos. After hearing the news of Dill's case, the boys planned to escalate their dive bombing campaign, while Dill gave Jake lessons in tactics and form.

On the Mountain, the children lived out under the stars. The elders, however, chose to live in cottages where they could keep a lot of stuff the children had no use for.

The children played games, explored everywhere, and swam down deep into the clear, bright river water grabbing handfuls of smooth, sparkling colored stones from the gravel bottom. The children swung from vines out over the water's surface and dove into the pools gathered along the way. When cool, they sunned themselves on the warm boulders lining the shores. They ran wild as if they were imagination itself. Indeed, they were the wind.

The children lived all the way along the streams that ran down the slopes of the mountain. And every day, the boys had adventures, pretending to raft down in search of MiKahl, meeting many people, both rivals and friends, along their way.

One holiday, Dill saved Jake from falling into chaos on a trip they made to the Edges . . . but that's a story for a different time.

In all their games of adventure, both Dill and Jake always played MiKahl. You see, MiKahl is the holy warrior. From him the emanation of reason brings order and predictability. MiKahl, at the head of a great army, guarded the borders of the mountain and patrolled the foothills that rolled out to the vast horizon where the Edges fell and Chaos began. MiKahl kept back Leviathan, the monster from chaos, anchoring the roots of the Mountain. The boys rarely thought of anything else except meeting MiKahl someday.

But there was another who lived in the kingdom who'd have a greater impact upon the two. His name was Morningstar because his charm sparkled like Venus in the promise of dawn. Morningstar was self-organized and the role model for those who strove to bootstrap themselves up the Mountain. He was a man of commerce and helped connect the lower and upper kingdoms, holding them together in a web of interconnecting trade. Although small in stature, he was in charge of a vast administrative bureaucracy and to him it was to sort and transport what was needed by the people of the upper and lower kingdoms. He did this with great skill as he was an extraordinary facilitator and manager.

Morningstar settled in the middle of the kingdom near the heart of the mountain. He could feel its pulse from there and react quickly to changing interests. Around him had grown a marketplace. Peaceable and organized trading was good for all the elders of the kingdom, hence he and his cronies and their

273

assistants and assistants' workers could be seen all the way from Chaos to the Temple.

Through Morningstar's sense of commerce, he'd become rich in praise. It was often rumored one day he'd be called to the Temple and elevated to "Overseer of Paradise." Often he fantasized about this and quietly encouraged such talk.

He built a home he called the Station because he thought it was just a stop along his way. The Station was brilliant and burnished with rich colors. It sparkled across the river so bright people began to call it "Morningstar's Star" or "The Star Palace." This pleased him, too. He said to himself that it was a good thing and sought ways to increase its luster.

In addition to his administrative abilities, Morningstar was also clever at inventing and building. It was he who first built large sized buildings. They facilitated his work as large spaces were essential for warehouses and distribution sites, office complexes and communication centers.

One day, Morningstar announced he'd build a lake or more precisely, a great dam in the river to form a lake in front of the Station. He presented his plans, had facts and figures drawn on blueprint paper for public scrutiny and oversaw the digging on the mountainside himself. He built the dam exactly to his own specifications.

When it was complete, it made a barrier for the passing of the water downstream. But this was only a temporary stoppage until the lake filled in behind the dam. Then the flow of the river was regulated by the gates Morningstar controlled.

The lake was unlike anything ever seen in paradise before and the word of it spread rapidly up and downstream. Light from above radiated upon its waters with such luminance it reflected onto the hillside directly above. All those who dwelt below could see the reflection on the hillside sparkle like a bright spot light.

Besides increasing his status among the people by improving the allure of his Station, the lake aided Morningstar in many ways. It facilitated commerce and assisted greatly in the

274

ease of communication and the projection of his control. Around the edges of the lake, industry began to develop, which made more products for Morningstar's people to move. Business boomed, as did Morningstar's wealth, reputation and control.

It was then Morningstar began to think of himself as separate and distinct from others, as special. He often found himself thinking, I'm different; I'm made to be better. These thoughts of his were the birth of ego or the little man. This ego is also called the small and common "i." Separation was begotten in Morningstar's thoughts of himself.

At about this time, the boys first noticed the new light above. Dill became aware of it first and called it a diamond. He told Jake and then, on the sly, they watched its light increasing for over a week. They told no one about the diamond but kept track of it day and night as it grew brighter. Between themselves, the boys continually speculated about it. In the end, they agreed it might be something MiKahl would want to know about.

They convinced themselves that if they could find out about the light and bring that information back to MiKahl, then they'd get a reward or perhaps even meet MiKahl himself. This fueled their imaginations and desires. So just about the time other people in their neighborhood began to notice the light for the first time, Dill and Jake were on their way upstream making a journey to its source.

Canoeing wasn't good because the river was low in spots, even a raft was too difficult, so Dill and Jake walked on trails away from the river itself. This was better because the elders kept chiefly near to the river. The boys wouldn't be noticed as they were steadily drawn upstream by their curiosity. They neither tired nor became afraid.

In due course and through many adventures, Dill and Jake finally reached the level of the dam. As they climbed over its edges onto the banks across from the Station, they saw it for the first time, gleaming like a new sunrise. It was beautiful and unusual in a way that excited their curiosity even more. They studied it for a long time. Finally growing tired, they decided

275

they'd cross over the next day. They found a soft, hidden spot and talked themselves to sleep.

By the time the boys reached the lake, many other people were flocking there. Many of them were children like Dill and Jake. Twice a day, Morningstar was given reports concerning the crowds descending and ascending into his territories.

At first, he thought this a benefit, a blessing to commerce and trade. But then he noticed there were too many people to benefit his businesses. There were too many to handle and not enough goods to vend. They got in the way of re-supplying and restocking. The sheer numbers hindered his work, so Morningstar started to quietly resent them. They interfered with his attempts to organize his lakefront realm. All he really wanted from them was to leave his regions in short order. When almost alone, he was rumored to say, "Give homage and go," for Morningstar had hatched a new plan and didn't want them in the way.

Of his new plan, he'd told no one. It was his secret of secrets and distracted him constantly. He loved to go over it again and again, all these dreams and schemes of his.

All the people coming to view his work were a continual interruption to it. They kept interfering with his most precious occupation, business. His time and attention was now spent overseeing traffic control; he grew increasingly impatient, irascible and isolated. He kept to himself within his Station because there he would not be bothered as much. His cronies took control of the immediate district surrounding the Station and heavily patrolled it.

But this didn't stop Dill and Jake. They were small, quick and, in their stealth mode, could easily out maneuver any elder or crony. The next day, the boys made it to the Station unseen.

However, with fewer places to hide, negotiating the long corridors inside was more difficult than the neighborhood outside. The boys took their time sneaking through the gilded labyrinth. They crept farther and farther into the palace until they were just outside Morningstar's private quarters.

Then, for some uncertain reason, Jake became afraid and wanted to go back. But Dill insisted they go forward. Dill was hard to sway from his purpose when determined. But Jake refused to go farther. They grabbed each other and pulled, totally at an impasse. Jake told Dill they should turn back; Dill insisted they go on. They fussed with each other until finally both became afraid that they were making too much noise. So, they compromised. Jake would wait there, where he could be the look-out and Dill would go just a little farther by himself.

Dill turned down one last corridor. It was richly ornamented in the most Baroque fashion conceivable. Even the decorations had decorations, all in gold leaf. Romanesque arches overhung the lofty hall. At their end was a huge pair of double golden doors.

As silent as he could, Dill scampered to them. He grabbed and slowly pulled down on the bejeweled handle. The hinges were mute as he inched the door open and peeked inside. What he saw in the room was so curious it made him want to laugh. But he didn't dare.

An odd little man with a small, square mustache and dressed in a funny suit covered with brass buttons and ribbon marched up and down in front of a gigantic mirror. The mirror was huge and filled the south wall of the enormous room. This made the man's appearance seem even smaller.

Peeking farther into the room, Dill saw that all four walls of the room were covered with mirrors. The room was essentially bare, thus, nothing reflected back to nothing in an endless corridor of illusion. But Dill understood that the man in the center of the room saw the images of himself in an infinite procession, passing back and forth between opposite, reflecting walls. He looked as if he loved to watch a never-ending progression of himself. Morningstar even had mirrors installed in the corners so he could see himself in 360 degrees.

He was animated in his monologue to these images of himself and gave orders to the countless figures. Here, with this army of shadows, he imagined his dearest and most secret thoughts of seizing the Temple and making it his own.

277

But all that the curious, brave boy saw was a huge empty room with a tiny FLM talking to himself in loud tones and gesticulating wildly. The man shouted rather vigorously, so his mustache twitched oddly as he articulated his words. Evidently, he was completely engrossed with himself. He didn't notice the boy listening at the door.

"We must remove these people or control them and keep them out of the way. I need more space to build. We need resources to work. Yes, these halls are lofty but they are only a tiny part of my vision of what the Station will be!" He raised a finger as if pointing to the clouds.

Dill was engrossed by the short man and his tall words so rearranged himself to see better.

The man must've thought he was alone because he continued telling all his dreams and schemes aloud. "i'm better than this and i'll show everyone. One day when i'm high in the Temple, i'll reveal who i really am. i'm the one who makes things happen. i'm he who is really in charge. i must take my place in the Temple, by force if necessary!" Morningstar spoke his secret out openly for the first time. "i WILL take it and hold it and show all i'm in charge. And then i'll begin my glorious reign!

Even though he didn't understand much of this, Dill thought it sounded rather silly.

Just then another man, much taller, entered the room at the far end through an additional set of double doors that were hidden until the moment they swung open. He ran to the little man. The new man sputtered but eventually told Morningstar, the boastful little horn, after he'd sounded, demanding, "Spit it out!"

"There is news from MiKahl's regions," the taller one said and shook noticeably. "He's mustering his heavy cavalry at its edges. The defense council believes he's riding up river, beyond his frontier to take the lake from you and the people." The messenger leaned away and lowered his head between his shoulders.

278

"You think he'd attack me?" the little man blasted. "Prepare the company . . . we go to meet him." Morningstar pushed the man from his presence. Returning to the mirror he consulted, "i'll send my spies to kill MiKahl. How dare he come at me?"

Well this was too much for Dill. He jumped up from the floor behind the door and pushed his way into the mirrored hall. "No, you don't," he shouted. "You won't kill MiKahl. I won't let you, I'll tell!" Then Dill ran from the room at top speed. Behind him, he heard a shrill cry full of frustration and fury.

At once, Morningstar sent men, his minions, after Dill but Dill got away. Morningstar needed to call his council, send out his spies and make ready for war. He was too busy to chase little boys himself. He sent underlings and familiars to track and handle him. So while Morningstar completed his plans for revolt, his cronies went chasing "that boy."

Meanwhile, Dill found Jake where they'd parted and rapidly told him they needed to get out "now"! The boys dashed for the doors and were out of the Station before any guard knew they were there. They flew through the nearby district of abandoned settlements and woods, Dill breathlessly telling Jake what he'd seen and why they had to get to MiKahl lickety-split. The boys raced on as if pursued by demons that knew them personally.

But before the boys found MiKahl, battle broke out on the mountain. MiKahl was attacked as he approached the lake. His forces were taken by surprise in the bright shadow of the Station. MiKahl had simply come to find out about the light. That was all. But Morningstar was now too drunk with his egotistical thoughts of greatness. And he perceived every action by others as a threat. So he sent his people to attack MiKahl preemptively.

At first, Morningstar's underlings took a toll on MiKahl but the battle raged all day. MiKahl formed and reformed his troops and eventually prevailed with order and courage. In the course of the intense battle, Morningstar grew fierce and angry because his company was being beaten back. His anger grew and grew in his heart until inside he was a heavy fire, like molten rock.

What happened next was a great surprise. No one could've imagined it, too terrible and unexpected. You see the weight of Morningstar's heart, full of anger, full of heat and malice, melted a hole in paradise. It turned his insides black and he imploded. His darkness consumed him until he was literally nothing but a black hole, a dense, empty space in the fabric of existence.

In the room of mirrors, Morningstar's council saw him fall from paradise. It was odd. His form changed into a heavy, hard, coal-like substance. For a micro-moment, he stood there with a look of astonishment and rage upon his face, turned pitch black and then was gone. It was as if someone had cut him from the room, leaving only emptiness behind.

All that remained in the space he'd occupied was a tremendously heavy nothingness, a black hole. And into the emptiness everything was sucked as if by great gravity. The counselors were swept away first, falling into the darkness that had been Morningstar. The doors and corridors were next. Then all the gilded decorations vanished into the growing darkness.

The Station, the lake and then the whole region rushed over the edges of the expanding oblivion, creating an enormous fissure in the mountain, a bottomless pit that swallowed everything around. And any who drew near to peer over its edge were also pulled into the abyss. And with every part of paradise it devoured, the pit grew in size, weight and power.

The heaviness of Morningstar's heart eroded a sinkhole in heaven and, on that day, one third of the host of paradise was thrown into darkness. One third of the children and grandchildren of the great I AM were swept into the ultimate gloom of a frozen, eternal and empty ego. The people of the mountain were lost in shadow, cast into Gehenna, the outer spaces which are the heart of Morningstar!

The boys never made it to MiKahl; they were overcome by the pull of the pit. Jake was taken first. He remembered how Dill kept him from falling into Chaos and, at the last moment, used all his might to push Dill forward. Jake fell backwards, grabbing for a low tree branch for a moment more. Then he was gone. A short time later, Dill too was lost in a rush of wind.

They fell into the pit, unable to hold onto paradise. It felt like they shattered into the countless slivers of a broken mirror. But they didn't die. They found themselves in an infinite, icy and lifeless darkness, unable to move, pursued by demons, eternally frozen in fear and stretched in all directions by the endless vacuum in a universe of nothing.

A third of the people of the Mountain were flung into the nonentity of Morningstar's heart, a third lost by his self-absorption. And, as his barrenness didn't discriminate, the grandchildren of the great I AM were hurled down into hell as well.

In silent terror, the lost children cried out to their Grandfather as the light of heaven shrank into a sphere, a dot and then a pinpoint, which fell away until they couldn't see or remember it at all. They were blinded by the blackness and for a time eternal they existed without a frame of reference, completely alone and powerless, sightless and frozen, as they fell into the pit, while seeming not to move anywhere at all. In the middle of universal nothingness, there is no time or motion.

But their silent cry was felt in paradise as the Spirit of Heaven brooded over the deep . . . over the formless void. Then a message was received within the vacuum, "Let there be Light." And with that unspoken voice the heavens and the earth were created in a great, big bang, an explosion of light. In an instant, nine-hundred-billion galaxies came into existence and began to form. And countless gas giants have illuminated obscurity from that first day until now.

The waters parted; water above, water below and dry land appeared as a place to stand so the children didn't need to keep falling. By grace, they were given position and time to align and orient their now limited perception while they searched for some way home.

#

Dill and Jake approached a tiny, blue planet. It was wet and warm and it amused them to see it sparkle like an illuminated blue marble on black velvet. They drew near and felt drawn to swim within its waters.

Dill was tired and came along slowly, still chased by personal demons. Jake went ahead excited but stopped. He didn't want to lose Dill. He waited some and then, unable to stop himself completely, he went ahead a little and then anxiously awaited some more. Eventually, they slid near together into the waters of birth, Jake just a little ahead.

So . . . almost unnoticed, a boy named Dylan was born. He was born into chaos and handled roughly when handled at all. At five months of age, he was placed into foster care. I didn't meet him during that initial foster-go-round. First other things came. . .
THE BEGINNING

Appendix 2: What is a Memoir in a Myth?

Most cultures have myths of origin. These are stories that people tell about themselves, how their society was formed and to what ends it exists. The stories in the Book of Genesis; Homer's Iliad and Odyssey; Brahma reborn in a lotus flower floating on an infinite sea, and George Washington chopping down a cherry tree are all examples of myths of origin. What happens in the myth is important to people in their time because it teaches them about their life, explaining why things are the way they are and passes down a system of personal and social values.

Individuals also have myths of origin. We make them up from what we've heard at home and what we remember from our early childhood. We connect these stories to our larger culture so that we know where we belong and what our purpose is. These stories come in many different forms and traditions but they are exactly the same in function and effect. We all have them, or at least, most of us do.

My son, who came to us through foster-care when he was five years old, had no such story. This became painfully obvious in the second grade during the week his class studied timelines. They had a big project but my son wouldn't participate. Instead, he was oppositional, disruptive to others, and generally "a conveyer of chaos" as his teacher described when she called that Wednesday.

284

Some Way Home

"What's the project?" I asked.

"A personal timeline," she began and I cringed inside. "The kids were supposed to bring in pictures from home, pictures of themselves at all different ages from baby pictures until now. Then, they were to order them along a line on poster board and that'd be their life." I told her he had none of these.

It was obvious that my son had no personal story but that everyone else did. He had no myth and this lack made him stand apart from his peers, alone and without an anchor. When puzzling over this, his therapist made the suggestion that I start a journal for him, beginning at the time he came to us. She said that this journal, this memoir, could be his story and I could give it to him later in life. I thought this was a good idea, so I began writing what later became part two of **SOME WAY HOME**.

But there were still two things wrong. First, he needed his story right then not when he was older. He needed that foundation to build upon. And second, the memoir wouldn't be a whole story. An incomplete account wouldn't work. He needed the entire tale from its beginning. And he needed it right then.

So, I took the short list of facts that I knew about his early childhood from official reports and combined it with the early memories he shared the first year he was with us. With this I constructed a complete story by filling in the gaps with characters and situations that made sense from the results I knew.

At bedtime, I told him a child's version of this story embellished with giants, water spirits and such. Bruce appeared as a Cyclops in these early tales. Dylan felt free to correct me when he thought the story was wrong. This lead to a series of playful bedtime adventures he still remembers to this day many years on.

SOME WAY HOME: A memoir in a Myth is an adult version of that myth and that memoir combined, edited, and written down with the purpose to teach both the effects of and cures for childhood trauma. Therefore, as a mixture of both fiction and fact, it is not meant to be a biography, even though so much of it is taken directly from our lives. But the distinction

285

between fact and fiction means nothing in mythology. In a teaching story, it matters little if a cherry tree was really chopped down. That's not important at all. And, in fact, is often not the case.

I narrated Part One of **SOME WAY HOME** as if it had been told to me by my son's former caseworker, Adam McDonnell. This is a fictitious character constructed to act as a literary device to help the narrative and act as part of the dialogue between adopted parent and the child protection system.

SOME WAY HOME is my son's history now and has helped him understand, giving a complete foundation on which to build his life.

\#

Back when this book was conceived, several things converged in my life that made stories and myths important. At work as a school psychologist, I was successfully using the Mutual Storytelling Technique by Richard A. Gardner, to work with angry adolescents. Also, as a father I was engaged with bedtime storytelling. With all my children's learning problems and emotional sensitivities, I often found it easier to tell them something difficult about themselves or their behaviors with a short narrative like a modern day Aesop's fable. A structured lecture was almost always counter-productive. When I told them stories at night, I felt a solid connection with both of them and the ancient storytellers who transmitted culture and wisdom down from one generation to the next through multiple millenniums. To me, telling stories began to feel like a real church experience.

At this same time, my studies in Christian literature led me to the Gospel of Thomas, which then led me to study early Christian Gnosticism. Gnosticism had a very strong base in personal mythology. Teaching stories were an important part of the Gnostic school's curriculum. In fact, in many places, Gnostic schools required their acolytes to develop their own myth as they advanced in the study of mysteries and the gaining of knowledge (gnosis). The point was to teach the insights learned through spiritual struggles and growth using literature and literary forms.

286

It was in this sense that I approached the writing of **SOME WAY HOME.**

Mythology is all about symbolism. To understand the meaning of a myth you need to "listen with two good ears" (namely your physical and spiritual ears) simultaneously. A most famous Gnostic myth is called, The Hymn of the Pearl (see: http://www.gnosis.org/library/hymnpearl.htm). On its surface, it seems to be a fairly innocuous tale similar to to the prodigal son. It is a story about the son of a great king, the King of kings, who is sent to Egypt to bring back a pearl of great value that is captive by a giant serpent. Well along the way, the boy is seduced by the Egyptians and falls into a deep, drunken sleep, forgetting about who he really is and his mission. After a long time, the King of kings sends a messenger to bring a letter to the boy. When the boy receives this letter he awakens from his stupor, remembers himself and continues on his mission to retrieve the pearl for his Father.

If you don't understand that the King of kings symbolizes God, Egypt represents the physical plane or the "world", that the pearl represents the memory of heaven and at-one-ness (atonement), sleep symbolizes the mindless existence we often live in the physical world, you cannot understand the real meaning of the Hymn of the Pearl. Understanding the symbols in Jacob's myth is essential to knowing the meaning of his story.

Finally, a Gnostic is literally "someone who knows". So in **SOME WAY HOME** the father is the Gnostic because it is he that knows the whole story. Jacob's writing of the Gnostic's Tale symbolizes the whole book, **SOME WAY HOME,** as an attempt to understand the relationship between father and son and why an innocent, like Dylan, suffers in this world. On the surface, Dylan's misery appears to be meaningless. But this book was written to understand the ultimate reason.

Ultimately, the answer Jacob discovers for himself is that Dylan suffers because he unmasks the ego (Morningstar) and its war against reason (MiKahl). Dill Fin (or Dylan) exposes our belief in 'specialness'. What Dylan is in effect doing throughout the course of the book, is testing everyone around him by questioning and confronting their selfish motives. This is the "test" that he presents to all the characters he interacts with and the reason so much anger is directed to him. He acts as a mirror that reveals the personal facades people make to convince the world that they are special and good.

Dylan reveals the truth that these facades are petty and vicious. Dylan reflects back to people the ugliness of their self-deceptions. His oppositional behavior ("No, no, no, no) threatens everyone's self-image. Depending on how they respond to this challenge, they either help Dylan heal or hurt him more. And this is the true secrete to healing, to love without specifics.

dK

Appendix 3: <u>*About the Authors:*</u>

David J. Kenney is a seasoned speaker having presented to parent and professional groups at colleges, universities and educational in-services on topics such as healing trauma, stress management, anxiety reduction, helping children with attention deficits, behavior as language, general parenting and achieving success in our schools.

David has been a school psychologist for over twenty eight years in a diverse group of educational settings, from rich to poor, from one of the highest ranked school in the state to one with much less success. He has worked in urban, suburban and rural settings

. As an undergraduate student, David was invited to the 1985 National Fairweather conference to present a program he developed using creative writing with chronic, schizophrenic patients. This project was spotlighted in the Detroit Free Press on August 30, 1985. In 1986, David graduated, magna cum laude, from the University of Detroit with a Bachelor's degree in psychology and again as a Specialist in School Psychology in 1989. He served as President of the Michigan Association of School Psychologists in 1997-98 and was liaison to the Michigan State Board of Education from 1995 to 1997.

But all achievements pale when compared to raising traumatized children to a healthy maturity. Children wounded by the world have been given little reason to trust it, so there were no guarantees of successful outcomes. Through his committed efforts, David learned strategies to heal harmed children. His expertise and insight has been noted by colleagues, who continue to seek him out for mentoring and training.

Barbara Kenney began her career by counseling emotionally disturbed children. She earned a Bachelor's degree in Human Services in 1976 from Ferris State followed by gaining her Master's degree in Administration from Central Michigan University.

In 1977, Barb helped establish a locked program for delinquent girls at Vista Maria. Barb was instrumental in program development for this secured facility, designing and establishing structure and treatment for residents. From 1979 to 1993, Barbara was a case manager for schizophrenics at an innovative agency that provided services to the mentally ill within the community. While there, she was recognized as an exemplary public speaker and trainer.

Fifteen years later, Barb left social work to tend to the needs of our adopted children. While they attended elementary school, she was an active and positive influence on the whole community. For three years, she acted as president and vice president for the Parent-Teacher Association. In the recognition of her substantial efforts and clear vision, she was conferred a distinguished service award in 1997.

In the next phase of her career, she taught at a local college and university where she instructed in the areas of health science, humanities, and social work for another 15 years. Currently, she is the Marketing Director for Kid-Epics Consulting.

24706115R00163

Made in the USA
Middletown, DE
04 October 2015